OASIS

THE TRUTH

Tony McCarroll currently lives between Ireland and Manchester. He still drums regularly and also teaches at his own drum clinic. He is the father of two children and lives with his partner, Sue.

Richard Dolan started to write when he was aged four. He hasn't stopped since. He is currently residing in Cheshire after travelling the globe for many years. Richard has somehow convinced a beautiful young girl called Jane to marry him and has three wonderful children. Well, two and a real Wrong 'Un.

TONY McCARROLL

OASIS

THE TRUTH

MY LIFE AS OASIS'S DRUMMER

JOHN BLAKE

Published by John Blake Publishing,
80–1 Wimpole Street,
Marylebone
London W1G 9RE

www.facebook.com/johnblakebooks
twitter.com/jblakebooks

Published in hardback in 2010
First published in paperback in 2011

Paperback ISBN: 978-1-84358-499-5
Ebook ISBN: 978-1-84358-818-4

British Library Cataloguing-in-Publication Data:

A catalogue record for this book is available from the British Library.

Design by www.envydesign.co.uk

Printed and bound in Great Britain by Clays Ltd, Elcograf S.p.A.

9 11 13 14 12 10

John Blake Publishing is an imprint of Bonnier Books UK
www.bonnierbooks.co.uk

For Willie O'Donnell and Mark McCarroll.
Sleep tight, boys.

CONTENTS

PREFACE

It was the winter of 2008 and I was back in Levenshulme, Manchester. My old friend BigUn thrust a copy of *The Sun* towards me, with an instruction to turn to the 'Bizarre' showbiz page. I did so, expecting the usual. And I wasn't let down. Noel Gallagher was blessing the pages again on his promotional drive for what might possibly be the final Oasis album, *Dig Out Your Soul.* I had been a founding member of the band.

He was rattling on about my unsuitable haircut and piss-poor drumming once more, but by now I was accustomed to those insults. Over the previous six albums, my hair had been a major marketing tool for him. I'd had 15 years of such treatment. I looked at the photo of Noel in the paper and realised he was shaping his own hair upwards in an attempt to gain a little extra height. Some things never change. I was not sure why he was so fixated with hair. I wasn't even in possession of my mop any more. But it was time for Noel to flog an album. And that's where I get involved.

OASIS – THE TRUTH

My name is Tony McCarroll and I was one of the original members of the rock 'n' roll band Oasis. I formed this group with my childhood friends and spent five years in it. I am often referred to as The Nearly Man, a Mancunian Pete Best, The Stupidest Man in Pop Music, alongside a host of other derogatory terms. Time to put the record straight I guess. Hopefully, this insight into my life, the Gallaghers, Oasis and the well-oiled machine we all know as the music industry will go some way towards putting those insults to bed; then again, maybe not. That, I suppose, is for you to decide.

What I can state with absolute certainty is that the story told by Noel Gallagher – be it through him, the other band members or sycophantic rock journalists – will not tie in with my version of events: that he stepped in and took control of a hopeless band of misfits, armed with a bag that contained hit record after hit record. It will not tally with his being the voice of an underclass, the working-class generation. And it certainly won't tally with his story of the events that surrounded my unceremonious exit.

Now I hear your alarm bells ringing. But don't worry, this isn't going to be a vicious swipe from a rejected band member. Hopefully, you will find it an honest overview of the formation of Oasis, and a reflection on the pitfalls of life – in particular, the ones that litter the music industry. It is also a recollection of times past, which I hope you will be able to relate to and enjoy once again. But most importantly: it's the truth.

Tony McCarroll
October 2010, Manchester, England.

CHAPTER 1
HE BANGS THE DRUMS

I was born at seven o'clock, on a typically grey Mancunian morning, in the summer of 1971 at St Mary's Hospital, Hathersage Road, Victoria Park, in Manchester. My parents are Tony and Bridie McCarroll – Irish immigrants and dream-makers both. I was their first child, and as my dad held me aloft on the ward he was already making plans for my musical upbringing. Whether to pass times on long cold nights across the water or to commemorate a fallen hero or freedom fighter, the Irish have always held musicianship in high regard. Guitars, accordions, keyboards, whistles and drums were like toys in our house. Combined with a record turntable constantly on the go, it made for a great place (and time) to grow up.

I was the first of three boys. All three of us would become addicted to playing and enjoying music. We lived in a traditional red-bricked two-up two-down on Wetherall Street, Levenshulme, 3 miles south of the centre of Manchester. The city had become a second home for many

Irish since its rise as an industrial power. My dad ran a construction business, which left my mother to chase us around the house. I had a very loving and happy upbringing – though if we stepped out of line, there would be the whoosh of the brush to dodge. I guess it's easy to look back on bygone days in a misty, wistful kind of way, which can be misleading, but I can honestly say I enjoyed every challenge or dare that came my way. I was that type of kid.

My first challenge in life came early on, when I was only five years old. An old wooden World War II demob hut still stood on Chapel Street in Levenshulme. The building had been turned into a dole office first, then a nursery. I was busy minding my own business at this nursery one day when I was plucked up and sat in front of a television camera. The cameras had arrived, along with a group of oddly dressed strangers who didn't dress and talk the way my mum and dad did. They laid in front of me an array of toys and games and a very nice young lady told me I could play with whatever I wanted. I immediately grabbed a pair of wooden drumsticks that lay on one side and began to hammer away on anything within striking distance. The film later appeared on a flagship BBC children's programme called *Playschool*: when the camera shot through 'the square window', I was revealed clutching that pair of drumsticks, banging away. A spark had been lit.

* * *

The sun beat down on the street outside my house, transforming the tarmac to a warm, pliable liquorice. It was the summer of 1976 – famously, a scorcher. I was using the melted tarmac as paint to daub my name on the baking pavement when I first heard the noise. Boom-boom-thud.

Boom-boom-thud. Boom-boom-thud. The noise came from a very large drum strapped to a teenage member of the Boys' Brigade who was ferociously beating out his rhythm despite the blistering conditions. Behind him came the rest of the boys, marching in time while completing rolls on the snares. I was amazed. A Boys' Brigade band, kitted out and in full uniform, and marching down those tight Mancunian terraced streets on such a hot day – did they actually *want* them to faint, or what? The sight of that large bass drummer had left me captivated, though. Each blow delivered to his skins directed and drove the other musicians wherever he wanted to lead them. Like the Pied Piper, he would speed up the tempo when they were marching through some of the area's more dangerous spots, then slow down if the route was lined by the more senior citizens of the community, who would wave and reminisce around the days when the British Empire still meant something. I ran behind the drummer and shot questions at him: 'How can I play the drums? Who taught you to play? Will you teach me?'

Now, I understand that the combination of the pressure of leading the band and trying to stay hydrated – not to mention staying conscious, and keeping in time – can lead a person to become somewhat short tempered. But still I don't believe it justifies cracking a six-year-old kid in the face with a fucking drumstick! It stung, but funnily the main thing I remember now was that he never lost the beat; he simply slipped the assault into a break in the music.

Despite this potentially off-putting attack, I was totally transfixed. The love affair had begun. I immediately raced home to tell my mother and father that I had abandoned my ambition to become the Six Million Dollar Man and instead was intent on forging a career as a drummer. I reminded them of my first TV appearance, as if it had been destiny. They smiled, as they always did when I came up with one of my grand schemes, but after a few days they sat me down and counted out the jam jar money that sat on a shelf in the kitchen. With just enough to cover the deposit, we made our way towards Manchester city centre, where I was to choose my first set of drums. Although this gift meant nothing at that time to an excited six-year-old, it was a sacrifice for my mother and father: after all, they were giving up any 'spare' cash they might have set aside.

Peggy, an Irish friend of my mother's, stopped us as we made our way to the bus stop. After being told the details of our impending journey she seemed very happy for us to take her son's old drum kit. (I'm not so sure her son was as happy.) The joy on my father's face seemed to light up the whole street. In those days, the Irish community in Manchester was a very strong one and the offer was gratefully received.

Such generous moments notwithstanding, times were extremely hard back then. Levenshulme was a very poor working-class suburb of Manchester. The Irish had descended upon it in their droves during the fifties and sixties, to the extent that it had acquired the name 'County Levenshulme'. By the seventies, as in most deprived areas, crime was rife; you learned fast to take care of yourself. I was no exception. I guess the drum kit was my parents' way of trying to keep me away from the violence and crime – and to be honest, at first it worked. The drums became an obsession for me and I played morning, noon and night. This led to the inevitable complaints from the rest of the street and eventually to the police visiting and enforcing a curfew: no drums after 7pm or I'd be lifted. So: during the day, I would attend St Mary's primary school on Clare Road, across from Errwood Park, where I spent more time running drum patterns through my head than learning maths or English. Each evening, I would sweat until the appointed hour, banging away on my kit like a little man possessed. Afterwards, as instructed by the police, I would stop hitting those skins and see just how much trouble my friends and me could manage to find. I guess that was proactive seventies policing for you.

* * *

My musical Mancunian life was brought to an abrupt halt in 1979, when I was told that I would be moving to Ireland. No arguments. No negotiations. My dad had landed a contract there. At first I simply refused. I could not understand why I could not stay in Manchester and take care of myself and the cat. I had a really strong set of friends there, and the thought of leaving filled me with dread. After nearly 10 years in my rainy northern city, I found myself suddenly transported to a remote corner of County Offaly. It was as far removed from the tarmac streets of terraced Manchester as I could get. For the next two years I would spend most weekends beating out the pheasants for visiting American tourists, or ploughing fields and delivering livestock. One constant throughout, however, was the music. I loved the fact that music can translate all languages and connect all cultures. Every evening people would gather around the peat fire in the cottage where we lived, with an assortment of instruments. My brothers would sit with their guitars while I would sneak off to a caravan at the end of the garden, where my old drum kit from Manchester sat waiting. I would listen to the distant sounds and shiver. The cold soon left, though, after I started to drum along. I taught myself to play songs by lots of different artists, The Beatles and Johnny Cash to name but two.

The village was situated at the bottom of the Slieve Bloom Mountains, the oldest mountains in Europe. They were covered by caves and log cabins and their slopes were lush in a carpet of beech trees that reached towards the sky. Naturally enough, they became our playground; it was paradise for an adventurous young boy and his two brothers. The sort of place, in fact, that Roald Dahl is probably much better qualified to write about. From trying to catch rabbits with pepper and rocks to shooting foxes at midnight with my Uncle Patsy, it was all one crazy adventure – and I loved every minute of it. The only thing that brought me down to earth was the fact that I had to attend the local school. We were taught only in Gaelic, and the Mancunian twang of my previous classroom was soon gone. I struggled with my own version of the language, as it didn't exactly sit well with my accent, but I had enough to get by.

For two years this was my home and I loved it; I had almost forgotten Manchester. Then, one evening, my mother and father announced that his contract had ended and we were to return to the city. I still remember the dread that filled my stomach at this announcement. Funnily enough, the last time I'd had such a feeling was when I left Manchester, and this took a bit of the sting out when it came to saying goodbye. I had grown to love the village and the simple way of life that it offered. But we live our lives in the city. There ain't no easy way out. I made myself a promise, though, that one day I would return to this place for good.

* * *

By the summer of 1981, I was back in Levenshulme. We moved into a new house on Lonsdale Road, just up the road from where we used to live. My timing was impeccable: the first night of our return saw the beginning of the Moss Side riots. The riots were Manchester's turn in a Mexican wave of violence that had the people standing up, arms raised, in Brixton, Liverpool and various other parts of the country. As an act of support, Levenshulme decided to have not so much a riot as a profitable tantrum. My mum and dad had decided that such an event probably wasn't the place for me, so I was confined to my bedroom. I watched enviously from my window as my friends made their way down the street armed with hammers, bricks and pieces of wood. The solitude and tranquility of the Irish midlands had been well and truly banished. In the distance, over the terraced houses, I could see a faint orange glow emitting from Stockport Road, where the people did not need much encouragement to start fires and cause general unrest. I waited by the window for the rest of that evening until, a few hours later, I saw my friends returning, with shopping trolleys full of goods removed from now windowless shops. They waved at me as I watched, their faces lit with the intoxicating activities of the evening. I've always thought that those riots heralded a change of culture in Manchester. Afterwards, everything seemed to become that little bit more dangerous. Reports of knife and gun attacks in the city began to appear in the evening papers and gang names were whispered on the streets. These events would lead to the organised formation of armed gangs, which went unchecked by the police for the next couple of years. It would also lead to a feeling of distrust against the forces of law enforcement, and a belief that if we were bold enough we could get anyway with anything.

After my return to Manchester, old friendships had been resurrected and after a month or so it felt as if I had never been away. That was when I first spotted him. I didn't know the fella's real name. I just made sure I stayed out of his way. Everybody did. He was five years older than us and he was huge. 'He's a fuckin' psycho, he kills cats,' whispered my mates.

I had finished my evening session on my old drum kit and wandered across to catch up with my friends in the park. On the way, I had found a dog-chewed golf ball, which I was bouncing and catching, rather clumsily. As I reached the park gates, I hurled the golf ball as far as I could. I watched as it sailed gloriously through the golden evening summer sky. It landed on a piece of concrete that the council had recently sunk as foundations for a new six-seater, state-of-the-art, horse-headed see-saw. The concrete threw it back up in the air at a ferocious speed and over towards the swings. This was when I first noticed the Cat Killer, who was pushing his luck there with a local schoolgirl. As he sat next to her on the swings, the golf ball arrowed towards them. Ping. Like a microwave oven – a new sight back then – that announces when its work is done, the golf ball connected with the psychopath's head. I was confused by the metallic sound. Was he a fuckin' robot? His head slowly turned and his angry eyes focused on me. First my legs started to shake and then, as he released a guttural roar, the rest of my body followed. I managed to pluck up all the courage I had and ran towards home as fast as I could. I was approaching the bottom of my street, only to realise that the Cat Killer had raced around to the top end. As I turned the corner, I spotted him 200 yards in front of me. We stopped and stared at each other, like two gunslingers in the Wild West, weighing each other up for potential weaknesses. I was 11 years old, 5ft 4in and 8st if fully clothed with bricks in my pocket. The feline slayer? Sixteen years old, 6ft 4in and a trim 16st. Taking these statistics into consideration, I decided to make a run for it. The only problem here was the fact my house and safety was a hundred yards away in the direction of the raving lunatic. I pondered the dangers of the situation in which I found myself until, with another roar (he liked roaring), he set off towards me. In a state of panic, I decided to make a dash for home. Who knows what went through the Cat Killer's mind as he saw me hurtling towards him, rather than away? He slowed at first, and then picked up speed again. As he neared me, the anger on his face became more apparent. I could see the spit on his screaming lips. He was at full charge and full volume as he tore towards battle. I kept running at him until we were less than 10 yards from each other. Then, with a nervous smile and an almost apologetic look, I darted to my right up the garden path and through my front door, which was slammed shut behind in one movement. 'DAAAADDDDD!' I slid to the floor behind the door, happy to have made it safely home.

It was a Saturday night and, as usual, my mum and dad were on their way to the Carousel Club on Plymouth Grove in Longsight, Manchester. This is where those who had made the journey across the Irish Sea would congregate to enjoy themselves. They would sit in large groups normally defined by county of origin and dance to frill-shirted show bands that reminded them of home. With my mum and dad would be Peggy and Tommy Gallagher, who had travelled over at the same time from Ireland.

Normally, Kathleen, the daughter of one of my mother's friends, would babysit, and after a bagful of harassment from me and my two younger brothers she would let us stay up late to watch *Match of the Day*; we couldn't wait to take the piss out of Jimmy Hill's chinny-beard-and-pullover combo. It seems that she couldn't make it that week, but she had arranged for her younger brother to stand in. Mum and Dad headed out as the new babysitter was hurried through the door. My dad shouted that the babysitter's name was Jimmy the Butt. Jimmy the Butt? I was thinking that maybe Jimmy the Butt should consider a name change if he wanted to further his career in babysitting when the living room door opened to reveal...the fucking Cat Killer! He casually entered the room, an assassin's ease about him. I'm a dead man, I thought. My throat immediately dried as I tried to squeak a warning to my parents that I was about to be murdered. Nothing came out. The only sound was the slam of the front door as my parents left. This sound perfectly masked the noise of the small fart I omitted as I sat in my skin-tight *Muppet Show* pyjamas, staring up at the gigantic man. He moved towards me ominously, but then gave me a big, lunatic smile. 'We need to talk,' he said.

And talk we did. The first part of the conversation had me stuttering an apology for hitting him on the head with a golf ball. Jimmy laughed it off. We then talked about anything and everything. He explained that he wasn't a psychopath and had never killed a cat, which reassured three very wide-eyed young brothers. 'Just a tramp,' he added. Jokingly.

And then he had me and my brothers in awe all night with his tales of chivalry and adventure. Well, if adventure involved fighting at United away games and chivalry came in the shape of fingering the local schoolgirls. He also explained how he had been attacked the previous year outside a boozer. Jimmy had argued with a couple of lads over something or nothing. They had lain in wait for him and then repeatedly stabbed him in the head. After they had finished, though, Jimmy had set about each of them. Although hampered by the blood pouring from his head wounds, like a blind bear he managed to pulverise each of his assailants before staggering off and collapsing. After days of surgery, the doctors decided the only way Jimmy would survive was if they inserted two metal plates at the front of his skull. This was groundbreaking surgery at the time and in a matter of months a new, stronger Jimmy was released back on to the streets of Levenshulme.

He immediately tracked down the gang responsible for the stabbing and although he had already hospitalised them once, felt it fair that he repeat the process. This time, though, he used his newly acquired weapon. The news of Jimmy hammering this gang by sitting on them and crashing his heavy metal-plated head into their faces soon spread across Manchester and a new name was being whispered on the streets: Jimmy the Butt. 'He's like the Six Million Dollar Man,' we laughed the following day. In our eyes, technology had rebuilt Jimmy the Butt and now he had superhuman capabilities. Fuckin' hell, he'd actually achieved one of my childhood ambitions. Jimmy taught us a few things over the next few years. Although he was a solitary figure, he never affiliated himself with one gang or another, but he taught us the meaning of loyalty and friendship. Once you were on Jimmy's side he would treat you like his own flesh and blood. First sign of any mither and Jimmy would be in. His steel skull would flail around, destroying everything in its path. 'If they are willing to fight then I think they're fair game,' he told us.

That was the reason for his fortnightly football excursion;

it was the perfect tonic for Jimmy. He would release everything, with no guilt, on his day away and the streets of Levenshulme felt that bit safer for a couple of weeks after. It wasn't for kudos or notoriety that Jimmy fought. Firstly, it came from a strong belief in right and wrong; and secondly, because of 'a buzzing in me head that goes away after I've kicked off'. This noise had started after he had been stabbed. His hearing was slowly deteriorating as well. It was not that he was disrespectful when others gave their opinion. He just knew that the way he thought had always been different to the way other people thought. He had learnt that arguing his point inevitably led to a fight, so had taken to saying what he had to, when he had to, which was not very often.

Jimmy continued to babysit for us and over the next couple of years I'd grow to admire him. Away from group pressures, he was a completely different character and would open up and be vocal. He also encouraged me to dedicate more and more of my time to the drums. 'It's a way out,' he would say. 'Don't want to waste your time on the streets.'

He had a friend who ran a football team and one spring evening in 1983, he brought me down to meet him. The friend's name was Vinny, and he was the polar opposite to Jimmy. Where Jimmy was a standalone guy, Vinny was probably the best-known man in the area. This was due to his larger-than-life personality, which was not constrained by normal social pressures. If Vinny had something to say, it got said. From the boys at the match to the men about town, everyone knew Vinny. That included the police and the priests. Jimmy and Vinny made quite a double act. Vinny, the staunch City fan and willing to let everyone around know it. Jimmy, the quiet United fan, but heaven help anyone who challenged him. The team that Vinny ran was called the

Northern Rebels. They had started a junior side and I was desperate to play. They trained on Greenbank playing fields, which was – conveniently – at the bottom of our street. One evening, we lined up against the outside brick wall of the changing room ready to undergo trials. There were about twenty local boys there, of all shape and sizes. The head coach sauntered over and started pointing and laughing at the group, singling out inadequacies as a way of determining which ones had the strongest character. You had to be tough in Levenshulme. His way of weeding out the less socially skilled or confident was brutal but effective, though he would probably be jailed for it nowadays. Next to me was a quiet lad who I recognised as he lived across the road from the local baths. He was a touch overweight, which led to some direct ribbing from the coach. I could clearly see that the insults were starting to have an effect on the poor lad and so I whispered, 'Tell him he's got big ears.'

The kid looked back with shock in his eyes; he seemed a touch unsure of my advice. He had a large mop of black hair shaped into the most enormous flick I had ever seen. There was an air of innocence about him. I can understand why he was unsure, but I knew that if he defended himself the coach would respect him for it and all would be well. I nodded at him and raised my eyebrows. 'Trust me. Just do it,' I urged. He turned and faced the head coach.

Suddenly he screamed at the top of his voice, his face exploding with rage. 'Shut your stupid fuckin' face, you ugly, jug-eared cunt!'

I nearly choked. I thought he had been a bit fuckin' harsh – and I was the one who had told him to do it. The head coach looked proper angry at the venom of those words. What the fuck must he be thinking? We quickly found out that he was thinking of kicking the kid's head in, as he stormed over with a vicious snarl on his face. The rest of the group went deathly silent. The poor kid was in for a right beating, so I moved myself between the oncoming coach and the little fella next to me.

'Don't go near him.' I squeaked. 'It was you that started it.' My words of protest didn't seem to register with the approaching coach. Something else did, though: Jimmy the Butt's booming voice

'Go near that kid and I'll put the fucking head on yer,' he informed him.

The coach came to an abrupt halt and stood glaring at me and the kid behind me. I nodded my appreciation towards Jimmy, who had spotted the commotion and made his way over. As usual, Jimmy defended the weak or vulnerable. One saying that Jimmy used a lot has always stayed with me: 'Right is right, even if everyone is against it; and wrong is wrong, even if everyone is for it.' I suppose these words gave you a good idea of just how Jimmy's mind worked.

After saving both mine and the kid's bacon, Jimmy then turned to me and in no uncertain terms very loudly told me never to get involved in anyone else's business like that again. 'But you did well,' he whispered, with a smile.

I then took it too far by trying to add about 'right being right, even if...' but Jimmy quietened me down by threatening to hide my *Muppet Show* pyjamas the next time he babysat. I was 13 years old and knew I shouldn't be sporting Kermit and Fozzy Bear across my chest. A shame that Auntie Dina in County Offaly didn't see things the same way. So, in front of the whole group, I went redder than a Royal Mail postbox. If Jimmy had threatened to beat me, then at least that threat would have given me some credibility among the rest of the team. To have my pyjamas outed in public was quite different. Seeing my crimson shade, the whole group began rolling about with laughter and, with everyone now relaxed, there followed a successful trial both for the fat little kid and me.

At the end of the trials, the kid came and thanked me for sticking up for him. 'Not a problem,' I told him.

'My name is Paul McGuigan, but people call me Guigs,' he replied, offering his hand. Guigs, pronounced as 'Gwigs', was the first member of the future Oasis I met. Although short in stature, he had a wide pair of shoulders from which he would hang thick Starsky and Hutch-style cardigans. He seemed like a good kid. Guigs lived on Barlow Road, Levenshulme, a stone's throw from the local baths. This was less than a hundred yards from where I lived. Unlike most of the local Irish youth, though, Guigs was Protestant, so he attended Burnage High School. I guess that's why our paths did not cross earlier. After a couple of practice games our friendship grew and we were soon spending time listening to music in the shape of Joy Division and A Certain Ratio. His bedroom became our main place of musical enlightenment.

We went to watch both Manchester City and United in an attempt to form a sporting allegiance. This helped Guigs integrate himself into the Levenshulme mob that I had grown up with. He was a friendly and unassuming young fella, always ready to listen and offer good advice. Some might say he was a lonely lad who relied heavily on those around him. I didn't feel that Guigs's neediness was an issue, though. We all need someone sometimes.

Guigs was always interested in what other people were up to, and he took particular note of my drumming. I had now been banging those skins for some seven years. Guigs would sit in my bedroom and watch as I practised roll after roll. He was always trying something new, something different; I called it the Mr Benn syndrome. One day he would be a cricketer, the next day a boxer, and I guess in that mode he sort of just carried on until in later years he became a scooter boy, then a practising Rastafarian. If a notion crossed his path, then Guigs would have a go. He had a strong character, though, and would try harder than anyone else when he had a new project, even if he didn't actually possess a talent for it. That attitude would serve him well when he met Bonehead a few years later.

We also started boxing around this time. Another constant in my life. The old dole office on Chapel Street had finished its days as a nursery and had been reborn as Levenshulme ABC. The whole of Oasis, bar – not surprisingly – Bonehead, would pass through this gym. It was always full and you had to make sure you arrived early if you wanted to train. A family of six brothers, all ex-professional boxers, ran it. The first time Guigs and me went along, it was a dark November evening. Outside, there were two people arguing. They noticed us and lowered their voices, but we could still hear the anger. As we passed, the taller one smiled at us. 'All right, boys?' he asked, in a flat northern accent. He was 6ft plus, with strong shoulders and long, powerful arms. His hair was blond and cropped close to his head. His friend was slightly shorter, with dark hair, also cropped. After we were inducted into the gym, we sat on a long bench in the changing rooms. I slowly pulled the horsehair from the ripped boxing gloves I had been given on my arrival.

'Oi!' I sat up, startled.

'What are you doing to those gloves?' asked the large blond-haired fella from outside, who had just entered the room.

'Nothing,' I stammered. 'Sorry.'

'They don't come fucking free, you know,' he said, as he pulled the gloves from my grasp and slapped me over the head with them, playfully. 'I've been told to look after you little fuckers, so listen up. No fucking about in the gym. No fucking about in the changing rooms. No fucking about anywhere. Simply no fucking about. Understand?'

Understood. We all nodded our heads as we looked up from our positions on the bench. There was definitely something intimidating about the man.

'Who the fuck is that?' someone asked, after the blond man headed off to spar with his friend. 'He's a policeman. My brother told me,' came the reply.

I later found out that this wasn't strictly true. The only connection to the police force was in the shape of a desk sergeant who had a football scout's nose for criminal talent. He was convinced the blond fella had serious potential. He presented both of the boys to one of the brothers with a request that they be given a purpose in life and something constructive to do. But the name stuck and we would always refer to him as the Policeman.

* * *

My old drum kit was a roll away from total capitulation. I realised I needed a job to fund a replacement, so on a winter's day in 1984 I walked down Stockport Road in Levenshulme, stopping at each shop to ask for work. There was no joy at the bakers or the candlestick makers, but the butcher was a good fella and asked if I could be up and ready for work at five the next morning. After my time on the farm in Ireland, I considered this a lie-in. I was offered the job and with it the means to earn enough to get myself a proper drum kit. I was ecstatic. The butcher shop was called Needham's and had been trading since the turn of the century. Good times were ahead. And cheap sausages.

I was there every morning before going to school and every evening after I had finished. I thought nothing of picking up entrails and bollocks, brains and eyeballs, which seemed to impress the butcher. One freezing cold morning, I was emptying a bucket out back, my breath visible in the air, when I spotted a body lying motionless next to the tunnel that led to Levenshulme train station. Fuck me, it's a dead man, I thought. Ever since the Moss Side riots, local drug wars had been raging and I expected this to be a tracksuit-clad casualty. I cautiously made my way over and the first thing that hit me was the pungent smell of urine-soaked clothing. In front of me was a tramp lying motionless on the ground. Horrified, I fled back to the shop to raise the alarm. The head butcher immediately ran over to examine the dead body, only to find that the tramp was still breathing. 'It's Trampy Spike,' he told me. 'He's a local celebrity.'

A local celebrity. I was learning to like my life full of characters. Nowadays, Trampy Spike would probably be followed around by a film crew from some cable channel. That morning they would have captured some strange footage. It transpired that a culmination of morning dew and urine, mixed with the sub-zero temperatures, had left the celebrity tramp frozen solid to the cobbles. He could not move an inch. Someone fetched a bucket of hot water and we slowly poured it round him, watching in amazement as he came back to life. After we provided the Lazarus-like vagrant with a hot cup of sweet tea, he revived sufficiently enough to tell me his name was Spike, adding as far as he was concerned he owed me his life. He swore that he would repay me somehow. Without wishing to sound heartless, this promise didn't fill me with excitement. After all, the only possessions he had were his piss-soaked clothes and a rusty wheelbarrow. In due course, though, I would find out that life's gifts can come in many different guises.

My eagerness to work had left me with a few quid in my pocket for the first time in my life. Although the majority of it would be banked in my attempt to get a new drum kit, what remained went on cider and weed that would be consumed in the park at the weekend. I guess this was typical of the era we grew up in and happened in parks countrywide. It was Thatcher's Britain and rebellion seemed right. As Greenbank and Chapel Street parks were right next door to the boxing gym, me and Guigs decided to move our drinking parties to Errwood Park in South Levenshulme. This, we thought, would give us some privacy and also stop any of the boxing brothers spotting us. After training all week, we felt it was a weekend reward. They (quite rightly) looked on it as a total waste of all the previous week's work. I guess one thing that the gym taught me was to respect your body and yourself, something that could only be brought about through self-discipline – which, in itself, was a great attribute to have.

Errwood Park was as typical a city park as any, founded by the Victorians – though the pomp and circumstance of their day was now nowhere to be seen. The bandstand still stood, although it was now dilapidated and played host to the local glue-sniffers rather than any brass band. The bowling huts were still in good condition, as were the bowling greens themselves. Both were maintained by members of the bowling club who, if their beloved lawns were invaded, would exit the hut in a military formation and attempt to capture and punish any unlucky teenager. At night, the swings and roundabouts moonlighted as lounge bars and shabeens for the local teenagers intent on inebriation. Running through the middle of the park was the boundary between Levenshulme and Burnage. This was a point of conflict long before we had arrived.

After a quiet first weekend in the park, we arrived the following Friday evening with carrier bags full of grog from the local off-licence; the only identification required in those days was a picture of the Queen on a crumpled bank note. After an hour or so, a firm of about 15 arrived in the park. Darkness had arrived, and with no one else around they made their way towards us. They were fronted by two skinheads, both wearing sheepskin coats and both named Peter. They were referred to as the Two Peters. Said a lot about the group, I guess. They then made us an offer we could not refuse.

'You've got a sixty-second start. Get out of the park and get home. If we catch you before you reach home, we'll put you in hospital. Do you understand, you Paddy bastards?'

The group was a couple of years older than us and we were at an age when that really made a difference. This statement of intent was not good news to us, as we were of mostly Irish descent. I looked at Guigs, who was terrified by the prospect of a beating. He was also upset at being labelled 'Irish'. He had recently taken to wearing a small Union Jack badge and in vain tried to point it out to the gang. They weren't having it. We had seen this mob beat two young men under similar circumstances, leaving one in the Manchester Royal Infirmary. It was no fucking joke. These boys carried and were not afraid to put their tools to use. They also had the use of vehicles, which could make an escape difficult. It's funny to think how prevalent such prejudices were, even two decades ago – and even that they still persist today in places. But these were the days when the IRA were conducting their most ferocious campaigns ever on the mainland and everybody seemed a little bit nervous and defensive.

We all headed out of the park, intent on making it home. Through stealth and caution, we very nearly made it. Three of us had split from the main group and were using the back entries of Levenshulme as a safe route home. Suddenly we stopped as dark figure appeared at the bottom of the alley we were in. We turned to go back on ourselves, only to find somebody else moving down the entry from behind us. Decision time. I sized up the guy in front, who looked smaller than the guy behind, and decided to make a run for it. Upon nearing the end of the entry I was surprised to see my would-be capturer was a lad I knew, called Noel. I knew him as Paul Gallagher's younger brother. I knew Paul Gallagher as Tommy and Peggy Gallagher's son. So I knew that he came from a strong Irish background. One of the two friends with me also recognised Noel. 'What the fuck are you doing trying to catch us? You're as Irish as the rest of us, you nugget,' he said.

'I'm English. I was fucking born here,' replied Noel.

'Yeah and you're gonna die here as well if you don't fuckin' move.'

Noel was a few years older than us, but my friend had been attending the same boxing gym as me and was becoming known locally for his ability to fight. As Noel slowly recognised him in the gloom of the entry, there was a visible change in his stature. Sure enough, he shuffled to one side and we burst past. I remember Noel whispering, 'Don't let them catch you' as we did. I thought it strange that somebody from the same background as myself would be in such a gang, but nevertheless he had helped us to escape – even though he had also had a hand in making it necessary in the first place.

Fast forward to 2008, and a very different Noel spoke to the Irish times:

> *I feel as Irish as the next person. The first music I was ever exposed to was the rebel songs the bands used to sing in the Irish club in Manchester. Do you know, I think that's where Oasis songs get their punch-the-air quality – from me being exposed to those rousing rebel songs. It was all rebel songs and that god-awful Irish country and western music. I grew up an Irish Catholic. I remember my mum would only buy Irish butter and milk. But then, during the 1970s with all the bombings, our local co-op wouldn't stock Irish produce, so my mum went elsewhere. I clearly remember my parents coming back from the Carousel Club in Manchester, the Irish club, and telling me about how all the cars in the car park had been vandalised by an anti-Irish crowd. It was scary.*

During the following weeks, we slowly integrated ourselves into Errwood Park, through a combination of football and Merrydown cider. Even the rest of the gang that had originally run us from the park seemed to have forgotten that evening and suddenly new friendships were born. Thursday, Friday and Saturday nights would never be the same again. The football games were fast and furious and sometimes downright hostile. Paul and Noel Gallagher were an ever present. As my dad was a friend of their dad, it was natural that we also became friends. Paul was the confident, cocky one, with Noel standing somewhat in his shadow. I liked Paul: he had a sense of loyalty about him, and you could trust him. He also had a quick wit and would fire sarcastic one-liners around that kept us all entertained. Noel was more withdrawn, but still a likeable fella. He always looked well dressed and obviously spent more time on his appearance than Paul – which, to be fair, wasn't difficult. We would play football, drink, smoke, manhandle young women, fight and then play some more football. After some while, though, it became apparent that Noel was starting to spend time up the trees that hid the railway track. A strange place to sniff glue, I thought: surely there was a danger of falling out of the tree? Over the next three months, I would watch them all as slowly they all fell out of the trees, one by one. It could be a dangerous spot for dog walkers...

'Bostik, Bostik, over here,' came the shout from his teammates.

Noel giggled across the bowling green, with the football at his feet. He could only move sideways, it seemed, and it wasn't long before he reached the bowling ditch and found himself in a crumpled, giggling heap.

Although he was quiet, you always felt there was more to him if you could scratch at the surface, but more often than not he simply wore that vacant look that a glue-sniffer develops. On the occasions when he wasn't, I would discover that Noel's upbringing wasn't that far removed from mine, from six weeks a year in Ireland to the copy of 'Four Green Fields' on the record deck. I looked back at our first meeting, and thought he was a confused fella.

One evening, Paul Gallagher brought his younger brother

to the park. Actually, I'll re-phrase that. Paul's younger brother accompanied him to the park. Immediately, it became apparent that the kid had more front than both his older brothers combined. When Paul tried to introduce him to the group, he was told to fuck off by his youngest sibling. After doing so, the young kid went round each person present and introduced himself. 'My name is Liam. My name is Liam. My name is Liam.'

He stood weighing the group up as a whole; already taller than both his brothers, his head was freshly skinned and he wore a long raincoat. He had a huge cow's lick on his hairline and a quick reply for everyone. Liam was already making an individual statement. I laughed to myself. I'd never met a kid with so much attitude in all my life. He stood in front of a group of 20 kids, all older than him, most with violent reputations and yet not a flinch. In later years, people would accuse Liam of being a celebrity 'act'. Surely nobody can be that destructive and belligerent? It must be just an act for the cameras. Well, I first met Liam when he was 13 years old. The boy I met that day was as loud and as brash as Liam the man today. His whole ethos is: what you see is what you get. Even people who dislike him must recognise the honesty in that.

Liam started to frequent the park intermittently. I wouldn't say he was part of the group, as he was too young, but he would turn up from time to time and play football. He was always loud and opinionated, but then again you had to be just to get heard. I liked Liam for his confidence and also the ability to get on with everyone. He made a point of talking to some of the more quiet and unobtrusive members of the group. I remember a football match during which a young, aggressive Liam came off second best to a larger, stronger lad named Chris Hutton ('Huts', for short). Liam reacted furiously to the challenge and showed that he had a fiery temper to match his personality. People ushered Huts and Liam away from each other, which I'm sure was to Liam's benefit as Huts really could handle himself. This altercation would be repeated on the same pitch but in different circumstances a few years later.

A particularly hard winter had left the stalwarts heating themselves by means of alcohol in Errwood Park, while the majority of us decided to warm ourselves by kicking a ball about. We left Errwood Park and made our way back to Greenbank playing fields, where Guigs and me had met. The council had just built a red-brick five-a-side court there, complete with floodlights. The floor was red tarmac and offered a slightly more comfortable landing than solid concrete. The lights were on a timer, but with a bit of ingenious tampering one smart-arse had overridden the controls and we now had the power to turn the light on and off ourselves. Most nights we would switch off towards midnight, which would be followed by shouts such as 'Have you put the cat out?' in the darkness. This move away from Errwood Park served Noel well, as he moved away from those who were encouraging him to sniff glue and fall out of trees. In turn, this helped him to come out of his shell more, and he developed into a likeable friend. He would shuffle along the red five-a-side tarmac, heavily weighed down by his knee-length mohair cardigan; he had an eye for a good pass and would work as hard as anyone. Noel was one of the oldest kids in the gang and was known for his verbal putdowns. For that reason, I suppose you'd be careful if you ever thought of taking a pop at him, even if in good spirit. Noel always had a sarcastic turn of phrase at hand, the humorous venom. He would put it to use very successfully later in his life.

The year was 1984 and the prospects for the older lads in the group were not great. Thatcher had tightened her grip on the country, and it was particularly hard felt in the North of England. Most kids I knew, including Noel, had taken to working at Benjey's, which was a government-funded workshop in St Peter's Church, Levenshulme. It was a furniture makers, and local lads would expect to perform the minimum amount of work possible, just so as to match the minimal amount of money they would be paid. Most of them could not pass the amusement arcade nearby without parting with their money. Paul Gallagher was on the roads, while Guigs was stacking shelves at the local supermarket. Others simply worked the city centre, stealing from stores or targeting businessmen. There seemed to be a real sense of indifference towards the authorities at that time. No one was really concerned, even if they did get caught. In those days, although if the prison system was a lot harsher than it is now, life on the out was also much more difficult. Thatcher had created a rebellious underclass. I've always believed that this detachment was what drove Oasis as a group in the early days and these streets were where that detachment was born.

Manchester had been hit hard over the previous decade and riots and unrest were commonplace. I suppose 1984 was important to me for another reason, though. This was when I first heard The Smiths. Until then, I guess I had always considered that the music I listened to belonged to another generation. Another time. Suddenly there was a band that not only hailed from Manchester but said something to me about my life. The first album I ever purchased was the Smiths compilation *Hatful of Hollow*. I hunted it down in a shop on Oldham Road. Sixteen songs for a fiver. Bargain. It sat revolving on the turntable in my mum's front room for months. It also joined the growing list of credible bands we listened to in Guigs's bedroom. Bob Marley and New Order had company. The Smiths sang about trivial and mundane things in a unique style somehow made northern and acceptable.

When Noel discovered my fondness for The Smiths, he lambasted me. 'The fucking Smiths, you faggot. What's wrong with you?' It seemed that although Noel had a passing admiration for the lead guitarist, the lead singer was not to his liking. I guess Morrissey's irreverent and humorous songwriting was a bit too 'gay' or 'student' for him. Years later, Noel would cite The Smiths as one of his first musical influences. I certainly don't remember him showing such reverence at the time.

CHAPTER 2

CONTEMPT BREEDS FAMILIARITY: A MANCUNIAN CONCEPT

We don't deny the fact that we take drugs such as cocaine, marijuana and ecstasy. We've been doing drugs since we were 14. In Manchester there are only three things you can do when you leave school – play soccer, work in a factory or sell drugs.

NOEL GALLAGHER

Noel's career advice may sound like simply a useful sound bite for the Oasis cause, but it was not that far removed from the truth. We decided a life of crime was the only way for us to pull ourselves away from the violent streets. In an attempt to find a bit of peace, we formed a hooligan gang. (I know.) As a tribute to The Smiths, we named ourselves the Sweet and Tender Hooligans. (Like I said, I know.) Each member wore a green survival jacket with attached hood. This hood had goggles stitched into it, and we would hide behind these when in action. The coats were purchased from the army and navy store on Oldham Road and must have been made in the early days of the Cold War. There were four of us in the gang: Guigs, Me, Crokey and Fantastic. Noel had told us we were off our tits and refused to have anything to do with it. Maybe it was the Smiths connection he didn't agree with.

Our first criminal enterprise was financial extortion. This dangerous-sounding idea was borne from watching *Once Upon a Time in America* on pirate VHS loop in Guigs's house. We first targeted a television shop on Barlow Road – the road that Guigs lived on. The shop was even visible from the house itself. First unwise decision. What's more, the shop was run by a bunch of Italians, who never seemed to spend time fixing televisions. They seemed to sit around and drink coffee and meet the different people who visited each day. You'd think that after we'd seen that video, this might have rung a few alarm bells. Oh no. So there came the second unwise decision.

One afternoon, Crokey was pushed through the shop door and mumbled some sort of demand in the dark and gloomy shop. When the large Italian lady standing tall behind the counter asked him to repeat himself, he turned on his heels and simply left. We all hurriedly returned to Guigs's house and asked Crokey what he had said. He told us he had got nervous and lost the plot, so he'd used a line from *Once Upon a Time in America*. The only one he could remember. What was the line, we asked, expectantly? 'Erm… "So what are you? You're filthy! You make me sick! You crawl up toilet walls just like a roach! So what are you?" '

'That's all you said? Just those words?' I asked him. He nodded. The quote he had used in the shop was uttered by a young girl in the film and was aimed at a peeping tom she had caught. I spent a moment trying to see the relevance and then realised there wasn't one; I shook my head in disbelief at Crokey and reckoned the old Italian lady probably had him down as a local lunatic. I was wrong.

Later that evening, we were sat in Guigs's house when there was a sharp rap on the full-length, glass-frosted front door. We poked our heads out to see the hallway darkened by a huge, lumbering figure hovering at the door. 'You get it,' Guigs whispered.

'Fuck that, you get it,' came the general reply.

We had a silent whisper argument for 30 seconds, until Guigs cracked and trembled up the hallway. It was his house, so he was in a difficult position. As he opened the door, we all listened.

'You come in the shop again we will come back with shotguns and give you some ventilation, *capiche* my little pig-like friend?' Said in the thickest Italian accent I had ever heard.

I was dying to crack up laughing, as it had to be a piss-take, so I poked my head carefully round the door. It was no piss-take. Standing there was the most terrifying-looking man I had ever set eyes on, a man made for nightmares. His face looked like it had seen the wrong end of a couple of hundred brawls and his dark suit was bursting with the 200lb of pumped muscle it contained. He emanated evil and pain and possible torture. Well, I might be being a bit dramatic there. It was more a crack with a baseball bat and a severe warning.

Guigs whimpered, 'Sorry, sir.' At that point, the Italian simply growled back and thrust his head forward, as if to attack. Guigs immediately hit the hallway floor and took up a hedgehog-like defensive position. This went unnoticed by the Italian as, after growling, he had swiftly turned on his heel and marched down the garden path, slamming the gate behind him. We slowly coaxed Guigs from the hallway with a saucer of warm milk. The lesson we learned here was: never try to enforce a protection racket charge upon a large Italian organisation that obviously had fingers even in little old Levenshulme. I guess the life of a racketeer was not to be an option, so it was back to being the butcher boy.

Over the next year or so, I continued to work at the butchers and saved enough to eventually get myself that new kit. I also finished my secondary school education at St Albans High School in Gorton and was now able to make a small boat out of balsa wood as well as a pretty good apple crumble. So, armed with those two amazing talents, I was released into the adult world.

The five-a-side court had literally started to crumble around us and people had begun to move on. The only activity that still united the group was the fortnightly away trip with Manchester City and, for those that could afford it, a night out in the boozer at the weekend. We normally drank in the Irish boozers in Levenshulme, but would sometimes travel further afield. The Horseshoe, The Midway, The Church and The little Vic were the designated watering holes; if we were feeling adventurous, we'd head upmarket to Stockport or Didsbury.

One Saturday evening, we made our way to a club called Shakers in Stockport. When we arrived there was a large queue, but we found ourselves being shouted to the front. Standing at the front was a beaming doorman. It was the Policeman. He had been taught how to fight by the six brothers, which inevitably led him into the murky world of door security. There he stood, hand out ready to shake, looking extremely professional in his monkey suit and crew cut. We had trained together over the previous four years or so and had developed a strange relationship. The Policeman had proved to be quite an adept boxer and had, not surprisingly, taken to the ring. His only problem was that when he fought he could turn into a wild man, which made him difficult for the six brothers to manage.

An example. I was sitting in a dressing room as four hundred or so boxing spectators were baying for blood outside. It was Levenshulme ABC's own show, so I was tasked with keeping an eye on the changing room and its contents. Easy work, I thought. If a thief were picking out a target, surely a boxer's dressing room wouldn't be that high up on the list? There was a right commotion going on outside. I peeked out of the door. The crowd was angry and was ferociously hurling obscenities toward the ring. The spotlights illuminated the wispy layers of smoke that hung over them. A loud, long booing rang around the old hall. Suddenly, the Policeman appeared, on his way back to the dressing room. He was sweating and scuffed, his face still reddened from the fight. 'Right, fuck this,' he snarled.

I didn't think the Policeman was very happy. It seemed he had once again gone a bit mental during the bout and had butted his opponent three times. This had been at the end of a fight that he was easily winning. Apparently, his opponent had pressed a button by whispering something to the Policeman, prompting the violent outburst. This, in turn, led to the referee disqualifying the Policeman; he did so, quite wisely, from the other side of the rope.

The Policeman was now swinging punches inside the

dressing room as if he were still inside the ring. 'Left, left, right,' he hissed under his breath. 'Left, left right.'

Suddenly the dressing room door opened and in walked the victorious opponent. He was smiling until he saw the Policeman at the far end of the room. The Policeman walked towards him, also smiling. But I recognised the smile and realised the victor wasn't going to enjoy his spoils for long. The Policeman motioned me out of the room with a simple look and nod of his head and as I pulled the door shut I heard the thick thud of his right hook connect. With perfect timing, the large brass bell rang out to start the next fight of the evening.

* * *

By the summer of 1987, Guigs had got himself a job at Barclaycard in Manchester. At around the same time, he seemed to become more and more withdrawn. This, I soon realised, was due to his fixation with marijuana. Back then, if he wasn't reading about it, he would be smoking or eating it.

I finally got myself a good number in a local insurance office in Burnage. Right on my doorstep and normal hours. All I had to do was answer the phone and point people who came in to the right adviser. All of this and out of reach of the Mancunian rain. I considered myself fortunate to have landed on my feet. I was 16 years of age and on my first day found myself overawed both by the job and by a young girl who blushed when I asked her name. 'Paula,' was the reply.

* * *

And then there was a large bang. In late 1988, an explosion of love hit the streets of Manchester. One little white pill had sucked the hatred and frustration from a scarred generation and replaced it with a weekend euphoria and a new belief.

One winter night in 1988 found me sitting in The Millionaires Club in Fountain Street, Manchester city centre, surrounded by two hundred perspiring and grinning lunatics. They filled the dance floor and none of them were millionaires. Everybody had a prescription and all were ecstatic. It was Saturday night. Both City and United danced a communal dance, while all the girls were suddenly less interested in themselves and more interested in me. Or so it seemed. That situation was good for me.

Not that night, though, as I had Paula waiting back at her house. I had progressed both as a insurance customer service adviser and in my pursuit of the young Paula, from Burnage. She was probably what kept me punctual and interested in work from Monday to Friday. After a couple of weeks of chasing, she succumbed to my caveman charm. Paula was a good girl and had a generous nature. Although I had only been with her for a few months I could sense something good happening. I was 17 years of age.

After hailing a cab I weaved my way through the rainy city centre and arrived at her place. I was still chewing, still euphoric. A new-found joy pulsed through me. Paula stood in the doorway, waiting for me. Her arms were folded.

'Hiya, Treacle,' I said with a smile as I paid the taxi driver and walked up the short path. She ushered me inside and sat me down. I had a bad feeling. Something was wrong. She looked me straight in my dilated eyes and said, 'You're gonna hear the pitter patter of tiny feet around here soon.'

'Why have we got mice?' I replied. She ignored the joke.

The cold light of the next morning brought the inevitable comedown and the sheer panic that the previous night's news had created. I was bringing a kid into the world. I realised that meant I would need a new job. Paula would have to leave the office and what I was earning alone would not cover us. But none of that mattered, because I was bringing a kid into the world.

I was still running around with the gang from the park. Not so much during the week, though, as I was in practice for the arrival of my firstborn. They had all shaken my hand when I told them I was going to be a dad, but celebrations were muted. We all knew that it meant a change. But I would still travel to City away games occasionally. Noel had broken his foot and had been shifted to the stores of the construction company where he worked. He seemed very happy about this. Guigs had given up filing for Barclaycard and was now filing for British Telecom instead. He didn't seem so happy about this. Liam had just been thrown out of school for having an altercation with somebody that resulted in Liam being hit with a hammer. Big brother Paul was still working the roads.

It was a bright Saturday morning in spring 1989, and I had a trip to Forest away. As usual, we met outside Johnny's Café in Levenshulme. From there we made our way to Levenshulme train station and, with family rail cards in hand, headed to our destination. Our family consisted of one adult and 33 teenagers. This family had been causing havoc up and down the country for a good three years already. That day it was Nottingham's turn. We laughed on the way down. The previous week, Vinny Collins, my football manager, had decided to have a pint in Stockport before City played them in a friendly. It had been a covert seek-and-destroy mission. His intention was to infiltrate County's hooligan pubs and then guide the rest of City's troops in.

Vinny, though, had drunk a little more than he should have and went missing in action. Nevertheless, the City firm decided to go ahead and storm the local boozers. Can you imagine their surprise when they arrived to find a right handy mob being fronted by Vinny himself?

'Get outta the fucking way,' they shouted over to Vinny.

'C'mon, shitbags,' Vinny roared back, at the top of his voice. Then he put his hands to his face and blew an imaginary horn while making a noise that you would normally hear at the start of a fox hunt. He moved forward and beckoned Stockport to follow, right into the front of City's firm, while he laughed. Back in Manchester city centre later on, some of the City lads weren't happy with Vinny's antics, but he soon had them turned round and laughing again. 'It's just a bit of pub fun,' he would say.

That morning, Vinny looked visibly excited about the trip. He asked if I'd seen Jimmy the Butt and told me to say hello to him. We all jumped on the train and soon arrived in Nottingham city centre. BigUn was leading the way, with his usual scallywag style. Burberry coat with collars pointing to the skies to reveal the trademark pattern underneath. At that time, it simply let everyone who mattered know you were a hooligan and ready for it. Now it seems it just lets everyone know you're a 'chav'. How times change.

'BigUn' was Paul Ashbee, who was about the same age as Noel. He was a local lad who stood 6ft 5in tall and 2ft 6in wide. I think he was best left described as entrepreneurial, although he was definitely a 'Spartan' (meaning 'well liked and respected'). Over 30 of us had jibbed the train without any hassle at all. Fuck knows how much the travelling away fan cost British Rail in the eighties. We had met up with Richard Jackson and Bad Bill from Salford. They had a tasty firm, so we decided to split into two groups; I was with Noel and BigUn and Jacko, and we marched off through Nottingham city centre. Across a busy street we spotted a group of twenty or so appropriately dressed Forest fans outside an amusement arcade. Space Invaders and Donkey Kong were to be an electronic prelude to mass violence, it seemed. BigUn immediately started to bounce and then, without even a word to anyone else, he screamed, 'C'mon, dickheads, let's have it!'

Not really part of the plan, but that never did stop BigUn. I'd always wish that he had been better at mathematics when deciding to start such things. The odds were already stacked against us as the opposing group started to rapidly increase as the inside of the arcade emptied onto the street. The Forest fans were now excited. Shit, I thought, I wish Jimmy the Butt was a Blue. We were the youngest of City's firms and way out of our depth. The Forest fans reached about seventy in number, then suddenly began streaming across the road towards us. I looked at Noel, who looked back terrified. 'Fuck this,' he shouted and was off on his toes.

His damaged foot apparently causing him no problem whatsoever, he was gone, a vanishing Mancunian flash. The rest of the group followed him. I panicked and looked around. As I turned to run, I saw BigUn in the middle of the opposing group. He was throwing his fists around, trying to stem an unstoppable flow of opposing supporters. Lunatic. I headed off into the more commercial part of the city centre, knocking shoppers out of the way. The Nottingham firm were buoyed by our retreat and poured after us. My cross-country training at school came into play and I moved from the back of the group towards the front. Then my 20-a-day habit kicked in, and I was soon being passed. As I glanced over my shoulder I saw Jacko run straight into a bus shelter and hit the pavement, scattering panic-stricken shoppers. He was quickly set upon by the following pack. I contemplated turning back, but there were just too many of them. Suddenly, as I rounded a corner, I spotted Noel and a couple of others slipping into a darkened doorway. A look of terror was pasted across his face. I followed and we headed down the dark stairwell into a cellar bar. We ordered a round of drinks and took a seat.

The pub had long wire-mesh horizontal windows, set at street level. Outside, I could see thirty or so pairs of Adidas, Nike and Reebok trainers. Oh and the occasional pair of Patricks. If they clicked where we were, we would be in for a right slapping. I sat and watched the stairway, fully aware that it was the only way in and the only way out. Time seemed to slow down. The rest of the bar sat looking curiously at the four out-of-breath arrivals. I looked to Noel, who was as white as a sheet and murmuring something unintelligible over and over to himself. I quickly realised that my hooligan days should probably end before they really ever began. After watching Noel slowly stop shaking, we finished our drinks and headed swiftly and quietly to the ground.

I was working my way down the tick list. I was no criminal. I was no hooligan. I had a moral issue with dealing drugs, so that wasn't an option. What options had I left?

Anyone seen me drumsticks?

* * *

She had arrived. As my father had held me aloft only 18 years previously, in the summer of 1989 I raised my daughter to the world on the very same ward. We named her

Gemma and sat in awe. I made some promises that moment. I will always love and cherish you. I will always be there for you. I will let no one harm a hair on your pretty little head. I decided it was time for a change. A new direction. If I was to look after the beautiful ray of sunshine that I held in my arms, I needed to find better work and a less chaotic place to live.

Gemma was one arrival that changed my life in 1989. The debut Stone Roses album was another. The arrival of that LP would send a new swagger down rainy Manchester streets. The detachment and frustration of a generation had a new beat with which to march. And fuck me, it was a cool one.

* * *

Spring 1990, and it had been a couple of months since I'd last seen Guigs. He'd rung earlier that evening, though, and said he needed to see me urgently. I was sitting in a Levenshulme pub called The Church, staring out the window at the insurance shop where I worked, which was directly across the road. I spotted Guigs slowly ambling up Stockport Road. It was good to see him. Two people accompanied him, one on either side. I recognised one as Huts, the lad who Liam had fought with in the park. I didn't recognise the other one. As they entered the pub I was waiting at the bar.

'Hiya, mate.'

'Hiya, fella.'

It was hugs and back-slapping between myself, Guigs and Huts. Standing silently behind them was a very happy-looking fella with an open face and eyes that seemed slightly unfocused. They then introduced me to one Paul Arthurs, better known as 'Bonehead'. He stood before me with his hand out and an odd look in his eye, which was exacerbated by a Max Wall-like hair do. It looked like The Church wasn't the first pub he'd been in that day. We shook and, after a short introduction during which Bonehead's unique style of humour became immediately apparent, we made our way to a booth in the darkest corner of the pub.

'We want you to drum for us,' said Guigs, before we had managed to sit down.

'We're the new Roses,' added Bonehead. With this outlandish statement, he swaggered off to the bar in an Ian Brown monkey-style slalom walk. I had been practising my drumming intensely over the previous 12 months and had rehearsed with all manner of different bands. My influences had diversified. I had been watching old videos of John Bonham in action, which had left me completely stunned and hungry to drum. I also found The Stone Roses' drummer Reni particularly inspiring, with his unique lazy beats. Guigs went on to explain that he had met Bonehead at a student club called Severe in Fallowfield a couple of months earlier. Bonehead was a childhood friend of BigUn. It seemed that he was a talented musician, too. Guitars. Keyboards. Mouth Organ. Radiators. You name it, Bonehead could get a tune out of it. He had been able to play the keyboard at four years of age, which had led to the local kids naming him 'Mozart'. He had encouraged Guigs to learn to play something and, as the bass could be played by a blind monkey, decided that that instrument was a good starting point. Guigs's Mr Benn Syndrome had, hopefully, finally paid off. I had always known that his attitude would serve him well. You had to admire Guigs for his desire to try something different.

Bonehead was a few years older than both me and Guigs and he had grown up in West Point. West Point was officially the 'west point' of Levenshulme, but like some rebel state, those there considered themselves a separate entity altogether. As if there wasn't enough segregation at the time. Although massively outnumbered, kids from West Point would frequently clash with Levenshulme as well as Burnage. That, in itself, gave them some respect with the surrounding gangs.

It didn't take long for me to warm to this mop-haired plasterer. He had the ability to down alcohol like no one else I had met, a talent that, it seemed, he had developed at an early age. As a 13-year-old, he would be regularly returned home unconscious from the park. Once it started to flow it just couldn't stop for Bonehead. Fortunately, he was that rare breed: a good drunk. His mother and father hailed from Mayo, but he wasn't your stereotypical Levenshulme lad. He had attended a grammar school but had not enjoyed the experience in the slightest. It had left him with a wry and eclectic sense of humour, though, somewhat Spike Milligan-esque. He was also as talented as any musician that I had ever come across. Sober, he was as witty and sharp as anyone. Focused, but funny. Drunk, he was like a one-man circus sideshow. Always fun. In the sober moments he would become a close friend and a source of trust and support.

He was standing at the bar in The Church, ordering drinks in fragmented German. The sturdy barmaid looked as if she was about to pot him, although Bonehead seemed oblivious to this. Guigs and Huts were obviously impressed with his musical nous, if not his mental stability, so I agreed to come to the Milestone boozer on Burnage Lane the following Saturday to see them in action. I watched as Bonehead frogmarched round the bar, his finger under his nose as a substitute Hitler moustache. It was like watching a mental patient on the loose. Luckily for Bonehead, it was the type of pub where you could easily have assembled a cast for *One Flew Over the Cuckoo's Nest*, so he carried on.

Guigs told me that Noel had got a job for the Inspiral Carpets as a guitar tech and was touring all over the globe, which seemed pretty impressive and also explained his recent absence. I wondered how the fuck he had managed it. Good on him, though. Noel had played his acoustic guitar in the park for us; he wasn't bad. Guigs and Huts were keen to get him on board with the band, or at least have a chat. I thought that Huts's bowling-green altercation with little brother Liam would have got Noel's back up, so even before they asked I knew it was gonna be a no-no. But I knew I had to make changes in my life if I was going to provide for the new arrival. Something already felt good about the band. Another kid that we had met through the park was Max Beesley. His father was a famous jazz drummer and Max was more than capable himself with the sticks in his hand. I asked Guigs to sort out a meeting for me with Max's dad next time he was round.

They finally left after Bonehead had got the whole pub in uproar with his antics. I liked him. After they'd gone, I sat staring out of the dirty pub window at the insurance office. Would this finally be a route out of my mundane, shithole job? Something good to break the monotony? I hoped my luck would kick in. Lord knows it would have been the first time.

* * *

It was a beautifully cold day. The crisp air followed Jimmy the Butt through the front door. He would often drop by for a cup of my Mum's sweet Irish tea.

'How's the music going?' he asked.

'Good mate, good,' I replied, and told him about Guigs and Huts and Bonehead. Jimmy beamed and congratulated me on my efforts, but he didn't look himself. There was a crack in the smile. As much as he tried to steer clear of trouble, it seemed it would always seek him out. It was difficult for him to be beaten one to one, so he was now finding himself up against two or three at a time. He had recently started a proper relationship with a girl and this seemed to be preying on his mind too.

'Do you understand them?' he asked. Must mean women, I thought, and shook my head. Now that I had a permanent girlfriend and a child, it seemed that Jimmy believed I understood relationships. If only. I told him to enjoy her and not think about it too much. Jimmy didn't seem to be listening to my advice and just sat staring into space. After a few moments, he grabbed my hand in his massive paw, gave it a shake and told me I was a good kid. He then told me once again that some things are right and some things are wrong. Act on them. With that, he gave me the grin of a wild man and he was off out the front door. As he left, a strange, uneasy feeling came over me. I shook it away.

A month later, Jimmy was gone forever.

* * *

I noticed the hastily designed poster advertising The Rain, who were playing the Milestone pub in Burnage one night in the summer of 1990. It had been covered in plastic to protect it from that evening's downpour. What a fuckin' miserable name, I thought. Who wanted reminding of rain in Manchester? Inside, the 'new' pub was full of chest-high tables and stools that you needed step ladders to climb onto.

At the far end of the pub, slightly off the bar, stood Guigs, Bonehead and Huts. The band. Next to them was every drummer's enemy: the drum machine. Chairs had been laid out cinema-style before the band and were filled by friends and regulars. Chris nervously shuffled from foot to foot. He was a good lad – somewhat excitable, but extremely enthusiastic and a good spirit. A definite Spartan.

The show started, and I began watching Guigs intently. He had told me that Bonehead had given him a crash course in bass playing and to his credit he was there and he was actually playing along, in time to the rest of the band. I was impressed. A couple of covers and an unmemorable original composition and they were finished. I thought that Bonehead was a truly brilliant musician and I was also impressed by the fact he could play while completely smashed out of his face. I knew that I would add something different to the group's sound, so afterwards I agreed to join the cause and rehearsals were arranged for the following week.

The practices initially took place in Huts's garage in Burnage. The set slowly evolved. As well as the standard cover, 'Wild Thing' by the Troggs, we also developed six or seven original compositions that were penned by Bonehead and Huts. As the weeks passed, we grew as a group. It was a good feeling.

Somebody mentioned a hotel not far away and a receptionist who I'll call Caroline – not her real name. It seemed they were both very happy to have the band in them. A rehearsal room was secured immediately. The hotel was an unusual place: a magnificent Victorian building sat back proudly on the leafy tree-lined road, but it ran on a skeleton staff. We rehearsed there for nearly a year, yet never saw more than a handful of guests. Not that we were complaining. A generous receptionist and a regularly unmanned bar led to free love and free alcohol. When we weren't rehearsing in the basements we would be leapfrogging the bar upstairs. Musically, we tightened the set we already had, but there were no more creative moments. After a few months, and minus a drum machine, we felt ready to unveil a less programmable version of the band upon south Manchester. Our first couple of gigs were pretty impressive and the compliments were good. We also had the usual 'never heard anything like you before' line, though I guess that may not necessarily have been a compliment...

Buoyed up, we decided that The Rain were going to make something of their efforts after all, and as a result we started gigging more. We also arranged for demos to be sent out to record companies and the local media, as all bands do. No fucking replies. It didn't stop us, though, as we had the spirit and attitude that was running through the Roses and the Mondays, who were then at their height. Unfortunately, that same spirit and attitude had also mobilised a thousand other young bands, so competition was tough.

We decided to approach Anthony H. Wilson, the founder of Factory Records and also a local television presenter. The problem was that Mr Wilson fell on The List. Let me explain about The List. Manchester is a unique city in the way it judges and treats its celebrities. If you are considered to be what is locally known 'as up your own arse', you are put on The List. If the locals might happen to discover a 'weakness', which could be something as minor as hair colour or shoe choice, they would also put you on The List. At best, the qualification criteria were random. This contempt and attitude was everywhere, so there was plenty to go round as well. It was contempt bred by familiarity on the streets of Manchester. Everybody had an opinion and rather than adulate 'celebrities' they would front them. There was no divide. The bricklayer or football hooligan. The insurance clerk or the student. Everyone had the 'Roses' attitude. Anyone on The List that you encountered would be in for a barrage of abuse. Some friendly. Some not. On The List in 1990, alongside Mr Wilson, you could also find the likes of Mick Hucknall, Peter Hook and Terry Christian. It didn't take much to get on it, but it was damn fucking difficult to get off. When they received a volley of abuse, different List members reacted in different ways. Peter Hook turned mute but one look at his hairy face would tell you how angry he was. Terry Christian laughed. Mick Hucknall scurried away.

Tony Wilson, though, would always turn and offer something equally as vicious back. His raincoat would flap wildly behind him as he would turn to leave, arm left hanging in the air, his middle finger giving some out. Tony was one person who, over time, eventually got himself off The List and instead demanded respect in those who had previously berated him on the streets of Manchester. And he certainly got it. I fell into that crowd. Anthony H. Wilson had a more radical view of the music industry than any of those around him. Just to have the notion that you could have a contract of trust with a band and then actually put it into practice was astounding. But that was Wilson all over. Astounding. The group of corporate types who, at one point, were interested in buying Factory must have stood with their mouths open wide as Mr Wilson explained that his record company had not a single binding contract with any of its artists. This was after he had invited the corporates round to buy the failing record company. Not surprisingly, they didn't.

Anyway, we drove round to his house in Didsbury, hoping he didn't recognise any of us from the street abuse. I reckon he did. Guigs knocked on the door. Tony Wilson himself opened it. The boot was most definitely on the other foot, as he brushed us away with advice to send the demo tape to the office. Can't say we weren't trying, but we just needed that break. So we cracked on with the gigs.

* * *

'JD and coke, please.' This had become my drink of choice. It still is. It sounded more rock 'n' roll than half a bitter. I had just finished setting up my kit on stage at the Times Square pub in Didsbury, Manchester, and was watching as the boozer filled. It was a strange mixture of old regulars, the new annual influx of students, and the usual crowd of family and friends who now followed us. Manchester was that year's most requested university, breaking the stranglehold of Oxford and Cambridge for the first time. We had all cheered the news. It meant more women in the city. There was an element of Me Man You Student about the locals' approach to courting at that time.

Suddenly, the door opened and young Liam swaggered in. As usual, heads turned at the sight and sound of him. He walked in front of BigUn, talking very loudly over his shoulder to his large friend behind. Typical Liam. Always wanted the spotlight. BigUn laughed loudly at what Liam was saying. He might have been nicknamed BigUn, but he was no lumbering Lenny. This man was as sharp as they come, and let's just say self-confidence was never an issue. He was a Levenshulme lad of the West Point variety who was always capable of creating trouble in situations where no one else possibly could. As a relationship, Liam and BigUn were a strange combination, but one that would provide endless laughter and adventure.

I was standing at the bar when Liam spotted me. 'Have a fucking good one tonight, Tony,' he shouted, over Northside's 'Shall We Take a Trip'. I smiled back and asked him if he wanted a drink. He shook his head and said he couldn't buy me one back. Broke. I bought him and BigUn one anyway and they both marched off to find a suitable seat.

Guigs was already on stage and was looking nervous. Back then, he had taken to smoking a field's worth of weed before each performance, which helped his nerves. This wasn't always good news to the drummer, who relied heavily on the bass to keep time himself. Bonehead had already downed a small vineyard and Chris was having an 'artistic' moment. 'I've changed some of the lines in "Wild Thing", so just go with me,' he shouted to us over the music, once we were into our set. His lyrical rewrite? 'Wild Thing, I think I love you. Let's go and smoke some draw.'

I shook my head in disbelief as we finished that song and moved onto our topical tribute to the Strangeways Riots. 'We're Having a Rave on the Roof' was in full swing as I became distracted by Liam and BigUn at the side of the stage, arguing with two large, red-faced men who had accused them of stealing their pints. After a few heated words, and I'm sure physical threats, the accusers made off, leaving Liam and BigUn to smile and raise their stolen pints in my direction. Some fucking babies, I thought.

After more rehearsals in the garage, we played The Boardwalk twice, but although we sold it out I couldn't help noticing it was mainly family and friends, and friends of friends. The support was welcomed, but we weren't exactly setting the world alight. We had been together for over a year by this stage and our initial enthusiasm was beginning to wear thin. We got on well as a group of people and had become tight-knit as a band, but Guigs wasn't happy.

'Huts isn't doing enough to be a lead singer,' he said. Now, I liked Huts. He was a Spartan and you knew where you stood with him. I wondered just what Huts's review of Guigs's bass-playing might be. But to be fair, Guigs did have a point. Something just wasn't right. I wasn't sure if it was Huts or not, but something wasn't working. It was decided that after an exhausting six gigs, we should take a breather. Spend some time apart. You know, clear our heads. It was obvious that Guigs had ideas about replacing Huts that didn't sit well with me. I'd never been any good at skullduggery. I had always believed in being upfront and honest. I tried to plead a case for the singer.

'We should speak with him, at least. He's one of us.' Bonehead had wedged himself firmly on the fence, which would become his resident position, while Guigs said we should go away and think about it. So we decided to take a few weeks out and see what time would bring. I couldn't help thinking, though, that maybe I had only delayed the inevitable.

My suspicions proved correct. Time would bring a fascinating revelation for me, and a slap in the face for Huts.

* * *

'We've got someone who wants to join as the lead singer.' An excited Bonehead was on the phone.

'Oh yeah? Who?' I replied.

Out of the handset came: 'Liam. Liam Gallagher.'

It seemed that BigUn had been mentoring Liam and had advised him he had the makings of a great frontman. As

BigUn was aware that Huts was living on borrowed time, he had put Liam in touch with Bonehead. I had a silent chuckle to myself. I thought about Liam as the face of the band. He definitely looked the part. But what about the aggravation? He was a right handful. Fuck it. If we were gonna be a rock 'n' roll band, that was exactly what we needed. Although Liam had started to style himself on Ian Brown, with his haircut and swagger, he could never be accused of not being his own man. I'd last seen Liam at a Roses concert and the aggressive, cheeky yet lovable boy had transformed into an aggressive, cheeky yet lovable young man. If you needed front to get by in the music business, Liam had enough to cover the country. Something tells me we're into something good.

'Has anyone told Huts?' I asked.

'Guigs is gonna do it,' replied Bonehead. I thought to myself that that conversation wouldn't happen in a hurry. In the end, I took the time to let Huts know exactly what was going on, because no one else did. Understandably, he was very unhappy and couldn't see where it had gone wrong.

'It hadn't,' I told him and expected the whole band thing to come to a halt there and then. I thought it was the end, yet funnily enough it was only the beginning.

* * *

We'd arranged for Liam to come and audition at my place on Ryton Avenue in Gorton, on a summer's day in 1991. The audition panel would consist of myself, Bonehead and Gemma, my one-year-old daughter. We were sitting eagerly in my front room, waiting. Liam normally entered a room like a storm. He'd be blowing insults and compliments, throwing out opinions and judgements. It was just humour and a little insecurity, though, nothing dangerous. As I already knew him, I had given both Bonehead and Guigs a rundown; they had both seemed impressed. Bonehead walked through the door, his eyes red and still slightly askew from the previous night's exertions. Then a rather nervous-looking kid appeared – Liam – but shit, he looked the part. Pair of brown cords ripped at the knee with a denim shirt loosely flowing. Desert boots and smart haircut. Liam had a talent for wearing clothes from Debenhams and still actually looking cool. I waited for the verbal onslaught. But it seemed the belligerent attitude had been left behind in Burnage. He stood rather sheepishly at the living-room door. Then, all of a sudden, he jerked forwards into the room as BigUn put his hand in the small of his back and pushed firmly.

'Let's get this fuckin' show on the road,' BigUn said, with a smile in his voice. He stood there, rubbing his hands together, as Liam threw a playful punch at him. I had warmed to BigUn. There was a spark about him. Never one to settle for his allocated lot, he was always on the lookout for an opportunity or opening. And he had a big heart.

A successful audition was guaranteed from the start, I suppose. The way I figured it, we hadn't got anyone else. Bonehead hadn't brought a rhythm guitar, so picked up a battered, out-of-tune bass I had lying in the back room. My drum kit was at the rehearsal room, so I made do with a set of bongos. Me and Bonehead started to bang out some old tune that was unrecognisable to us, never mind Liam. In turn, Liam hummed a tune that was also completely unrecognisable to us. During all this, BigUn danced from foot to foot, displaying all the rhythm of a rusty robot. It had to go down as one of the most unprepared, unprofessional and useless auditions ever. But then again, we finished with one Liam Gallagher as our frontman. So maybe it was the best.

After a few rehearsals, in which Liam introduced some songs that he had been working on, we started to get a feel. It was strange at first with Huts not being up front, but we all recognised the fact that Liam had something about him. It might have been menacing and slightly evil, but it was still 'something'.

We had all now decided that we were going to 'knock fuck out of anything in our way'. This mission statement wasn't exactly hung on the rehearsal room wall, but we all understood and suddenly the confidence started to show in our performances. We were still rehearsing at the hotel, although we had been warned that we would have to be gone soon. It seemed the money pit had been sold and was soon to be demolished. When the time came for this move, we temporarily took up residency in The Grove in Longsight. This was a snooker hall turned Irish club, the same kind our parents had visited a generation before, though the frilled shirts had now been replaced by cowboy-style equivalents. Paul Gallagher had 'sorted out' our tenancy with the owner. We were never quite sure of the terms; we just gave the cash straight to Paul. This was where we would finally gel and begin to feel like a real act. Rehearsals had once again turned into an alcoholic free-for-all, with the bar being raided regularly. BigUn would be on lights and the PA desk and our rhythm section really started to come together; gradually, we began to create our own distinctive sound. Unfortunately, although we really enjoyed our time there, the discovery of our alcohol theft led to us being told to move on. From The Grove we headed to The

Greenhouse Rooms in Stockport. This was a purpose-built rehearsal studio and had its own backline (gear, amps etc.). We were developing original material now; 'Life in Vain', 'Reminisce', 'She Always Came Up Smiling' and 'Take Me' were the stand-out tracks. Lyrically, these songs were a collaboration between Liam and Bonehead. Guigs's bass playing was still basic, but he was steadily improving and the rhythm section of the band had developed quite a unique sound. And then there was the way Liam delivered the songs. The rest of us almost seemed to fade into the background; all our audiences seemed to be transfixed by our lead singer. Even at rehearsals. His nasal delivery and fighting stare would leave people enthralled and threatened, both impressed and nervous.

From the start, I didn't think Liam was happy with the name The Rain. I guessed as much when he said, in one long breath: 'It's a dogshit name. Any ideas, anyone? No? Right, we'll call ourselves Oasis.' The whole dynamic of the group had changed with him joining. Why not the name? It later transpired that BigUn had spotted the name on an Inspiral Carpets poster hanging on Liam's bedroom wall the previous evening. It sounded good to me.

And so Oasis the band was born. We rehearsed and rehearsed for the next eight months or so, during which time we all got to know Bonehead better. Most of his friends we already knew through BigUn and this was when the Entourage was formed, a group of mates and acquaintances who would provide us with back up and support.

The band would always maintain a positive spirit and quickly developed an 'us against the world' kind of attitude. We knew that we had a distinct sound as a rhythm section and everyone in the band thought that Liam had the charisma and natural personality to take it somewhere. Everyone except Liam, that is. He wanted to invite his brother Noel to join the group. Liam had already played a demo of Noel in a band called Fantasy Chicken and the Amateurs to us. In truth, it was not very impressive, but he did know a lot of people in the industry so we put him on a back burner.

CHAPTER 3

A DEFINITE MAYBE

Our first public outing as Oasis was in The Boardwalk, on Manchester's Little Peter Street, in late summer 1991; along with other clubs such as The Hacienda and The International, The Boardwalk provided an important live venue for many local bands. It was a warm evening and we were expecting a large turnout. Sweet Jesus and The Catchmen were also on the bill. We were also expecting Noel. Liam had invited him down and seemed genuinely excited that his big (little) brother was coming to see us. 'Lets' fuckin' make it a good one, let's show him,' he urged the rest of us.

With this in mind, we headed out onto the stage. Liam was extra menacing that evening. The audience stared back, at first unsure, then unable to remove their eyes from the frontman. We played and we were tight, but the set was pretty uneventful. After we had finished, Liam went out front to see Noel and ask him what he thought. 'Fucking shit,' came the reply.

Liam returned backstage, his fringe still stuck to his forehead with sweat. He was deflated after his brother's cutting two-word review. Then BigUn entered the room, smiling. 'Hey, your kid fucking loved that,' he said with a laugh. Liam looked at him quizzically and asked, 'How do you figure that?' BigUn then told Liam that Noel had been engrossed, excitedly telling his girlfriend just how much potential the band had. Noel just couldn't bring himself to tell Liam that. That news changed Liam's mood instantly and we were back on track. This was the norm from Noel, who seldom showed any positive emotion towards Liam. It seemed that Noel was also impressed with the rhythm section. We all knew that he was itching to join in, but we decided to let him sweat. We were sounding tight and definitely had our own unique sound. We also knew that Noel had a couple of songs he had written, which would give us a grand total of seven. It was the perfect match and one that Liam had longed for. But it was fun to make Noel sweat. The Noel version of events – which sees him joining armed with a clutch of hit records already penned, assuming the nickname 'the Chief' and immediately starting to dish out orders – is utter nonsense.

Bonehead's brother, Martin, was a much more serious man than Bonehead. Then again, everyone was more serious than Bonehead. Luckily for us, though, Martin had a job fitting out recording studios. His grammar school education had seen a much better return than Bonehead's. Martin had negotiated a deal for us at Out of the Blue studios in Manchester city centre. If we could plaster a few walls for them. they would give us enough use of the facilities to create a four-track demo.

Liam couldn't make it, so the following week me,

Bonehead and Guigs turned up in the Bonemobile – a Mazda 1800 pick-up truck that had a moulded plastic roof. Bonehead had painted this roof in a Jackson Pollock-like style, as a tribute to the Roses. It drew some very strange looks. We gave even stranger looks back. We had to plaster three walls and as this was Bonehead's trade, he took charge. After a couple of days' work, the owner checked the job and said he was happy; we had our recording time. I was surprised, because I noticed the spirit level that Bonehead was using had no bubble in the middle. Nothing was ever quite what it seemed with the man.

Liam had mentioned that Noel still kept hinting at joining us. He said each time he did so, he would ask him why he wanted to join such a shit band. Noel would mumble some kind of reply, but he'd never admit he thought we were good. I thought Noel joining would be a good thing. I hadn't really seen him since he had joined the Inspiral Carpets. In fact, no one really saw Noel after he joined the Carpets. I also felt that Liam was pushing for him to join our outfit not only to be his bandmate but I suppose to be his brother.

During a chat one lunchtime in Piccadilly Gardens, I sensed he seemed to be skirting around something, until finally he came out with: 'Why don't we replace Guigs with our Noel?' My first reaction was surprise, because Liam was a Spartan and I didn't expect that of him. My second reaction was to get angry. Controlling my temper, I reminded him that it was Guigs who had first set up this outfit. To Liam's credit, he looked guilty, and almost immediately backed down and apologised – unusual for him. I suggested a compromise.

'Why don't we have Noel join as lead guitarist?' I said. As that was his instrument of choice it made sense. Liam's guilt instantly evaporated; now he was animated. 'I'll go and tell him where we are recording,' he replied. Liam was incredibly proud of the work we had done and was genuinely thrilled about Noel getting to work with us. I thought I had made the best decision of my life and good times lay ahead. I told Liam to speak to Bonehead and Guigs first before speaking to Noel. He agreed and ran off with an excited look on his face. It was the best of decisions, it was the worst of decisions.

It was good to see Noel. It had been a while and we were catching up over Jack Daniel's in The Square Albert boozer. He told me about his girlfriend Louise, who worked for a music promotion company. He was deliriously happy when speaking about her, which I thought was a good sign. After Jack Daniel's had become friendlier with us, I began to notice a few more changes in Noel. He seemed surer of himself than he had before. I guessed his time with the Carpets had broadened his horizons, but it wasn't just that. He looked physically different. I'd seen the look before. A pale look. He had been whitened by a chemical snowstorm, so to speak, and had lost weight he could ill afford to lose. His newly found confidence also left him with an opinion on just about everything. It was as if he had morphed into his big brother Paul without gaining the stature or the girth. The jibes still came thick and fast and his face would literally crease with laughter. We talked about the band and how great a musician Bonehead was. He told me he had a few songs of his own that he wanted to slip in. He was genuinely excited, though, and was desperate not to step on Bonehead's toes. We headed off to the rehearsal room together and I felt it was good to have him back.

We plugged in and started playing. Noel stood looking intense in the corner of the studio, nodding his head in time to the music. The large white, woollen jumper he was wearing made him sweat profusely. He picked his guitar up and started to lay down some backing riffs for 'Take Me'. No one had asked him to, but it felt right. After the session we all welcomed him onto the good ship Oasis and he suggested that we start rehearsing at The Boardwalk. The Inspiral Carpets had a permanent berth there and a small rehearsal room had just become available. We all agreed. It seemed that, without any questions asked, Noel had integrated himself into the group as our lead guitarist. It felt good. There was never going to be a problem with us liking Noel as a person, as we already knew him. And as for Noel, I reckon he realised he had just found himself the perfect vehicle for his songs.

The cellar room at The Boardwalk resembled a dungeon. New mould grew over the old mould on the damp brick walls and there was a puddle of water where the concrete floor dipped in the middle of the room. I reminded myself not to plug anything into a wall socket. We decided that the place needed brightening up and so the following week we set about whitewashing the walls. Me and Liam stole two tins of bright white from B & Q in Ancoats and the four of us set about slapping it on the walls. We then had to stick posters up to break up the colour a bit, as we would all have been suffering from snow blindness otherwise. We also painted a Union Jack on the wall as a tribute to The Who. Noel wouldn't turn up until after the work was completed, but then offered to brush up in return.

We were rehearsing twice a week. Thursday and Sunday. Noel was still working for the Inspirals, so did not attend regularly. It wasn't the initial rush we'd been expecting. When he did attend, though, he brought with him three songs: 'Must be the Music', 'See the Sun 'and 'I Better Let You Know.' The first two were a disaster, with the nature of the songs not sitting with the style of our music at all. Within a couple of days, though, we'd met on 'I Better Let You Know'. The song suited my lazy drumming style and the dancing wall of strings from Bonehead and Guigs. Liam looked comfortable delivering the lyrics in his own unique way. Noel would go through the songs he had written and sing them acoustically. He would then run through the bass chords with Guigs as myself and Bonehead went to work on the drums and guitars. That was one method we had for creating the songs. We would also jam for hours, and record the sessions, then sit down afterwards and review the tapes in the hope that we could pick a particularly catchy riff or killer melody. The sound that Noel came with was akin to that of Johnny Dangerously, aka Johnny Bramwell, later of I am Kloot. He had also taken to dressing like him. Noel had a fixation with Johnny that would lead to him writing such songs as 'Take me Away'. But I suppose if you're gonna be fixated with someone, Johnny Bramwell is a good place to start. I've always admired Johnny's songwriting skills and consider him an unsung Mancunian genius.

It was a fine period of my life. The fact I was playing music always made me feel good. To be in a band with the kids I had grown up with made it all that more special. Noel had begun to offer little bits of advice that he had picked up from his duties in the big, bad world of the music industry. It was as if we had an advantage over any other band due to our closeness. At that time, other bands had been listening to our ramped-up rehearsals, which literally shook the door to the room. Noel's ability to draw upon others' tunes was evident even in those days and if he heard anything worthwhile from another room it would be developed as a new piece for us. We would sit and giggle mischievously on the other side of the door while BigUn would deal with any problems. This led to a number of altercations with the other bands sharing The Boardwalk. One evening we opened the door to find a note sellotaped to it. 'Find your own fucking riffs,' it read. We immediately banged on every door in the place, but no one was willing to admit to leaving the note. Don't blame them, really. Our aggressive, up-for-it attitude was evident for all to see.

The rehearsals had left my kit in a right state, though. I'd fixed it up enough times, but now reckoned that enough was enough. I needed a new kit.

* * *

It had been four months since our last gig and on 15 January 1992 we were back at The Boardwalk again, with Noel on stage for the first time. We played 'Take Me', an acoustic song that was an originally named, erm, 'Acoustic Song', and 'Columbia' which was in its infancy and had no lyrics. 'Columbia' had been born in a late-night jam. When we had reviewed the tape of the session, we had discovered this deep, ominous riff that really had something. The audience at The Boardwalk that night in January 1992 didn't think so, though, and once again the reception was ambivalent. People talked between songs and laughed at jokes, which was winding Liam up royal. I could see him staring out into the darkness, trying to identify who was showing him such disrespect.

A few days later, we were standing outside the drum shop on Deansgate, Manchester. Me, Liam and Noel stood staring at the plush red Pearl export kit that sat in prime position in the front window. Everything about it looked fucking great, except the price tag. Six hundred quid. It was a lot of money. As it happened, though, I had just received a tax rebate – probably the largest cheque I'd ever received up until then. Fate was definitely playing its part, as the rebate was also six hundred. Was someone trying to tell me something? I had already promised Paula that the rebate would go on tidying up the house for my new girl, which at the time had seemed fair enough, but now had begun to look like the wrong decision.

'I think you should buy it,' Noel told me. 'Look at it as an investment.'

I explained that the money was already spoken for, which received a withering look from Noel and a rather more sympathetic one from Liam.

'Look, when we are signed you will realise that it was worth it,' Noel insisted. Fuck it, he's right, I thought, and we marched in to the shop and bought the kit. This emptied me out and with Noel and Liam already on empty we didn't even have the taxi fare back to The Boardwalk. We loaded ourselves up, the kit distributed equally among the three of us, and headed off back down Whitworth Street West on foot. I was excited about my new purchase, but not half as excited as an exuberant Noel. 'It's a proper fuckin' kit. It's gonna make the difference,' he crowed. We soon arrived back and in no time at all we had the kit set up and I was banging away.

Rehearsals continued. It was problematic, though, as Noel was still with the Carpets and not around much. Liam was scratching at the dole office every second Thursday as well as valeting cars for BigUn. Bonehead was plastering and getting plastered. Guigs was practising how to roll various styles of reefers and still living at his mum's. I had to leave my job in insurance and had taken to working for a construction company on Strangeways prison, in Cheetham Hill, completing a refurbishment. The hours were long and hard, but the money was better.

I was on my way to prison to work one day. It was just after six in the morning and the streets were still quiet. We drove through the city centre. The back of the dark van was filled with the rest of the gang, most still weary from the previous night's drinking. The drinking had created a strange odour that had become trapped in the enclosed van. Add to the atmosphere the secondary smoke of at least five continual strainers and you had a fucking toxic and suffocating situation. At first I was relieved when the van doors were suddenly yanked open, letting in the grey morning air. Not relieved for long, though, when six heavily armoured policemen pointed pistols at us and started to shout very loudly that we were to put our hands in the air. There had been a spate of bombings by the IRA at around that time, and a dark blue transit van full of Irishmen was, not surprisingly, considered suspicious. One of the older men decided to have a pop at the policemen and started a rant about persecution in a West Country Irish accent that we – never mind the police – couldn't understand. After the police looked us over they became aware of the stench of stale alcohol, hurriedly shut the van doors and let us proceed.

A couple of years previously, the inmates at Strangeways had taken control of the prison and staged a 30-day rooftop protest. They were having a rave on the roof. The burnt and smashed prison wings had been redeveloped and fitted with new cells and I had to cement a small fitting into each of them. It took half a day to complete a job and there were 500 cells. All the cells were identical to the last detail and I was becoming bored rigid. I figured I would be at this for the next 18 months. Fuck that. I might as well be in fuckin' prison. I was sitting having my lunch by the thick wire security fence when I heard someone shout my name. I looked around to see an inmate grinning at me. At first I didn't recognise him. After a few seconds his smile started to slowly fade, but then mine began as I realised it was a washed-down and shorn Trampy Spike. (The lack of bed mattress hair or stench of urine had thrown me.) He shuffled over to me, looking around furtively. After I'd, ahem, saved his life, Trampy Spike had appeared regularly in the park. He always told people he owed his very existence on this planet to me. I lapped it up. We would all drink together but wouldn't share a bottle, if you know what I mean. Behind his shabby exterior, Trampy Spike was one of the most educated and enthralling people I'd met. (Not sure if that says a lot for him or a little for me.) He seemed to have experienced a lot and always had a story to tell you. At the time you'd often see various tramps passing through Levenshulme, and they would normally be harassed and poked. They, in turn, would spit and swear and on occasion lash back. Nobody treated Trampy Spike like that. He was highly regarded on the streets by people of all social standings. A community tramp, so to speak. He'd probably get a grant nowadays.

'What the fuck you doing in here?' I asked him. Trampy Spike was up close to the fence now. His fingers pushed against the steel mesh, making the tips turn white. He whispered back, 'I was cold, so I lit a fire in a house. For this I was jailed. They might be able to take away my liberty but they can't touch my soul.'

As I said, he wasn't your average run-of-the-mill hobo. He

could be a touch dramatic. For an hour, we sat and a somewhat reflective (or maybe just sober) Trampy Spike told me a tale. The story revolved around a boy who was born into a moderately successful family. After a good education he was guided towards a career in the medical profession. While at Manchester Royal Infirmary, he met a girl. This girl stole his heart and taught him much more than any university could. Her curriculum included long, hot summer days near her home in Macclesfield, feeding the down-and-outs from the Saint Vincent de Paul kitchens in Manchester, Led Zeppelin concerts, Greenpeace and herb gardening. He had never experienced anything quite like her. They had planned a trip to Switzerland, but before it could happen she said she had to tell him something. She began to speak, but then broke down and confessed that she had been fighting a bone disease that had been getting worse throughout her life. A recent letter had confirmed the worst and within three weeks the beautiful girl had shrivelled and shrunk and wept, then finally left this life.

He simply could not accept that this had happened. He began to sleep at her rented flat until the landlord discovered him and had him forcibly removed. He did not go back to the Royal Infirmary or return any phone calls or letters from his family, friends or colleagues. He moved out of his own flat and brought all his belongings with him. He burnt them all at a spot where he and his girl would sit at sunset in the glow of the evening. He steered clear of any places where he was known and slowly he faded from view. He lived off favours from generous strangers and also used the soup kitchens where he had previously helped out. From the low point to which he had fallen, he now found himself looking at those around him differently, and with what he had learned from his girl, he could finally recognise the goodness in people and the happiness in life's smallest pleasures. This was his way of surviving. Of keeping her alive. After a while, he found he could not face returning to his old way of living. He felt too much hatred and greed and pain was still there.

When he finished his story, Trampy Spike had tears in his eyes. He wiped them away and the glint returned, as did the smile. He lifted himself to his feet, dusted himself down and winked at me. He then made his way back to the confinement of his cell. The story of all his many years had been condensed into my lunch hour. But something had stuck with me. This penniless tramp, unjustly jailed, with nobody or nothing waiting for him outside, was still happy. And even after this he was not complaining; rather, he was trying to help other people. What the fuck had I got to worry about? In times of hardship or self-doubt, I could think back on that moment to see me through. As he had promised on that freezing cold morning behind the butchers, Trampy Spike did repay his debt.

After leaving the prison that day, I walked to the rehearsal rooms, where I told the band about meeting our old friend. Upon which Noel told me he'd read in the paper that Trampy Spike had been locked up for burning down an empty three-bedroom semi. It was the seventh house he had burnt down in a fortnight. Lying, fucking smelly tramp, I thought.

Before we finished that evening, Noel revealed he had some good news. We waited eagerly to hear what was coming. 'We're going on TV,' he said. Oddly, Noel himself seemed only half-excited by his own announcement. I was worried at that. Surely this was a big thing for us?

'Smart. What on?' I asked.

'Granada. It's Red Nose Day and we're gonna be supporting Alvin Stardust.'

This explained the half-hearted introduction. Alvin fuckin' Stardust. Whoopee.

'Isn't that the silly cunt in the gold-glitter jacket?' asked Bonehead.

'He's a fucking genius,' said Noel, leaving the rest of surprised to say the least. Well, almost the rest of us.

'Yeah, a legend,' piped up Guigs and received a funny look from Noel, who was slowly learning to read him.

Anyway, fuck it. TV exposure could only be good, even if we were supporting Alvin Housedust. It seemed that Alvin was not Noel's only unlikely musical influence. He also saw Abba as one of the greats.

I told Liam he might have to dress up as Pudsey, the little sick bear, and he stormed out of the room shouting, 'It's never gonna fuckin' happen!' We all roared with laughter.

We rolled up on the day in the Bonemobile to find that we were to use Alvin's PA and drum kit, which saved a right load of mither. We were also told to mime the track, which would be a first. With spirits lifted, we made our way to the replica Rovers Return (we were at the Granada Studio Tour location, which had been opened to the paying public) and started on the bar. If we only had to mime, what was the harm?

'Right, this is it. Everyone will be watching,' Noel announced. He was trying to warm us up for the gig. 'It doesn't matter if it's two hundred people in the crowd or two thousand. Just enjoy it.'

We burst onto stage, ready to be amazed. The steel roadside barriers were in place to control the baying mob of fundraisers and Granada staff. All 12 of them. Alvin was still in the back, applying a tub or two of wax to his fucking massive hair and getting ready to coo-ca-choo. Outside, Liam faced the crowd. As usual when nervous, Liam became defensive and was stood staring wildly at them. Even at this early stage he was perfecting his glare. Rather than a stadium of testosterone-filled males as an audience, though, he had members of the Salvation Army, St John's school choir and a handful of technicians. They all looked nervously back at the aggressive singer with the long hair and face like a hooligan, all set to attack. I laughed, as I knew that Liam meant no harm. Not sure if the little girl who was crying at the front did, though.

The cameras began to record as the compère faced the crowd and began, in his big showbiz voice. 'Let us now welcome Oasis who have just flown back to be with us from their tour... OASIS!' He swept his arm around and stood facing us with a cheesy grin. A bead of sweat slowly rolled from his brow and down his forehead as he was met by silence. We all just stared at him.

'We've just come from Burnage, dickhead. We ain't on fuckin' tour,' snapped Liam.

The crowd erupted in laughter, from the school choir to the Sally Army, as we launched into 'Take Me' and Liam stared the compère down off the stage. We performed more than adequately and received as much a response as you'd expect from a mimed performance to a crowd full of kids and ambulance staff.

After rounding up BigUn and the rest of our decidedly dodgy entourage, we headed off back to the Bonemobile. Just as we reached it, a brand-new Cherokee jeep burst past us, narrowly missing Liam. 'What the fuck you doing, dickhead?' shouted Liam after the vehicle.

The jeep screeched to a stop at the security gates, where we clocked the driver was Simon Gregson, who plays Steve McDonald on *Coronation Street*. The window rolled down and a hand appeared from the side of the jeep, making the internationally recognisable up-and-down motion indicating that one might masturbate.

'We'll see who's the wanker in a minute,' said Liam, and jogged towards the jeep. There was a look of panic on the actor's face as he spotted the lank-haired hoodlum getting ever nearer. With a frantic wave of his badge and a nervous smile, 'McDonald' sat revving his engine as Liam closed in. Still the barrier was not raised. The security guard waited until Liam was just upon the vehicle before he pressed the button to release the barrier and Simon Gregson screamed off into the night. The guard was beside himself with glee by this stage and gave Liam a wink before he burst into laughter, already watching the replay on his little TV screen. He waved us in and we all gathered round and watched a fine piece of method acting by Mr Gregson.

Despite agreeing to play with Alvin Stardust, our performance was not broadcast. We were devastated. Our big opportunity had been stolen from us by some musical philistine who simply did not recognise just how brilliant we were. If somebody at Granada can dust down the old tapes, I'd love to see that performance. In the bar afterwards, the feedback we got from our showing was positive but there were also a few questions from the same security guard we had been laughing with earlier, regarding somebody breaking into The Kabin on Coronation Street in an attempt to steal cigarettes. The culprit hadn't taken the time to consider the fact it was not a real shop and security had followed the discarded (and empty) packets of stage fags back towards to our van. You couldn't write it. I stared at BigUn, who looked back indignantly. (We'd thought it odd that he and the rest of our entourage hadn't been around when we'd been performing earlier.) As usual, all present denied any involvement whatsoever.

Strangeways had finally driven me insane, so I had agreed to valet cars for BigUn, which meant that me and Liam would be working with each other as well as playing in a band together. At one point, the whole group worked for BigUn and we were all grateful as this helped pay for rehearsal time and equipment. I know there were times when BigUn lost money on jobs but he took the hit and he still paid us. My first day working for him took me to Prestbury, Cheshire, just south of Manchester. It was a very affluent area and home to many of the local football players and soap stars. After very carefully cleaning the car of Keith Curle, the captain of Manchester City, I returned to the van, my work done. BigUn and Liam were waiting. Before we left Prestbury, though, BigUn handed Liam an invoice and told him to drop it off at a large house that he pointed out. As Liam crunched his way up the gravel driveway, we sat outside in the van. BigUn had that look about him.

'What you up to?' I asked him.

'Just watch,' he replied. 'It's not an invoice, it's a fuckin' love letter.' BigUn had written 'I think I love you Curly. I'm gonna make you mine' on a piece of card and had stuffed it in the envelope. He thought this was funny. All that was left now was for Liam to innocently deliver it. Liam rang the bell to the large house and stood moving from foot to foot as he awaited an answer. Slowly the door opened and out stepped Mark Hughes, the Manchester United and Wales football player. His tight curly dark hair was instantly recognisable.

The gel on his perm glistened in the afternoon sunlight as he greeted Liam.

Liam's blue blood left him unsure as what to say, so he simply handed the supposed invoice to him. Hughes opened it and then read the contents as Liam stood waiting. He quickly looked up and spotted us pissing ourselves in the van at the end of his driveway.

Fair play, Mark Hughes laughed and he turned the card to show Liam what was written on it. Liam read the card in horror and then began to stammer that he had no feelings whatsoever for Mark Hughes and how there was nothing wrong with curly hair.

'I think your friends are taking the piss,' said Hughesy with a laugh, and nodded in our direction. With this, BigUn hopped out and loped over, chuckling. After a brief chat, BigUn returned and we headed off back to Levenshulme. That meeting would prove to be an important one for BigUn, as through Mark Hughes's introduction he would become the valeter for Manchester United Football Club, which in turn kept the band in work.

A few days later, we headed off to Abraham Moss studios in Cheetham Hill to complete our first demo as a five-piece. We recorded 'Colour my Life' and 'Take Me' but it was a shambolic session, as became evident when we slipped the tape into the van's cassette player on the way home. *City Life* reviewed the demo in their Christmas issue, though the reviewer wrote that he was not too excited by the band. Thanks for that.

We each fired the demo around people we knew in the city. Noel told his contacts he was not even on the demo, as if he was ashamed. Not the greatest sales technique to use, I remarked to him. He then told us he had given the demo out to the smaller local radio stations, who agreed to give it some airtime. When he said 'smaller local radio stations', he actually meant hospital radio. I suppose that isn't the greatest demograph to target, as most of the listeners couldn't even get out of their beds to buy a fucking record.

So we weren't even at the starting line with the rest of the bands out there. The demo was the trade's standard way of getting yourself heard. I remembered reading that one particular A & R department would receive 300 unsolicited demos a week. There were five A & R departments in that corporation. That's 1,500 demos a week. There were six other corporations in the industry. That's 10,000 demos a week. Five hundred thousand demos a year. The whole UK music industry would sign, at most, 200 acts in a year. Out of those, you might get 20 acts who 'made it': got on stage or in the press; released a record or toured the country. Out of those 20, on average 10 of them will recoup the money that the record company had spent on them in the first place. The remaining 10 should earn enough to effectively retire. But every now and then an act would really hit the big time. And that was what we were aiming for.

* * *

We had rehearsed the arse out of the songs we had. We had recorded them and fired them out there. We had played the local venues. We had harassed any local contacts. It was time to try further afield. We had managed to book ourselves a spot at Dartford University for 19 April 1992. 'Let's see how the students like us,' said Noel.

We pulled up in the van to be greeted by a right firm. 'Thought this was a fuckin' student gaff?' Bonehead asked Noel. The audience was made up of really pissed students interspersed with what could only be described as angry football hooligans who had been poked with hot sharp sticks. The feeling of impending violence was already in the air. We played our set. The crowd were throwing insults and beer at Liam. Liam was goading them as he paced the front of the stage, arms by his sides chin in the air as if welcoming them onstage. Noel looked edgy, but I was pumped up and ready for it. Anyone who came within an inch of my kit was getting the drummer's punch. Liam kept on winding up the crowd, pointing at the spitting and frothing lunatics who tried to shout back over the wall of sound. I knew I could rely on Liam in a punch-up, and did so on many occasions. Anyone who came on the stage throwing them around was fair game and this was a rule we took seriously. We had always had that edge. I suppose that exalting the virtues of cocaine and alcohol and cigarettes as a band would attract some wrong uns, and fuck me it did, but we always held firm. (When I say 'we', I don't mean Guigs, who would adopt his hedgehog position as we defended our ground.) We finished the set and hurried off stage to be met by the promoter.

'We can't pay you for tonight,' he mumbled.

'You fuckin' can and you fuckin' will,' exploded Liam.

Noel stepped in now, as Liam was on edge from the performance and looked liable to boot off. 'Why can't you pay us?' he asked quietly.

The promoter looked at us, already prepared for the inevitable outrage, and began. 'Well, for starters, one of your group has stolen the charity money box from the bar.' He looked at us, waiting for a guilty look or twitch. All he got was comedy silence, as we all looked round at each other, eyebrows raised.

Liam then asked, aggressively, 'Who stole the money? Did you see? Do you have proof?' The promoter shook his head. The rest of the entourage gave resounding noises of downright indignation at this, as Liam continued. 'Don't go fuckin' hurling accusations unless you can prove it.'

With this sudden turn in the mood, the now sweating promoter quickly backtracked and said, 'We don't have any money to pay you. It's as simple as that.'

'You should have just said so,' laughed Liam, and then jumped at the promoter, taking a wild swing. The promoter back-pedalled and threw himself behind the gathering masses, who stood in anticipation of fireworks. I noticed that the crowd was mainly the football hooligan element from inside and they were simply waiting for the opportunity to arise. Liam squared up to them and I was tensing myself, getting ready to go. I weighed up the front of the crowd as I tried to pick my first. Anybody who was screaming never caught my eye. There was one ginger lad in a brown cord shirt, though, who was standing motionless, his eyes fixed on Liam. He had that excited smile the real bad bastards have. You could see his mind whirring, waiting for the right moment. He was the danger.

Noel suddenly piped up in an attempt to control the situation. 'No need for any of this.'

His arms were outstretched and he raised his eyebrows and cocked his head to one side. Now was not the time for reasoning, I thought. We were clearly outnumbered, but we gave some out anyway which made the crowd back off in surprise – that was how we were. Away day. I banjoed the ginger in the brown shirt as he made a beeline for Liam. The crowd's initial shock at the fact we had kicked off had now passed, and they had visibly increased in anger and confidence. Slowly, they began to head in our direction. We turned and made a dash for the fire exit, slamming the door shut behind us and holding the bar in place as Bonehead fumbled with the keys for the van. After letting go of the bar we ran and threw ourselves head first into the back of the van. Bonehead feebly revved the failing engine and we were away. The group from inside had tried to cut us off. Each turn around the campus brought a new group of vigilantes armed with a 'dangerous' assortment of mops and rakes. We laughed at the unfortunate choice of weapons. With the final swerve of the van out of the campus, a stolen money box rolled from under a bench and noisily spilt its contents across the metal floor.

'Dickheads,' said Noel.

I wasn't sure if he meant them or us. We laughed, when maybe we shouldn't have. The next time it would happen there would be close to two hundred people chasing us, and they would be throwing bricks instead.

* * *

By the spring of 1992 we were stationed at the training quarters of Manchester United FC, driving around in Mercedes, Porsches and Beamers that were worth hundreds of thousands. BigUn hadn't even fuckin' insured us. We were a disaster waiting to happen. But Liam didn't like waiting.

I was holding my sides, as the laughter had reached the point where it hurt. I was not much help to Liam, who sat in the front of the van next to me, looking proper unhappy. He had just shown me how he had used wire wool to clean the wheel arches of Paul Ince's brand-new Mercedes. It was a right mess. A fucking disaster of monumental proportions. I couldn't believe what he had done. He's a fuckin' madman, I thought.

'What the fuck made you clean it with that?' I asked, perplexed.

'I was trying to get the shitty tar off them. Wanted to do a good job,' came back a depressed reply.

He'd got the fuckin' tar off them all right. And the paint. And the primer. There were even curled shards of car metal pointing out of the wire wool that he was still gripping.

I was happy. I mean really fuckin' proper, ecstatic happy. We had finally made it! We were in *The Manchester Evening News*. Penny Anderson had submitted a positive article about us, with a photograph to boot. We were Mancunian famous.

I'd come home from work to find a stack of the newspapers sitting in the hallway, ready to be posted across the Irish Sea. The *Evening News* was the main barometer of any success for my mum and she had that look that mothers get when you have done something to make them proud. She ruffled my growing curly locks like I was a six-year-old again and hugged me. For all the attention and bullshit back-slapping that was to come, this was a moment that I would treasure forever.

* * *

Me and Bonehead were laughing. It was the summer of 1992 and we were in The Boardwalk and readying ourselves. That day, we were off to BBC Radio's studios on Oxford Road, Manchester, to record for *In Session*. It was a big day for us. It had been sorted out by a friend of Louise, which had left Noel in a deadly certain mood. 'Just be nice. No swearing or kicking off,' he politely advised us. Noel told us that his missus Louise had pulled a few strings and there would be murders if we took the piss. He was deadly serious, though, and went off to ring Louise and confirm he had relayed the news to us.

'Liam's gonna cause murders on the radio,' I said, with a laugh.

'Nah he'll be as quiet as a mouse,' replied Bonehead.

'How much?' I asked, hand already out. Bonehead shook.

Noel and Liam duly arrived, followed by an out-of-breath Guigs, who had been running as he was late. We had an hour or so in the rehearsal room. The show we'd been asked to appear on was *Hit the North*, hosted by Mark Radcliffe and Marc Riley. As Mr Radcliffe was holidaying, they had asked Peter Hook to help out that evening. Bad decision. One of The List. After Tony Wilson, I thought The List was gonna bite us on the arse again. We walked the short distance from The Boardwalk to Oxford Road studios, set up our equipment and got ready for our first public broadcast. We fired out 'Take Me', to polite applause from the hosts. Noel and Liam were asked for a quick question and answer session and agreed. Peter Hook started with a welcoming opening question, but Liam wasn't interested and ignored it.

'What the fuck are you doing wearing leather trousers?' he asked instead.

I laughed and thought that once again the Kid had struck. Peter Hook was wearing the look he was wont to adopt for List abuse. Hooky then told Liam he wouldn't be welcome in the Hacienda if he carried on like that.

'Give a fuck, mate. It's shit anyway,' came the offhand reply.

His first ever broadcastable sentence contained swearing and an insult. Brilliant. Bonehead looked over towards me unhappily as he put his hand in his pocket to retrieve my money. We waited in hope that the broadcast might have alerted some eager record company who had a nose for obvious brilliance. It didn't. Manchester's In The City festival was approaching, though, so it was back to rehearsals.

On 13 September 1992, we played the festival, our first, at The Venue, which we had all frequented throughout our youth; we were on with Machine Gun Feedback. It felt like we were the home team, which would surely give us some kind of advantage. In fact, it seemed to have the opposite effect. 'Too much like the Roses' seemed to be the general consensus. This left us all feeling a touch dejected. Noel wasn't happy with Liam's words for the crowd either. Liam had called one of the audience 'a fuckin' nonce', which hadn't gone down too well. I didn't see how Noel thought the ensuing argument between Liam and himself on stage might help our musical cause either. It was natural for the rest of us in the band, but we tended to forget how shocking it could be for someone else to see. Nothing was held back. I always knew that all Liam wanted was some recognition from Noel. And I also knew that it was the last thing that Noel would ever give him. The fact that their father was absent from the family home certainly didn't help matters, but both young men were angry for different reasons.

Noel was not a happy chappy. We were completely ignored by the In The City crowd. We were all disappointed, but tonight Noel seemed particularly dejected. He was standing at the doorway to The Boardwalk's rehearsal room, seething. Earlier that day he had parted company with the Carpets.

'Fuckin' twats. We're rehearsing five nights a week from now on. Fucking thick Oldham cunts,' he spat.

The cocaine didn't do good things for Noel and I was considering having a word, but not that night. It'd only end up on my lap. We all liked and got on with the Inspirals, but that day Noel drew another line. Us or them. It was a side of Noel I had not seen before.

Anyway, Cunt Balloon's (this was Clint Boon's new Noel name) decision to flirt [Mancunian for sack] Noel might just work to our advantage. If you could pull any positives out of his hate and anger, surely it would be that we would be rehearsing more. So we turned up the schedule.

Me and Liam also turned up the schedule working for BigUn. It had been one disaster loping after another, but at least it was amusing. Charles Talleyrand was one of the greatest diplomats Europe has ever seen, a Frenchman who was exiled from his country due to his precocious behaviour and took up residence in Levenshulme, of all places, during the late 18th century. One summer day in 1992, BigUn, Liam and me were sitting outside the General's garage in Talleyrand, a part of Levenshulme named after its former high-profle resident Frenchman. The car we were sat in belonged to another displaced Frenchman: Mr Eric Pierre Cantona. The car was also slightly modified due to the fact we had the driver's door strapped with a piece of old rope to the roof.

The General stood in front of his garage – Bonehead's best friend and a true Spartan. So we had called in a favour. Cantona had just arrived in Manchester and had been befriended by BigUn. As Cantona's car had needed new tyres, BigUn had offered to help out. Then, in an attempt to make a few bob, rather than take the car to the approved and authorised garage, or even to the General, we had bobbed along to see a friend of BigUn who could do the job on the cheap. As they raised the car to fit the new tyres, however, it had fallen off the hydraulic ramp. BigUn had also left the driver's door open, which was ripped off in the fall and thrown across the garage floor. He stared at me with absolute horror on his face as the door rocked to a halt on the concrete.

'Oh my good fuckin' God,' he began. This started the first bout of hysterics from me and Liam.

So we turned up in Tallyrand, door on roof. The General, real name Jimmy Regan, looked at BigUn as if he had lost his mind. 'You want me to weld a whole fuckin' door on so that it looks like it has never been violently ripped off? On Eric Cantona's brand spanking new Mercedes? In the next hour?' he asked, with wide eyes.

BigUn replied, 'Yeah. If you could.'

'No. I fuckin' can't,' came the quick reply. Ten minutes of cajoling later, the General reluctantly gave in and took the car into the garage. After much banging and grinding and a hasty spray job, the car was returned looking as if the A fuckin' Team had fixed it up. Me and Liam started another bout of hysterics. Actual physical pain through laughter. BigUn, though, looked like he had been run down by a truck. He eventually righted the wrong, but would never ever tell us just what it cost him.

The band's rehearsals were going well and we were still playing The Boardwalk, but not actually getting paid. We were simply paying off what we owed in backpay for the rehearsal room. Each week we would flee using various exits and methods in an attempt not to pay for the room. We never considered the fact that all our equipment was still there, or that we would be coming back to rehearse again. Forward thinking wasn't a band strongpoint.

It was both mentally and physically exhausting, but it was in aid of something good. We were finding ourselves and the songs were getting tighter and tighter. Initially, I had wondered if the sound we had created would sit with Noel's songs. But rather than making them weaker, it seemed to add something extra. This, coupled with Liam's vocal, also changed the punch of the package. To Noel's folk-tinged sound, Liam added venom and danger.

Other bands had taken to hanging around our door. 'Whose song is that?' they would ask.

'It's an Oasis song,' we would proudly reply.

It wasn't that long ago they were trying to rip the piss out of the 'covers' band, as they dubbed us. We also now had a group of young women who had taken to hanging round the back. The group seemed to grow all the time, and they would hang on Liam's every word. Things were looking hopeful.

I had not yet realised my dream of a less chaotic place to live, though. I had taken to living on Fort Ardwick, which sat on the edge of the city centre and had become known locally as Baby Beirut. As in all such areas, they had good and bad. One of the good elements was a neighbour called Charlie Farley, known locally as the Rusk, who was friendly with a guy who was head of A&R for a local record label. Charlie promised that he would speak to his guy about the band I was in, although this was the type of promise I heard regularly. But Charlie was true to his word. He returned a few days later and told me he had organised it. A tie-slacks-and-shirt man and a stunning female colleague came down to see us at the rehearsal room one evening. They smiled and they left. They didn't come back. If they had returned in three months' time they would not have recognised the band. We were about to embark on a brief period that would shape us forever.

This was a critical point in the development of Noel as a songwriter. And us as a band. Up to now, we had a set that consisted of mainly heavy punk rocky affairs – 'Rock 'n' Roll Star', 'Columbia' and 'Bring It on Down'. Noel had met a band called The Real People through the Inspiral Carpets. They were as stereotypical Scouse as you could imagine and had a hit record called 'Window Pane' during the baggy scene in Manchester. They had used some of the money they made to open their own recording studio (called, logically enough, The Studio) in Bootle. In autumn 1992, Noel had asked them if we could use it and they had, rather surprisingly, agreed. In return, we offered to let them produce anything that they found interesting. Such generosity was typical of the band as people. And so we were off to Liverpool. Fucking bring it on.

There had been a violent and explosive rivalry between Manchester and Liverpool over the decades, but personally I had nothing but admiration for the Scousers. I think it all began when the Mancunians decided to build the Ship Canal, which rendered Liverpool useless as a port to Manchester, then the largest industrial city in the world. Over time, this ill feeling carried over to supporters of the football teams of each city and over the years many a pitched battle had been fought. It was difficult to get ambushed in Liverpool, though. The swish-swish of acrylic always gave the shellsuit-clad hooligans away. (Only joking, La...) As I say, I've got a deep respect for Liverpool. I can't think of another city in this country that has the ability to unite against any injustice that the rest of the country had chosen to ignore. From Thatcher to *The Sun*. And fuck me, they've paid for it.

We drove up the East Lancs in the van. Liam was already hypered and was jumping around excitedly. The road into Liverpool was lined by Edwardian houses long past their prime, a passing nod to a time when the city was a thriving port; they still stand derelict, to this day, a testament to Thatcher's regime and Blair's recent daydream. We arrived at a rundown shack near Bootle docks. The surrounding buildings were derelict, bar one. The To Let sign on that solitary building had been adapted to read 'ToiLet'. Appropriate, really. We parked up. Luckily for us, the van we were in wasn't worth thieving and the hub caps were already long gone.

We had soon unloaded and were in the studio. The Realies stood before us. Tony and Chris Griffiths were the two songwriting brothers who formed the nucleus of the band. Tony and Sean were the drummer and rhythm guitarist, respectively. They welcomed us with a blast of hashish smoke and four crooked smiles. I already felt at home. Tony Elson, the drummer, was a proper character and looked as hard as nails. We got on immediately, which I was very glad about.

We then got down to business in the eight-track studio. It wasn't long before Liam's personality had won the band over. 'Frankie Goes to Fucking Hollywood,' he said with a laugh. He was shaking his head as he reminded the band of the city's musical heritage.

'The Beatles,' came back The Real People.

'Fair enough,' said Liam, 'but what about The Farm?'

The band held up their hands in mock surrender and we all fell about laughing. The next three months would be spent educating ourselves around all things rock 'n' roll. The Realies had just come down from their trip as we were about to embark on our own. Their experiences and advice were drip fed to us over this period.

The next three months would see us change the way we rehearsed, the way the songs were constructed and the way

Noel composed his lyrics. The 'Real People' sound is probably most evident on tracks like 'Don't Go Away' or 'All Around the World'. It was a departure from the brash punk of 'Rock 'n' Roll Star' and 'Bring It on Down', but it was one that would change our fortunes forever.

It was our second week in Bootle with the Realies. We had that comfortable thing already and we just knew that we could produce something good here. Liam was frustrated, though. He wanted to write a song. One of our earlier rehearsals had developed into 'Columbia', a simple instrumental that needed finishing but we still rolled it out live. Liam sang a melody quietly to himself while Chris Griffiths plucked away on his acoustic.

Liam suddenly raised his voice: 'There we were. Now here we are. All this Confusion. Nothing's the same to me.' Chris Griffiths asked Liam to repeat this line over and over, then joined in, in a higher pitch, with, 'But I can't tell you the way I feel because the way I feel is oh so new to me.'

Crash, Bang, Wallop. Oasis and The Real People collided. It sounded bang-on, and in the next couple of hours it was completed. Chris threw in a few 'yeah, yeah, yeahs' as his Liverpudlian marker and Liam pleaded his Mancunian 'C'mon, c'mon, c'mon' and we had another new song. We headed back to Tony Griffiths and Noel and sang the new melody and lyrics to them. We told him that Chris had come up with it. Noel looked proper chuffed and was immediately repeating the melody. Liam then proudly told Noel he was involved in the writing as well. Noel's smile seemed to vanish as quick as the light after the flick of the switch.

We were duly introduced to the Griffiths family, which included his cousins Digsy and Steve. They were on another planet altogether. It was like a carnival when they were present and their banter and general comradeship was infectious. As a group of people they had a spirit and bonding like no other I had seen.

Liam still had his share of frustrations to bear, though. He was wearing cans for the first time in the studio. A set of headphones enabled you to listen to a backing track but would also relay your voice as if recorded. This could be quite unsettling at first. Chris Griffiths was standing in front of Liam, trying to convince him that it had to be done.

'I don't like the way I sound,' Liam said. 'It puts me off me singing.'

Chris replied simply, 'Just don't think.' It worked. In no time at all Liam was comfortable and started singing away. Insert your own jokes. Over the next day or two, Liam's voice underwent a transformation. He mimicked Chris's elocution and Scouse drawl in his own Mancunian style. The slightly over-pitched teenage warbling he had arrived with suddenly changed into a more growling and brusque delivery. It suited both the songs and Liam himself. This style would be encouraged further down the line by Creation Records boss Alan McGee, but it was Chris who first taught Liam how to sing that way.

As Chris worked with Liam in one part of the studio, Tony was mentoring Noel in another. The songs we arrived with were being torn apart and restructured in front of our very eyes. Chris had shortened every song we had. He also gave Noel advice on song structure, which became very evident in his writing from that point.

'It has gotta be no longer than four minutes, simple,' Chris Griffiths would drawl.

This had meant that we had to get rid of most of Noel's long guitar breaks, which we were all happy about – bar

Noel. Chris also devised bridges to lead the verses to the chorus, which instantly gave the songs more structure.

The songs that we developed in this period would make up the backbone of *Definitely Maybe*. We entered the session with a small set of songs, but we left with the first album nearly written. I can't give enough credit to Chris and Tony, who shaped not only the way Noel composed his lyrics but also taught us all to structure and enjoy music. We spent over three months with The Real People and without them we would never have created *Definitely Maybe*. Or *(What's the Story) Morning Glory?*. Or *Be Here Now*.

The Griffiths boys were like a musical factory. After each session they would invariably sit us down and play us something new that they had composed. I clearly remember a fantastic ditty that Tony had knocked together on his keyboard. It was a string arrangement and as catchy as anything. This melody would be later used by Noel as he constructed the single 'Whatever'. On top of this there was also 'Columbia', 'Rocking Chair' and 'Don't Go Away'. All songs that were 'inspired' by The Real People.

We left after three months of sheer lunacy, bedlam and mind-bending sessions. The band was tight and we'd never sounded as good. We'd had a new set of songs and Noel was still working on ideas borne there. We headed off down the M62 in the van unaware that we would be returning to record our first single, with The Real People, less than a year later.

We also started to travel a little further afield, with gigs at The Venue – which was 500 yards away – and the Hippodrome – which was at least 5 miles from Manchester. The new songs were warmly welcomed by the punters and we felt we had really been through a sea change. The excitement in the faces of people in the audience now looked genuine. We all knew we were onto something. One thing you were guaranteed on a gig night was an adrenaline- and substance-filled Liam. 'Like fucking Worzel Gummidge,' Bonehead had complained, 'Different head every night.'

One evening in rehearsals, Noel revealed he was ready to show us the song he had told us he was keeping under wraps in the Bootle studio. He then went on to play 'Live Forever'. When I say Noel could blow us out of the water with his compositions, I mean it. You know if a song has potential the first time you hear it. 'Live Forever' was a simple piece of brilliance and the best offering to date from Noel, in my opinion. Liam had a look of pride in his eyes and kept glancing at each of us with a broad smile on his face. It was his 'I Told You' face. And he had. He had shown faith in his brother. This was a completely different style of song to what Noel had come up with in the past. Enjoy the simple things in life, I thought, as I began to develop a drum pattern for these pieces of brilliance Noel called songs.

'Live Forever' was the icing on the cake of what would prove to this day to be Noel's most productive songwriting period. Since our arrival at Bootle and the work with Chris and Tony Griffiths, we had in the bag 'Whatever', 'Acquiesce', 'All Around the World', 'Cloudburst', 'Fade Away', 'Cigarettes & Alcohol', 'Up in the Sky', 'Married with Children' and 'Digsy's Dinner'. The Griffiths brothers would also contribute to 'Supersonic', but that was yet to come. Add to that 'Live Forever', which was born in Bootle, and we had an exciting and diverse body of music. From the moment we all sat and played back these songs, we knew something would happen. It was a matter of 'when', not 'if'. We knew it and the Realies knew it. We were good. Real good.

CHAPTER 4

ALL FOR ONE AND ONE FOR ALL

We were all thrilled about how good we now were and had decided to take the new songs somewhere new. When we heard of a possible gig in King Tut's Wah Wah Hut in Glasgow, we were well up for it. We had managed to hawk together £200 to hire a van. With the other three in the front and myself and Guigs sprawled across the amps in the back, we made the journey to Glasgow on the last day of May 1993. We headed a two-van convoy that, behind us, included BigUn and a right firm in a transit on loan from Salford Van Hire. This van would double as both transport and accommodation if necessary. We all had the same intentions: a good night out. I suppose at that point it was just another gig in another town on another day. Obviously we hoped to create some interest and see the audience reaction at an out-of-town gig, but I guess no one could have predicted just how fateful this gig would be.

Eventually, we found King Tut's, but we weren't greeted at the door as expected. The promoter told us he already had three bands playing and the line-up was full. We told him we were Oasis from Manchester, as if that meant something.

'Neva heed of ye, now feck off,' came the reply, in thick Glaswegian.

The wrong thing to say to a vanload of hooligans cum musicians who've spent their limited money getting there, and taken a day off to boot... BigUn starts the questioning. 'Who owns the club, dickhead? Get him out here now. Tell him his club is getting fucking razed. Don't be a smart cunt. Sort it out.'

A verbal barrage, the arrows of mob rule. The door staff were shocked by the onslaught. So, as if doing us a favour, they let us in. There was a small crowd present and we made our way to the stage and set our gear up.

We played our set to an ambiguous reception. Four songs. Liam was on form, though. His blue-and-white Adidas tracksuit top was zipped to the hilt and his stare was as intense as ever. Like a jungle cat weighing up its prey, he stared the audience down. Four songs, that was it. Polite clapping with the occasional overenthusiastic holler from our corner. Exit stage left. After a quick towel down, we headed straight to the bar. JD and coke, JD and coke, JD and coke. We were all intent on getting nailed as it was gonna be a long journey home. It went faster if you were smashed. We were standing on a raised section of the club, looking out over the dance floor, when a strange-looking guy with a flash of red hair stumbled up the steps towards us. He had obviously downed a few, although his eyes carried an alertness that suggested he was mixing the alcohol with bugle; he was older than us and was dressed like a pretentious twat. Standing in front of Noel, he started to talk. I could hear his thick Scottish accent, but not what he was saying. Noel tried to push our demo tape to him, but the ginger fella refused. Oh well, I thought, at least he's trying.

Noel sidled over after his chat and we hit him with questions. 'Who the fuck is he? What did he say?

Noel whispered, 'McGee, Alan McGee, head of Creation Records. He's just offered us a record deal.' He imitated McGee's Scottish accent as he said this. We all fell about laughing. Now, I would normally have taken this offer with a pinch of salt. We'd been offered all sorts previously that never came to fruition. But Noel's excitement was infectious. 'Right, he's coming over. Act cool. Act fucking cool,' Noel hissed through his teeth.

As we all stood there trying to figure out how to look cool in the dark of the club, McGee ambled over. He introduced himself and then started warbling about how we were going to be the biggest band in the world, bigger than The Beatles. These statements would be repeated like a mantra for the next 10 years. For some inexplicable reason, we all genuinely felt that this was a monumental moment. The beginning of something special. Even if the guy was half smoked, coked and poked and didn't want to accept our demo, we felt that something was right. With the help of The Real People, we had the songs. With the help of our upbringings, we had the attitude. But most importantly, we had the belief. Not a whimsical half-hearted belief, like so many other bands, but an almost certain one. Here we fucking go.

And it was no longer just us. We now had Alan McGee on the team. With McGee came an attitude and a mentor figure for Noel. It was McGee who put one arm around Noel's shoulder as the other painted the bright lights flashing Oasis in the air. McGee's influence over Noel Gallagher should never be underestimated. In the next few weeks, Alan McGee would reveal himself to be as imposing and influential a figure as I had ever come across. He would appear in dressing rooms, recording studios, at gigs, at aftershow parties. He would normally be on a cocktail of alcohol and mind-altering substances. He would always create a scene and proclaim us as the saviours of the English music industry. But more importantly, he would stir the imagination of Noel Gallagher, at whose he feet he would lay the glory. This acclaim certainly matched Noel's own ideas about himself and his ambitions, and so the new Noel was born. The introduction of a record contract and the financial allure was just all too intoxicating. The Noel of old had left us and a new one had arrived. I found out that I didn't really like the new Noel and I know now that he didn't much like me. In fact, he didn't like many people.

The first man Alan McGee introduced us to was The Man Who Can. The Man Who Can was under instruction to turn us into the most reckless and wild rock 'n' roll act in town. His name derived from the fact that he was the man who could provide everything we might need. The first ingredient he introduced to the mix was pure, undiluted cocaine. Not available on the streets of Manchester, but available to us on demand. He would cater for our every need and actively encourage us to party. He was an extremely likeable chap, which I suppose was a pre for his role. He got on with the whole band and could also be used as a barometer of popularity. He would divide his treats equally between the band and would always be on the lookout for you.

'Do you want a taxi? What about her? Do you like her?

Do you wanna key? Do you wanna drink?' At aftershows he would circle around us on constant loop, just to ensure we were sufficiently provided with an endless supply of vice and debauchery. Any subsequent fallout from all this drink and drug consumption would be leaked immediately to the papers.

We didn't actually sign on the dotted line; we were simply told we had a record contract. We were going to be invested in and would get to record all the material from the Bootle sessions. I was absolutely fuckin' ecstatic.

We arrived at rehearsals to find Bonehead missing, as he was packing cardboard boxes at home, all set to move house. This was the first rehearsal Bonehead had missed in three years. Noel was not happy. At first we thought he was joking as he himself had missed most of the rehearsals for the last 12 months. It seemed he wasn't.

'I don't give a fuck,' Noel told Bonehead over the phone. 'Either get down here or I'm gonna sack you.' His eyes then widened as Bonehead told him what he thought of him and also informed him he was on the way down to kick his fuckin' head in. Noel laughed this off, but you could see the fear darting away behind his eyes. We made our way outside to await the impending arrival of Bonehead. We waited in silence – but for the occasional fart from the ever-flatulent Guigs.

'You should stop eating at that takeaway,' Noel joked as he shuffled nervously, trying to make light of things. But you could see the tension in him. Liam told him that he shouldn't speak to people the way he did. Before Noel could reply, Bonehead rattled round the corner in his white Austin A40, which had been built in the fifties. His windows were down and he rolled towards us slowly. You could hear the intro of

House of Pain's 'Jump Around' screaming away. I was thinking that maybe Bonehead was gonna do a really slow drive-by, when the car pulled to a halt. He hopped out, his face red with rage.

'Who the fuck do you think you are?' he started. 'You can't fuckin' sack me.'

He then blasted Noel, who stood there wearing a sullen look. You could see that Noel was not really listening to him. He was just trying to figure out how to get away from a potential slapping. Bonehead was not a happy man and looked like he was about to start swinging.

Liam then jumped in and defended Bonehead, which gave Noel a timely and dignified escape route. 'Yeah, you fuckin' support him,' Noel hissed at Liam and turned on his heels. I suppose this was the first indication of how New Noel perceived himself. We were all shocked. Including Liam.

* * *

The 'masterplan' was first mentioned in Noel's flat; he had moved into India House in Manchester city centre with his girlfriend, Louise. Noel was extremely proud of his city-centre living, as it moved him away from Burnage. I would drive over after I'd finished work and we would hang around until it was time for rehearsal.

BigUn was already there when I arrived. From the speed and content of the conversation between him and Noel, I guessed they had already started on the white line. Louise, as ever, was at work. She worked in the music media and had met Noel through the Inspiral Carpets. She was a genuine and likeable girl who had time for everyone. I was thinking that there would be hell to pay if anyone else in the band turned up for rehearsals changed out of their minds but, hey, there you go. At that time, it was curtains if you missed a rehearsal – as had been proved in the Bonehead incident.

'I have a masterplan,' began Noel. When he said 'I', everyone present thought he probably meant Alan McGee. He then began to explain how we could guarantee certain success for ourselves. 'It's the media that sells records, not the band. We need to be more cocksure than the Roses, more fucking mental than the Mondays and at least make sure we've got better tunes than Cunt Balloon. And we've got Liam. It's a simple game, get with it, boys.'

It seemed that both McGee and Noel sometimes had a low estimation of the average music-buying fan. Noel often called them 'sheeple'. I laughed and told him that good music was surely the most important factor. Noel shook his head and replied, 'All we've got to do is give them something they can relate to. If we keep telling everyone we're the best band in the world, sooner or later they're gonna believe it.'

'What's the rest of the masterplan?' I ask, half teasing.

Noel went red and shifted on his feet. 'It doesn't matter,' he muttered. It seemed as if he had suddenly become defensive about what he had told us.

We made our way to The Boardwalk for rehearsals, but it seemed that Noel's mind was somewhere else. After a poor evening, when we drank and smoked more than we played, we decided that we should pack up and go for a drink in the boozer. We headed off to Dukes in Castlefield, where we scraped enough together for a session. When we'd spent the lot, we headed back to Noel's flat to finish the chemicals that had been started earlier.

After we finally stumbled through the door, Noel began to tell us how Alan McGee knew he was special. How Alan McGee had plans for him. How Alan McGee had told him that, without him, the band was nothing. I looked at BigUn, with my eyebrows raised. I suspected that Noel was divulging more information than he should due to the evening's drinking and coke consumption. BigUn smiled back and shook his head. He then urged Noel to continue. Noel told us how McGee was going to get him a Rolls-Royce and had talked about how mega stars (such as he would become) sometimes even got knighthoods.

It seemed that Noel and Alan McGee were now thick as thieves but I noticed that Noel had started talking about just him and not the band as a whole. I asked him, 'What the fuck would a working-class lad from Manchester do with a knighthood?'

Noel told me that I would never understand. He was probably right. Everything we stood for had been based on revolution and being against the establishment. We sang about drugs and fighting. All our lives. We were the underclass. We came from the north of Thatcherite Britain. From the city. We left the city centre in the early hours and through the familiar rain jibbed the train back to Levenshulme.

The transformation of Noel from a fairly level-headed friend and bandmate into a possible nominee for the Queen's New Year honours list had been a rapid one.

We were asked to read up on all things Beatle and to this end books were purchased and records continually played. Liam took the piss by telling Noel only to refer to him as John, as in John Lennon. He also talked in a Scouse accent for three days solid, which Noel didn't find very funny. The Beatle sound that McGee had jumped on was a direct result of The Real People's melodic Scouse influence.

The following evening at rehearsals, we laughed at Noel's

Above left: Levenshulme, Manchester, 1979 – already perfecting the vacant stare. With Ged and Adi McCarroll, my two greatest comrades. I'm the one on the right, Adi is in the middle and Ged is on the left.

Above right: Ireland, 1977. The Quality Street Gang. The McCarroll and Donnelly clans would create a proper racket with a host of impromptu instruments. That's me, banging on the empty chocolate tin.

Below: Levenshulme, Manchester, 1988. Dolan, McCarroll, Croke, McGuigan and Mannion. I guess the names give an indication as to why it was known as 'County Levenshulme'.

Bonehead and Dave Rayson in Corfu, 1984. *© J Regan*

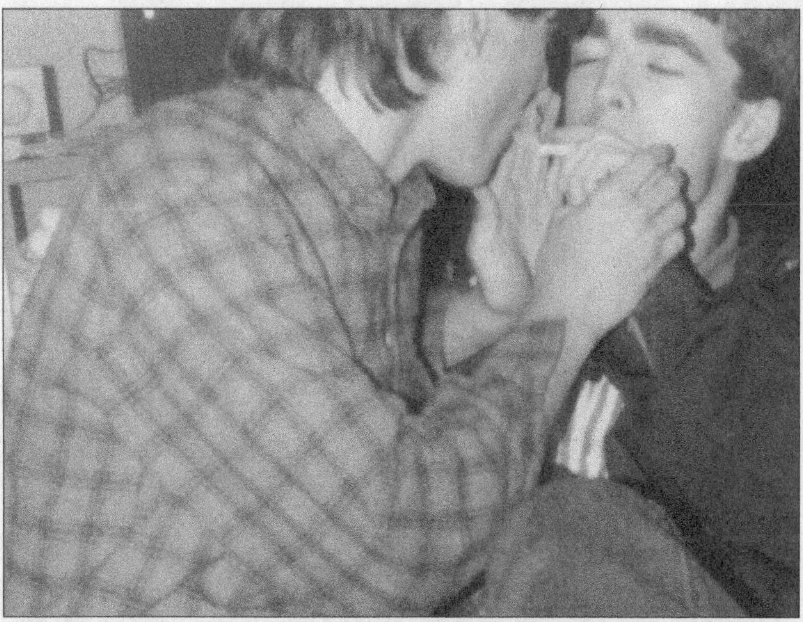

Above: The famous Breshnev Blowback. © P Ashbee

Below: Bonehead and the General – Didsbury, 1986. © J Regan

Burnage, 1993. Liam outside his mum's on his beloved scooter.

Liam with Evan Dando, who became an honorary member of the band, at his own insistence.

Above: The Fleece and Firkin, Bristol, March 1994. The happiest place in my life. Behind my kit, that is, not Bristol. © Paul Slattery

Below: Another inspired performance at The Venue, New Cross, London. © Paul Slattery

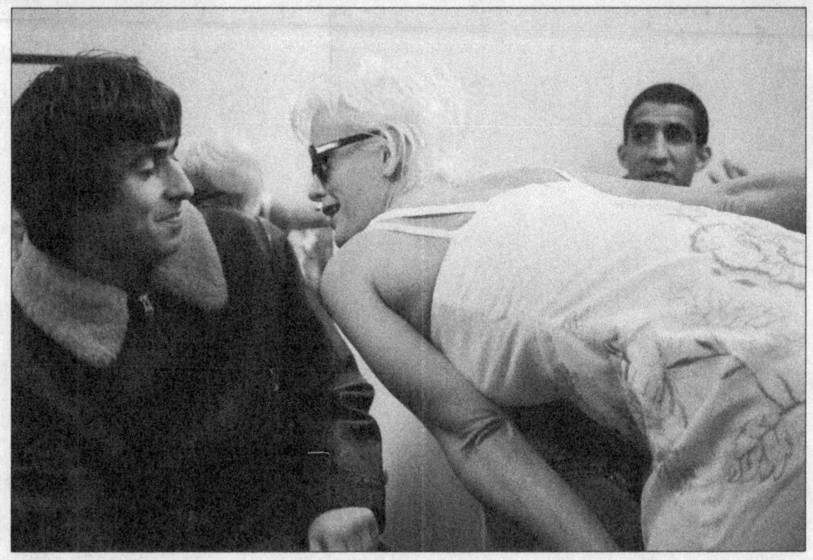

Above: *Top of the Pops*, June 1994. The looks are up front for once. I sit coiffured and heavily plastered in make-up as we perform 'Shakermaker'. My rather pasty-looking colleagues got at least a month's worth of piss-taking out of this. The piss-taking stopped as soon as *Face* magazine made us all wear eyeliner for a photo shoot.

Below: Back off, tiger. There was a definite chemistry between Liam and Paula Yates.

The Columbia Hotel, London, 1994. A few hours after this photo was taken, we were banned from the hotel after the contents of our room landed on the hotel manager's car below. We all took the rap but no prizes for guessing who the real culprit was.

fragile state and referred to the chat about the masterplan. I poked fun at his desire to get himself knighted and declared my admiration for LS Lowry, a local artist who had turned down more honours than any man in the history of this country. Liam asked what I was talking about, so I began to recall the previous night's conversation.

Liam listened and then we started to sing 'Matchstalk Men and Matchstalk Cats and Dogs', maintaining the LS Lowry connection. Everyone roared with laughter.

After the success of the first two Oasis albums, Alan McGee partly fulfilled his prophecy by buying Noel a chocolate-coloured Rolls Royce, as promised.

If I was ever to refer to the masterplan again in the future, 'Shut the fuck up' would become the standard response from Noel. I guessed we were right in thinking that he had never meant to give so much away.

By nine that evening, we'd polished up 'Cigarettes & Alcohol' and it was now a great fuckin' song to play on. We'd laughed our arses off when we'd first started rehearsing it in Bootle. Bonehead had shouted, 'Whoah, whoah, we can't play that!'

Noel stood in the corner, looking indignant. 'What the fuck do you mean, we can't play that?' he asked.

'It's T.Rex, for fuck's sake. Everyone's gonna rip the fucking piss.' Noel stared Bonehead down and then started the riff again, only louder. He did not take any notice.

After rehearsal Noel said that he wanted us to stay out of Levenshulme. No drinking there and no socialising. The band and the entourage were from Levenshulme, so this would cause murders. But Noel knew that. I thought that I shouldn't have poked fun at the masterplan, and we definitely shouldn't have sung the Lowry song.

Alan McGee planted the seed, but couldn't be around to watch it grow. For starters, he got himself caught up in the Los Angeles earthquake, which shook his equilibrium in more ways than one. His energy had driven the band on no end. His work had left us with different Noel, though, and with this there would be casualties aplenty. The first indication of how things now were came quickly enough. Creation had fronted us £1,000 for equipment. Nice one. I was told that Noel had his eyes on a new guitar. When Noel asked me if I needed anything I simply replied, 'Skins.' Twenty quid's worth. That was it. He continued to ask each of the group what they wanted. Liam wanted a microphone, Bonehead needed his amp fixed. Guigs didn't ask, but it was suggested that he needed a new pair of shoes. I thought they looked good. When Noel turned up at rehearsal that evening, he was clutching a new £800 guitar. He looked ecstatic. I asked if he had managed to pick up my skins. He laughed and told me, 'I've arranged for a gold-plated drum key to be made instead for you. It's in the post.'

Liam had his microphone and Bonehead had a working amp. Guigs even had a new pair of fuckin' shoes. It was a silly argument, but it was one I had to have. I told him to stop being a prick and it was not long before things got out of hand. We ended up outside The Boardwalk. I was straight into Noel's face. 'What the fuck is your problem? Gold-plated drum key? You offered to buy me something and it's not the fact that I can't have it, Noel, it's your attitude.'

I suppose I was the first to react to New Noel, which in itself was inevitable. Bonehead had stepped back from confrontation since his argument with Noel and had diplomatically placed himself back on the fence, while Guigs seemed to be siding with Noel. You can't count Liam, who had been clashing with Noel on a daily basis for the previous 20 years. New Noel or Old made no difference to Liam. The rest of the band stood with their mouths wide open at the situation. It was one of only two times me and Noel had a serious confrontation. This one was not as fatal as the next.. I told him that right is right, and Liam suddenly voiced his agreement. 'It's my money and I can do want I want with it, dickhead,' Noel shouted back at Liam, the attention deflected. He continued, now with a more composed look on his face. 'Alan McGee says I'm in charge.'

If this was Noel's way of backing off, it wasn't working for me. I would not have him try to get the better of me. I stood and looked at him. The record company had only just waved a cheque book under his nose and he'd already hit the rock 'n' roll cliché trail. I wondered what was happening to him. He had been such a good lad. But I would not back down. Right is right, even if everyone is against it; and wrong is wrong, even if everyone is for it. After Jimmy the Butt's departure, this had become even more important to me.

'In charge?' I reminded him of Liam, Bonehead, myself and even Guigs. I reminded him of Tony and Chris Griffiths. I reminded him of BigUn. 'It's not just about you, Noel. Why do you have to be such a fuckin' miserable twat?'

For a moment, he seemed to crack. There was a look in his eye and he opened his mouth. Then, as quickly as it had come, the moment passed. He simply turned away and left. He cut a forlorn figure in the Manchester drizzle, guitar case in hand. As he faded from view, the rest of the band stood and looked at each other with raised eyebrows. As the great Mr Dylan once said, the times they were a changing.

They were changing at home as well. The rehearsals and time spent away from home had finally taken its toll. Paula had simply had enough. I could understand her frustrations at my absence but never believed it would result in us splitting. But it did.

Noel rang me a few days later. 'Look, I'm not ringing with my tail between my legs but can we just get back to rehearsing tomorrow and getting this right? I know how important you are.'

Things were beginning to move fast now. It seemed that Noel had handed our demo to Ian Marr. Ian was a likeable chap who turned up regularly around Manchester gigs and was an actor. To be honest, though, the only thing I'd ever seen him in was Tesco's. Ian's brother was Johnny Marr from The Smiths. After Johnny had listened to the demo he had sent back word he was impressed enough to organise a meeting with Noel. During this meeting, he had recommended a manager by the name of Marcus Russell. Noel was relaying the events in an excited manner. He told of his drinking session and a trip the next day in Johnny's car to visit a retro guitar shop in Yorkshire. I looked at him in admiration. When Noel had a sniff of an opportunity, he would be on a full-blown Mancunian charm offensive. You had to give him credit for front.

Noel had met Marcus and considered him savvy and good for us. He had told him about the verbal offer that Alan McGee had made us and this interested Marcus enough for him to agree to represent us. It would prove a shrewd move. On both sides. Marcus was Welsh, but despite this he was a good fella. His unimposing shuffle and crumpled suit made some people underestimate him. But his day-to-day management of what was going to be a full-on rock 'n' roll hooligan band was bang on. And his conduct as a human being was even more exceptional. Marcus was born in

Ebbw Vale, deep in the heart of Wales. The town was heavily reliant on the steel factories they had built and the coal seams that nature had provided. Marcus was a blast furnace operative in one of those steel factories until he removed his helmet and decided to educate himself. After teaching economics up and down the country for a decade or so, he moved into management by chance. A friend from the valley wrote lyrics for a band called Latin Quarter, who would eventually release seven albums. Marcus agreed to manage them. From his sterling work with them he had attracted the attentions of Johnny Marr, Bernard Sumner and the Finn Brothers (of Crowded House). As Noel had McGee for his fatherly influence, so Marcus would fulfil that role for Liam.

* * *

We were at rehearsals and Guigs was running off about the Policeman, who had been arrested by the local bona fide constabulary. It seemed they had picked him up and warned him about his behaviour and criminal activity. He had simply asked them if they had any evidence to substantiate those accusations of criminal activity. They told him they hadn't, so he told them to fuck off and left the police station. He was not happy about being picked up, so he arranged himself a holiday. While in Tenerife, he then allegedly coordinated a series of fire bombings across Manchester and Stockport. Cars of rival criminals, shops and schools were all targeted. It was a highly organised affair. Over £55,000 worth of damage was caused and the story ran on that night's BBC *Nine O'Clock News*. When he returned to these shores, he sported a relaxed air and an all-over tan. The police once again wanted to interrogate him over the fires, but his solicitor said he would only agree to this questioning if the police had some evidence linking him to these fires. They didn't. So the Policeman had made his point. He then made a charitable contribution to cover the damage caused. I was worried for him. His rise to power had been quick and ferocious and he had left many beaten and angry people behind him. He had now taken to taunting the police as well. In the national media. Could only end in tears, as far as I could see. I made a mental note to see him.

I had lent Noel a videotape of our first performance at The Boardwalk, from the days before he joined. Liam had asked to watch it, so we went round to Noel's flat in town. After we explained the reason for our visit, Noel looked extremely awkward. 'Erm... You can't watch it,' he said.

'What do you mean we can't watch it?' Liam asked.

'It's not here,' Noel replied 'I've lent it someone.'

'It's not yours to lend out. Get it back,' Liam shot back, angrily.

We never did get that tape back – it disappeared off the face of the earth. It was the only video footage of the band prior to his arrival.

* * *

It was time to meet Alan 'Ginger Bollocks' McGee in London. This was an important day, the day we'd waited for. Three years of hard work rewarded. We were signing our record deal. Finally. A proper record contract. With Sony Records. We never actually signed to Creation Records. That was mainly due to the fact that Creation Records and Alan McGee had no money. McGee though, ever the shrewd sweggy, had begged and borrowed to finance what he (and we) considered the best demo ever created. Self-belief was running sky high again. On the back of this demo, Sony agreed to sign us and then immediately licensed all UK sales to the penniless Creation Records, making Mr McGee a very wealthy man indeed. But more importantly, it gave us that record deal we had worked all these years for. We would finally get to record the body of songs we had worked on with the Realies.

On 22 October 1993, Liam picked me up in a battered old Nissan taxi and Eugene the taxi driver sang Elvis songs as we headed to Piccadilly train station to meet Bonehead and Guigs. They stood waiting outside. Bonehead raised a half-demolished bottle of red. Guigs was red-eyed and his mind was clearly elsewhere. It was eight in the morning and they were already under the influence. We paid Eugene and as 'The Wonder of You' faded off towards the suburbs of Manchester, we hit the station bar in an attempt to catch up with Bonehead and Guigs. After we boarded, we cracked open a bottle of Jack and set about our business. Everybody was wearing that look. The smiles just waiting to burst. The mood was one of extreme jubilation. Punches were thrown playfully before Liam started to rip the piss out of a group of suits in the far end of the carriage. It was only playful banter, though, and the suits looked on bemused by the strange, hairy creature. Guigs had given us some of his weed, so me and Liam retreated to between the carriages and stuck our heads out of the window. Like a steamer of old, the smoke billowed along the side of the carriage before disappearing into the English countryside as the train sped its way along the tracks. Liam looked at me.

'We fuckin' done it. We fuckin' done it.' His smile was infectious. 'Got to stick together now,' he told me. 'Gotta be strong.' I guess that the feeling of comradeship was never again as intense as it was that day. We had always been so anti everything that it had made us tight as a unit.

We returned to sit smirking, full of self-congratulation and elation. We had achieved what we had set out to do. It had taken three years of perspiration and arse-ache, but that was irrelevant. We had indeed fuckin' done it.

We arrived in Euston and were met by a sleek chauffeur-driven Mercedes that whisked us to Soho Square. There were bottles of champagne to be consumed quickly. We exited the vehicle to be met by the sight of Sony headquarters' impressive facade. Staring up at the glass-fronted building, we noticed that each floor was lined with people, all of whom seemed to be clapping. We looked quizzically at each other before realising they were actually clapping us. Fuck me. We raised our half-drunk champagne bottles upwards and then headed towards the entrance, swaggering our way in and making for the top floor. The smell in the lift was a strange mixture of wine, champagne, marijuana and sweat. We all fell about laughing as the record company staff looked on, unsure of how to join in. We fell out of the lift where our bottles were removed from us only to be replaced with more champagne in glasses, and schnapps to boot. We were already well done from the train journey and this tipped us over the edge.

In particular Bonehead.

'Where's the wine?' he shouted, while he poured his champagne into a plant pot. Like clockwork, the Man who Can appeared with a bag that was bursting and simply sailed past us into the nearest toilet. Not a word was said, but we all followed in line.

An hour or so of party later, we were ushered into a room and told that the document we were about to sign would leave us indebted to Creation and Sony for the next 18 years. Sounded good to me. We were given more champagne, and there was wine for Bonehead. A record company solicitor then rattled on for an hour or so in a language that occasionally resembled the same one that I used, though the rest of the time it sounded like Latin. We all stared at each other, smiling mindlessly.

Finally it finished and then: 'Tony.' They waved me to the front. Fuck me, I was up first. I started my inebriated slalom to the boardroom table and tried to focus. On the desk in front of me lay a pile of paper that seemed to reach a foot off the table. Fuck me, I thought. Do I have to read all this? One of the legal team pointed his finger at the top sheet and I was simply asked to add my signature there. I read down the signatory list. In clear black print, it read Noel Gallagher, Liam Gallagher, Paul McGuigan, Paul Arthurs. Then my name. But not in print. Instead, it had been added in biro, with a less-than-straight dotted line beneath.

'Are you happy to sign this document here and now?' asked another member of the legal team. I now wished I hadn't drunk all the champagne, glasses of which were still being thrust at me. I couldn't tell anyone that I just had a 'bad' feeling about this, so I reluctantly scrawled my moniker where requested and moved off to let the next man up. The rest of the band made their way up to the table and finally we stood together as the flashbulbs exploded and the office applauded.

Next, we headed off to a large Mexican restaurant in the centre of London, where we stared at the food momentarily and then ordered more drinks. The toilet was most definitely busier than the kitchen in that restaurant.

'You happy?' I asked Noel, as we sat with a plate of

untouched burritos between us. I thought back 10 years to the summer days in the park and how that unremarkable kid had transformed himself and us to the band we now were. I had to hand it to him, he forced all the issues and, with the help of The Real People, we really had a collection of songs to be proud of.

'As happy as I've ever been,' he replied.

The draft contract that I'd seen gave Noel all the songwriting credits, which was fair and just, and then we each received a 20 per cent split of the rest. There was no key member agreement and the band owned the rights to the name Oasis. Standard stuff. As I said, this was agreed on and everybody thought it fair. But, as I was to find out later, the contract that had been signed that day also gave him and Liam the name Oasis. What's more, it had given him the power to fire any member of the band he thought unfit for purpose. Myself, Bonehead and Guigs had been relegated to the sidelines. It seemed that I had signed a document that was different from the draft agreement but I would not come to realise this until I had finally left the band.

In our ignorance and drunken state, we ploughed on to the Falcon Pub in Camden. We were on our second wind now, and Liam was shouting at us from the bar. The band Whiteout were playing, and they were a good set of lads.

'C'mon To', we'll get up and play,' he slurred, crashing into people at the bar. After he laughed this off, he headed towards the stage. I looked at Bonehead, who crossed his eyes and put his fingers in his glass of red and then blessed all around in wine before following me after Liam. We were all fucked out of our minds and I couldn't keep rhythm. Bonehead was spinning a 360 while playing the guitar. Liam had forgotten who he was, let alone the words to the song he was singing. It was shambolic but funny. And after all, it's not every day you sign a record contract.

We partied on, with the Man who Can showering us in appreciation. Noel was not at all impressed by our musical outburst and spent the evening at Alan McGee's place.

* * *

We were feeling good. The news of our signing had spread like wildfire across Manchester and there was a real buzz of excitement in the air. All sorts of merchandise was now being thrown our way. Three huge boxloads of Adidas trainers were delivered. They were stored in the back of the transit and would later prove a vital commodity.

Things were hotting up. In early November 1993, we jumped once more into our trusty white transit and headed off towards the M6, to perform in London for the first time. Someone needed to speak to Marcus about the transit vans. The backbone of England they may be, but it was *my* spine that was being rattled and thrown around the country. As usual, Liam was excited, although by the time we reached Newport Pagnell service station, various substances had exacerbated that natural excitement. This now made him dangerous.

'Fuck you, Noel.' This was thrown from nowhere. Liam's eyes flashed danger. Noel gave him a little smile, which he knew would only serve to wind him up further. 'What the fuck you smiling at, you little shitbag,' continued Liam.

Noel's eyes lit up 'Sit down, you prick, before you fall down,' he sent back.

Liam sent an arc of Holsten Pils lager through the air and it caught Noel full in the face. As he wrung his eyebrows and stared down at his lager-stained lucky shirt, anger spread across his face. 'You're nothing short of a prick,' he hissed.

This had become the norm. I guess it was pretty obvious that the media had latched onto the fiery relationship between Noel and Liam. Or rather, they were being force-fed juicy morsels by the record company. Before we had even released a single, the record company had already started marketing the image of the warring brothers and their rampaging rock 'n' roll band. It was the beginning of an age of celebrity-obsessed culture and the two battling brothers were just perfect for the times.

In truth, the media attention was having an adverse effect. In the past, a confrontation between Noel and Liam might sometimes end in threats of violence. Now they always did. Noel was very aware that the barbs thrown today were the soundbites in tomorrow's papers. It was like a running commentary on our very existence. The machine had started to warm up. The chief stoker of that machine, Alan McGee, was jumping up and down at the front of the audience a few hours later. We were midway through 'Shakermaker' when I noticed his bright-orange hair bouncing up and down as he pogoed.

In the dressing room afterwards, Liam began smashing a plastic chair against a brick wall. Shards of it were flying around, which made everyone back away. He had just read a review that Johnny Cigarettes had written for *NME*. He was not very happy. It read:

> *If Oasis didn't exist, no one would want to invent them. For a start they look and sound like they are a long overdue product from a bankrupt scally*

> *also-ran's factory. Vaguely trippy guitar, almost tunes with vaguely late sixties rock tendencies, vaguely Ian Brown as Tim Burgess slob of a front man, singing in vaguely tuneless half whine, vaguely shaping a tambourine, vaguely... well you get the picture. But most annoying is the fact that they're too cool to have a personality or be more surprising than the dullest retro indie fops, too well versed in old records to do anything new, and evidently have too few brains to realise any of the above is true. Sad.*

Liam had marked Cigarettes for being rolled in a carpet. 'Dead man,' he said.

NME reviewed another Oasis gig almost immediately. This time they allocated reporting duties to Calvin Bush, who wrote: 'Oasis are frankly incredible. They leave, I gasp and ache. The thought of having to wait a whole ten days before they play here again is already cramping my lifestyle.'

We seemed to have created something of a difference of opinion down at *NME*.

* * *

On 4 December 1993, I headed down to our gig at Warwick University in the van with no Noel or Liam. Noel had had enough of travelling in the transit and drove down in a hire car instead with Coyley – Mark Coyle, who'd worked with the Roses and the Inspirals. (More of him later.) Liam made his own way on the train, for some reason, and did not arrive until we are just about to go on stage. Noel hadn't seemed concerned about Liam's lateness until Liam actually arrived. Then he screamed at him and threw a plastic chair in his direction. It seemed that Liam had started a trend for hurling plastic chairs. Noel looked around afterwards, though, to make sure that all the relevant music journalists had recorded this altercation. We then headed on stage and played a blistering set.

December 1993 saw us head for Liverpool's Pink Museum recording studio. We literally had a welcome party waiting for us. The Real People were in town. Even before we'd unpacked the instruments, the recreational had started. The Real People had a way of lifting a room. Their non-stop banter and lunatic behaviour left everyone in a good place. Chris Griffiths was already wrestling with one of his group, who had decided to steal the goldfish from the tank in reception. He had brought the little tank to our room, then held it aloft and drank the unlucky little fish right down. I'm not making this shit up. Chris had tried to stop him, but was too slow, and now he was rubbing the other guy's back and holding the now empty bowl out. All of sudden there was a hurl and a whoosh and the kid threw everything back into the bowl. His stomach contents now swirled in the bowl as a very shaken-looking goldfish started to eat away at it. Chris looked at us apologetically before he returned the bowl back to the receptionist with the words, 'I've give him a bit of food, love.'

We all laughed and were glad to be back. The Real People were ecstatic for us and for our success. I told them that if it wasn't for them we wouldn't have achieved anything, but I think they already knew that. We'd still got no money, so I began to unpack my kit, which had not stood up to its recent hammering. I started running a sound check and practising a lazy beat I had been working on. Chris came up and told me to keep my head up with Noel; he had also spoken to Guigs and Bonehead. Then: 'Get your arse out there, La, and give it some. Just jam away,' he said, with a smile. Out I went. Chris's attitude and big fuck-off zest for life really rubbed off on all those around him. He was a true musician and a true Spartan.

I started to drum. Boom-cha, boom, boom-cha. Bonehead quickly began nodding his head in tempo and began to play his rhythm guitar over my beat. The rhythm kicked in and I adjusted as Bonehead changed chords. Noel started to pick at his lead over the rhythm guitar while Liam rattled his tambourine. Guigs nodded his head in time. Soon Noel was humming a melody over the rhythm, but then called the jam to a halt as it was time to start recording.

The door to the studio suddenly flew open and an incredulous Tony Griffiths burst in. 'What you fucking doing?' he asked, his Scouse accent as high pitched as humanely possible, leaving every dog within a 3-mile radius howling.

'We're gonna record "Bring It on Down",' replied a surprised-looking Noel.

'Like fuck you are,' Tony Griffiths replied, with a chuckle, informing us that our 'jam' had the makings of a hit record. 'Bring It on Down' was shelved and thirty minutes later, after a brief interlude during which Noel scribbled furiously in the corner, we were almost ready to record a new song. Tony Griffiths guided Liam through the tune and provided backing vocals. 'Supersonic' had been born – and it really was that easy. We didn't even remix it. When we got it right, we got it right. That moment of that evening would be our first-ever offering to the public. The Realies were having their effect again. They were producing us, as agreed. Life was beautiful. Now, I know that Noel is the main songwriter for Oasis, but there were many instances like this where the band as a whole – and The Real People too – were integral to the composition of a song.

We were sitting in the ever-reliable transit van. The radio was blaring out an advert for a musical festival... then we heard the recognisable intro to 'Columbia'. We all looked at each other in astonishment. It had been released as a white label but had been given airtime on Radio One. As the advert faded the volume of the song increased, and Bonehead started jumping up and down, forgetting that we were in a vehicle. His head was leaving dents in the tin-can rooftop. The rest of us cheered. The only member not joining in was Noel. I guess for us it was a different trip. Noel seemed hardened by his time with the Inspirals and we used to tease him when he delivered his daily statement: 'Done it all before.' We used to tell him he had not 'done it all before'; he'd only carried the instruments as the Inspirals did it all. But this did nothing to encourage his enthusiasm.

* * *

Liam and BigUn had had a falling out. It seemed that none other than Sir Alex himself had pulled BigUn into the office at Old Trafford. He wasn't very happy, it seemed. Liam had blurted to all the papers about how we had fixed Cantona's car when he was working for BigUn. He had gone on to talk about having cocaine for breakfast, dinner and tea. Sir Alex was unhappy with the comments and BigUn was given the heave-ho – for which he blamed Liam. Liam made a call after the gig and they sorted themselves out. Lucky, really, considering Liam was lodging at BigUn's gaff.

But we had bigger things to occupy us: we were off to Monmouth to record at Monnow Valley recording studios. The Stone Roses were making *The Second Coming* a few miles away at Rockfield. Mani had told Noel which pub the band would be drinking in while they were in Monmouth and suggested we might like to meet up. We'd found the boozer and it seemed to suit every taste we might have. There we were, in the middle of Monmouth, and we were to find out there were more drugs on offer than in Manchester. Me, Liam and BigUn were sitting at the bar. Behind us some locals were fighting over a card game while others danced, spaced out, to the Super Furry Animals. A Welsh band for a Welsh pub.

Suddenly, we heard: 'Fuckin' hell, it's The Stone Roses.' We all spun round, hoping to find the full Mancunian crew. Instead, the rest of the pub were looking at us.

'Are you Ian Brown?' one inquisitive local asked Liam. It was the thickest Welsh accent I had heard. After Liam finally interpreted what the question was, his face changed.

'No I'm not. Now fuck off, cottage burner,' he replied. Liam was quite to the point with people. Always had been. The United Nations had not missed out when he had decided on a career in music. But this was not a good place for it.

'Who the fuck do you think you're speaking to, bollock brains?' came back the immediate and aggravated reply, in an even thicker Welsh brogue.

Once again it was time for me to start my peace-keeping missionary work. First I calmed the Welsh boy down with the customary placation pint and then turned my attentions towards Liam. 'How would you react if a Welshman told you to fuck off in front of all the boys, Liam?' I asked.

Liam took the top from his pint, contemplated for a moment and then asked, 'Do you think they've got any gear?'

As usual, if Liam didn't understand, or simply didn't have an answer, he ignored the question. As a drug transaction might broker peace, I decided to ask my new Welsh friend if he could help us out. Within moments we had an array of goodtime in front of us. Acid, weed, MDMA, bugle and crack. And we were in fucking Monmouth! I shouted Liam and BigUn over and since it had been a while for all of us we decided on the acid. After we necked a couple of tabs each we sat by the door and awaited the ride. Yet another person approached Liam and asked if he was a member of The Stone Roses and then wanted to know what he'd said about the Welsh earlier. He was obviously picking for a fight. The warmth and comfort of the acid had taken hold now, though, and Liam actually began telling people that yes, he was Ian Brown, and no, he wouldn't dare call someone a cottage burner – followed by a roar of maniacal laughter.

After an hour or so, we decided that it would be a good thing to see if we could find Ian Brown at Rockfield recording studios. This decision was unwise for a number of reasons. We didn't know where the studio was. It was pitch black with no streetlights and we had no transport. Liam was talking about voices telling him to burn down the village. Ian Brown was probably asleep in bed. It was two-thirty in the morning. We were out of our heads.

So with all this in mind, we threw open the boozer doors and headed out into the thick black night, intent on finding the studio. After what seemed an eternity we had left the glow of the town and were in the heart of the countryside. Liam was to the side of me with his arms outstretched, trying to find his hands in front of his face. He was studying them intently, oblivious to the cold and dark surroundings.

'I don't think we're moving,' whispered BigUn from the darkness behind me. I tried to figure out if I was moving and although I was aware that I was putting one foot in front of the other, I had to agree with BigUn. The darkness was not doing the trip any favours and enveloped me like a dark blanket. It was suffocating.

'I think, therefore I am,' shouted Liam, who had become invisible in the darkness in front. As if to prove this profound utterance, he suddenly walked into something and let out a cry.

'I've just fuckin' smashed into something. Twat.'

He kicked out in anger and connected with some power. Liam barked his pain into the blackened night. BigUn sparked his clipper and produced a pool of light. Liam was hopping around in the dark next to an old beat-up tractor that was sat on a verge at the side of the lane. It was an ancient model with the two headlights sitting on top of the rusty body like bug's eyes. I was immediately transported back to Kinnitty in County Offaly, Ireland, where I would spend whole summers riding these tractors round farms and fields. Without a moment's hesitation, I jumped on the tractor and with a quick twist and a turn the engine roared to life. The stillness of the night was shattered by the pumping pistons. With another flick, the lights illuminated the narrow country lane in front of us. Liam and BigUn screamed in delight, hopped on and with some difficulty we headed off, laughing and tripping, shouting and swerving our way through the Welsh countryside.

We arrived at Rockfield Studios after a 2-mile ride. It was a long horseshoe-shaped barn building with a farmhouse attached. We jumped off the tractor when we spotted the lights and crept up the gravel driveway. Our stealthy approach was marred only by the crunching gravel and our continuous laughter as the trip reached its zenith. The barns had been converted to house a number of recording studios, which were attached to a large farmhouse. It was nearly three in the morning as we knocked on the door. No one answered, so we tried the door and to our surprise it opened. Inside, we saw a table tennis table.

'Ping pong' roared Liam, and then started to laugh hysterically. This had obviously caught somebody's attention, as we heard an inside door swing open and then crash shut followed by heavy footsteps on the stone flagged flooring. 'Shit! Hide!' shouted BigUn and even though we hadn't done anything wrong (besides taking a vehicle without consent and consuming illegal drugs), we each dived behind one of the many stone pillars supporting the barn roof. Whoever had come to investigate had brought with them the power of light and after flicking a switch we were all illuminated in the courtyard.

'What the fuck are you doing?' enquired a voice from the doorway. I suppose we should have moved, but instead we stood firm in the crazy belief we couldn't be seen. 'I'm phoning the Old Bill if you don't leave.' With this, we sheepishly returned to the courtyard. I put my hands up in the air in mock surrender and the other two followed suit.

'We're here to see Ian Brown. We're in a band called Oasis.' As was becoming more common, the namedrop worked. We were ushered into the building and pointed towards a door at the far end of a long corridor. As we opened the door we saw a slouched Ian Brown sitting in a leather chair. Behind, working away at a mixing desk, was an engineer. BigUn shouted, 'Fuck me, it's Ian Brown'; me and Liam looked at him and told him to shut up.

'Morning,' muttered the lead singer, who was surrounded by a cloud of smoke as he pulled on a fat one. 'Come in, sit down.' Nobody moved. We just stood in the doorway and stared. This was the man who had inspired most of the band to become musicians, and in particular Liam. Liam had a cartoon surprise face on. I suppose this was due both to his meeting an idol and the LSD that was still rocketing around his mind. We took seats either side of Ian Brown, who then started to talk like talking was about to be outlawed.

'I'm a fly in the ointment, you see. But I don't want to be no fly in the bottle. They ain't got anything to pin on me. It's not just swings and roundabouts, there's also the slide to consider. The paling of the shadows are a sure sign of the morning light.'

What the fuck? I guessed with this dialogue it made the weirdness of the trip even more intense. I was burning up and all I really wanted was to speak to Reni. Drummers' union, so to speak. I was waiting for Liam to start monkeying around, but it seemed it was all a little too much for him. Whether it was meeting Ian Brown or being on the trip I'm not sure, but he was simply sat there, staring straight at the Roses' singer but unable to say anything. The mouth was firmly shut and he simply nodded as Mr Brown started to confuse everybody again. As I was sat immediately next to him, I bore the brunt of most of his questions. So I just smiled and gave him a kind of weird trippy look. Didn't stop him talking, though.

'Is Reni around?' I ventured after he finished another four or so sentences that, when stringed together, didn't actually mean anything to me. Ian Brown looked at the clock on the wall. I was wondering what the fuck sort of reply I was gonna get. I thought the answer would probably be space and time related.

Instead: 'He'll be here in a couple of hours, but we'll have to be gone by then. The rule of one cannot be the rule of all.'

He's a right fucking weirdo, I thought to myself. It took me some time to figure that it wasn't the trip making the whole event surreal, it was Ian Brown and his gobbledygook. If this was the end result of being in a band, I was thinking we should all reconsider. Anyway, it seemed that Reni recorded his tracks for the album between five and eight in the morning. This was so he could be alone and, to be honest, after a few more of Ian Brown's ramblings I understood the solitary part. We managed a sort of conversation for the next hour, which mainly consisted of one of us asking a question that was followed by an unrelated prophetic or bizarre answer from the right honourable Mr Brown.

Ian did not take up the offer of any of our drugs as he 'preferred to stick with the coffee and the weed. Why don't you change that song to "Cigarettes and coffee"? It sounds better.' This was his final piece of advice. Not a peep out of Liam all night. Strange, that.

Shortly before Reni was due in, we had to leave due to the fact we were semi-conscious. So we headed back to Monnow Valley on our tractor with the Welsh dawn accompanying our comedown.

* * *

'Get the fuck up. Get the fuck up. Get the fuck up.' This was the voice in my head as I slowly opened my stinging eyes and readied myself for the aftershock. It was not a bad one, though, and within an hour I was dressed, shaved and washed and downstairs in the rehearsal studio. We were getting our photo taken for the 'Supersonic' single. I was grateful for my position at the back of the shot, as I was still spinning from the previous evening and early morning. There was still no sign of Liam. He finally trudged into the room looking downcast. He was wearing the same denim shirt and jeans as the previous night.

'Fuckin' smile, you miserable twat,' ordered Noel.

'Fuck you, dickhead,' came back a half-hearted reply. Shit, Liam wasn't even rising to Noel. He really must not have been feeling that good. I thought that maybe his meeting with Ian Brown wasn't what he had expected. The argument was interrupted by the sleeve designer, Brian Cannon, who asked us to take up our instruments and look rebellious. When the resulting shots were shown to us, I noticed that depressed, vacant stare still on display across Liam's face.

Brian's company, Microdot, had worked with The Verve and an introduction was made. They turned up a few days later at the studio. We bonded immediately as bands and always got on well from then on. It was a relaxed and playful atmosphere built on mutual respect. After we signed our deal, we played a number of gigs with them.

The producer had us recording our individual pieces in separate rooms away from each other. It just wasn't right. For three years we had rehearsed and recorded together. The eye contact and feel was as important as the music itself. It was what we had become accustomed to. Without this energy, the music sounded soulless. Day after day we would record, only to be bitterly disappointed when we played back the results in the evening. The downing of too much goodtime and a continual overindulgence in Jack Daniel's hadn't helped either, I suppose.

After 18 days of hard work and sweat, we only had 'Slide Away' in the can. Although having said that, it wasn't half a good song to have in the can. I'd loved 'Slide Away' the minute I'd heard it. Mr Melody strikes again. The version of the song that we'd just finished is the version you can hear on *Definitely Maybe*. It was the only thing that Dave Bachelor, our producer, got right. Dave was a good guy who had in his time produced The Kinks, among others, but he just wasn't the right man for us. Or so we told the record company. Easier to explain that than admit we just got mindless for a couple of weeks. Don't think Creation bought it, though. In an attempt to get back on track, we were off to see Coyley at Sawmills Studios.

I'd better formally introduce you to Coyley at this stage. Mark Coyle had been the sound engineer for both The Stone Roses and the Inspiral Carpets and had struck up a friendship with Noel that lasted until only recently. He was rapidly losing his hearing even in the early days, which was an unfortunate occupational hazard, I suppose. He had offered to work the desk for us in the early gigs at The Boardwalk. This sounded great to us all, as Mark had the experience of touring with the Carpets, so was sure to improve us. He would also swagger with our attitude. On many occasions he would have fisticuffs with angry club owners intent on turning us off after we had overplayed. Mark was also responsible for the musical intake while on tour. He would bring along an eclectic mix of music tapes, from Burt Bacharach to The Creation, Ennio Morricone to Neil Young. Noel would namedrop these artists if he was ever asked to recount his own musical influences. Funnily enough, he never mentioned Alvin Stardust or Abba. I always found Mark good company and his importance to the band in the early days should never be underestimated.

Sawmill Studios sat on an island in Wales. We arrived by a small engine-powered boat. This was a first for us. They told us it was the only available recording space, but we soon found out that the decision to record here was more down to its seclusion than any availability problems. It was a 3-mile trek along a darkened railway track to the nearest boozer and a police sniffer dog couldn't have found any drugs. Creation had obviously decided that the experiences at Monnow Valley were not to be repeated. Their plan had the desired effect. During the next week we recorded again as a band in the same room, unlike in Monnow Valley. It was a re-creation of the set-up we'd had in both the rehearsal room and Bootle, and we had that feel back, that understanding a nod or a wink could bring, that spark. We began to trawl through the new batch of songs and laid down 'Shakermaker', 'Up in the Sky', 'Digsy's Dinner' and 'Rock 'n' Roll Star' in quick succession. It was obvious that it worked when we played as a unit and it didn't when we didn't, so we ploughed on. Next we completed 'Live Forever'. The song was a joy to record. That evening, me, Liam and Bonehead sat on a grassy riverbank, fishing. Wrapped in warm coats, we waited on the fish, who stared blankly at our bait, which was made from tinned pineapples. We all agreed that the sound and structure so far had been bob on. We finish the last two days with 'Cigarettes & Alcohol' and 'Married with Children', and everyone was excited about the recording. We really felt that this was the one. When we finally heard the album mixed down, though, we were all a little deflated. Although it was good, there was something not quite right. Once again that 'oomph' was missing. When we played live, we blew people away. There was a distinctive roar that seemed impossible to recapture in a recording studio.

By this stage, the only track that we hadn't completed was 'Bring It on Down'. Noel wasn't happy with the recording we had, and highlighted the drum track as the reason. I had received a phone call from him: 'I'm bringing in a session drummer to record "Bring It on Down". We need to have the album finished and we can't waste any more time. Or money,' he told me. I was gutted. I couldn't see what was wrong with the original recording, but I wasn't going to argue. I knew just how important it was that we finished the recording quickly, so reluctantly agreed.

One day back in Manchester and then we are all aboard the spaceship transit van, which hurtled (at 50mph) towards the Big Smoke. The trip to London had become more familiar now. We had the Realies on board again and the mood was electric.

We arrived at the studio to find the session drummer already sitting in a tiny, dark, sweaty room. The intensity was immense. I keep rattling the various patterns of 'Bring It on Down' through my head. Then I was off, my hands held invisible sticks, my mind with a kicking tune. I was beat perfect, I felt. I listened as the session drummer started to play my drums. It was not a nice feeling. His first take was poor and his second was even worse. It was a difficult song to drum. After two sessions of banging away, he was still no closer to it than he'd been on the first take. That song was always about the feel. It didn't matter how technically good you were. Noel was looking well fucked off and went for lunch in a mood.

After he had left, Tony Griffiths pulled me into a side room and looked at me with real anger on his face. 'Listen,' he said, 'you're gonna get your sticks and you're gonna do exactly what I say. You are the fucking drummer in this band, not that fucking cockney wide boy out there. Remember that, La.'

After these words, he went and whispered something in Bonehead's ear. He then thanked the session drummer for his time and as he shuffled out I took my place behind the kit. Bonehead looked at me and laughed. 'I've been slipping your missus one for the last twelve months, you know, Tony,' he said. 'She's good, real good.' The rage descended. but I quickly realised what Bonehead was doing. I started the song with the image of Bonehead writhing around with me missus planted in my mind. The anger transposed itself and I blasted the fuck out of the kit for the next four minutes. Everything else was irrelevant as I banged away and finally finished, to cheers from Bonehead and Liam. I'd fucking done it. Like, the first take.

Tony Griffiths returned and gave me the thumbs up. He told me that he was going to deal with Noel and suggested that I go and grab a Benson. Upon Noel's return, Tony asked him to listen to the latest recording. Noel listened and smiled as he realised it was beat perfect. Rather craftily, Tony didn't tell Noel it was me. I was sitting outside, finishing my cigarette, when Noel joined me. He told me he had just listened to the last recording and commented that it was perfect. 'Just how the drumming should be,' he added, with a smile.

I looked him square in the eye and agreed. He looked confused until I explained it was me on the recording. Then he began to look irritated.

Also present that day was a new producer we had brought on board. Owen Morris had been a sound engineer at Spaceward in Cambridge since he was 16. He was given 'Slide Away' and asked to see if he could do anything with it. It was a fantastic opportunity for him, which he duly grasped. After a couple of weeks, he returned with his mix.

We all sat and listened. Afterwards, we simply sat and looked at each other. Owen had found the 'oomph' that had been missing and had amplified it five times. He had also ramped up the drumming, which suited me fine. We finally had our producer for *Definitely Maybe*.

We took Owen out on the drink as a way of celebration, which turned into a messy one. At one point, he was telling Noel that he sounded like Slash from Guns N'Roses and that he ought to cut it out. That pissed Noel off, but not as much as when he told him to turn me up. Owen's brilliance with *Definitely Maybe* led to him being inundated with offers and his next and second job was to produce the critically acclaimed *Urban Hymns* for The Verve.

We were later told we were to attend a very important Sony showcase in Amsterdam. It seemed that the global leaders of Sony Music were gathering to hear their new acquisition perform. The day itself, we marched on to the ferry already well on our way, due to the copious amounts of powder that we had shovelled up our noses. Once again, Noel wasn't looking happy. He later tried to pass off this unhappiness as some kind of professional thing, but the rest of the band knew it was just him being sulky. Even Liam had noticed the change and was intent on getting hammered. With Liam it was as much out of embarrassment as frustration.

This was the real thing. We were going to Amsterdam. In the transit van we all huddled down, trying to be inconspicuous as we parked in the belly of the vessel. It was never going to happen, and we were under constant scrutiny as soon as we embarked. After more drinks at the bar, and after banging some more down in the toilets, we were confronted by Noel. He was still sore from the previous time we'd ignored what he had asked us to do and warned each of us that if we fucked up he would rub our noses in it when we got to Amsterdam. You'd better believe we'd be rubbing our noses in it when we got to Amsterdam, I thought. I had got talking to a German lady who was sat in the bar. Her English was very good, so she fully understood the nonsense I was spilling out. Within a few minutes we were upstairs on the deck. A few minutes later, we were riding like teenagers, her tights ripped and torn due to the urgency of the situation.

When we returned to the bar, it was in uproar. Liam had insulted a German guy who was looking for his wife and there had been a proper kick-off. I vanished sharpish as the crew gathered together to round up the culprits. After some chasing down, me, Guigs, Bonehead and Liam sat surrounded by ship crew. As well as being blamed for causing an affray, we were also being accused of stealing champagne and Jack Daniel's as well as using forged money. There was still a definite attitude about us, which did not help the situation. After the Dutch police had arrived, and before McGuigan could point out anybody who might be Spartacus, I stepped forward and offered the explanation that the man that had instigated the riot was surely the German who had been mouthing it rather than us.

'We shouldn't be held responsible,' I finished. I had no defence for the other allegations, though. That was because there was no defence. It was us, guvnor. Fair cop. We were then handcuffed and frog-marched off the boat.

I remember Noel in the port, standing the other side of a rusty chain fence, simply shaking his head in disbelief. One by one we passed him, our heads hung in mock shame. His disbelief soon turned to anger as we all fell about laughing. Yes, it was unprofessional but fuck this, we weren't pretending to be a rock 'n' roll band, we were fucking *being* one. Once again we made the pages of *The Manchester Evening News*. We also made the *Ten O'Clock News* on national television. My mum wasn't as proud that time.

* * *

March 1994. We had to be at Channel 4's studios for three o'clock; we were to appear on *The Word*. Noel was smiling and genuinely excited. He had finally got over his disgust at our behaviour on the ferry.

Noel's girl Louise worked with *Word* presenter Terry Christian's girl and Noel had mithered Terry sufficiently enough for him to organise a slot on the show for us. This was our first television appearance after the Alvin Stardust debacle and we were all happy-nervous again. Liam was itching to add some substance to his life, but Noel was adamant that we all stay clean until after the show.

We all headed off for a show that at least this time was guaranteed to be broadcast. We hoped. Terry Christian was hosting. Although he was on The List, we all found him to be a genuine and likeable chap, just doing his thing. We slammed out 'Supersonic' as a psychedelic backdrop gyrated behind us on screens and scantily clad young ladies danced round my kit. It was an electric performance and Liam's cocksureness came right out the bank of TV screens behind me. Although we hadn't got Tony Griffiths on backing vocals, I knew he'd be watching us. We finished as Bonehead wrapped his arm round Hufty and licked the top of her head with his tongue. It was then time to hit the bar, where we had a gaggle of giggling girls waiting for us.

When I think back now, we sort of went round it in an upside-down way. Most bands will meet and over the next five years will rehearse, sign a contract, appear in the media and then fall out. Oasis? Before we got a record deal we had been together for years. Before we released a record we had appeared on the national news, we had appeared in the national papers and had now performed live to nearly three million people. Everybody had heard of Oasis and Liam and Noel Gallagher. The machine had begun working overtime before we even started. How could we fail?

CHAPTER 5

BONEHEAD THE VIKING: UK TOUR

PERSONNEL LIST

BAND
Liam Gallagher, vocals
Noel Gallagher, guitar
Paul Arthurs, guitar
Paul McGuigan, bass guitar
Tony McCarroll, drums

CREW
Margaret Mouzakitis, tour manager (joined 7 May)
Jason Rhodes, production manager
Mark Coyle, sound engineer
Phil Smith, backline technician

So we gave them what they wanted. Full out rock 'n' roll lunatic behaviour. The chief culprit of this lunacy, though, was without doubt Bonehead. I guess at first I was a willing participant, but I soon learned to restrain myself. The money for smashed TVs and windows and cleaning and minibars would be deducted immediately from our pay. That very week. It was leading me to the point where I had no money to eat. Bonehead's enthusiasm knew no bounds. Noel would be locked away readying his 'we're off our heads us' quotes for following day's paper and Liam would be busy with the local female talent. Meanwhile, Bonehead went on a one-man tirade across England with full endorsement from all those surrounding him.

28 MARCH 1994. JUG OF ALE, MOSELEY, BIRMINGHAM

We arrived at the gig and as Guigs headed for the toilet the rest of us tried to find the dressing room. It turned out that the toilet Guigs was urinating in was to double as our dressing room. We all crammed in and our faces were centimetres from each other; then we laughed and decided to use the back of the van instead. We had begun this tour with a band I mentioned earlier, called Whiteout. Unfortunately for them, though, the hype surrounding us was escalating madly and after our set the venues would empty. Now, if this was a night when Whiteout were headlining, that would leave them playing to an empty room. We decided, therefore, that it would be better if we headlined the tour.

30 MARCH 1994. FLEECE & FIRKIN, BRISTOL

It was a cold night and I was glad I was a drummer. Five minutes into the set and the blood was coursing around my veins as I pounded away. I was soon warmed up. It was another good shift and the fans seemed to be getting more hysterical by the day. Afterwards, Mani from The Stone Roses arrived in the dressing room, which led to a mammoth drinking session. This was continued back at the hotel, where Noel suggested we adopt Mani as the new Oasis bass player. Guigs didn't see the funny side of that suggestion. I'd always found Mani to be a proper chap, a good guy. His musical knowledge was immense, as was his ability to party. Both those talents saw him held in high esteem by the whole band. He also provided a lot of banter, due to his being a United fan. If drummers had their traits, then so did bass players. Their trait came in the shape of borrowing £20 every time they met you in the boozer, which they never give you back. It seemed BigUn had the same problem with Peter Hook. Only joking, Mani!

11 APRIL 1994. 'SUPERSONIC' RELEASED. REACHED NO. 31 ON THE SINGLES CHART

Our first recording was unleashed on the British public. I know it sounds easy to declare after the event that we were sure we'd make it, but that is how it was. We knew we were good. We knew we were better than good. The first-ever aural offering from the band was my hi-hat and bass drum. The same beat that had been a simple soundcheck jam in a room full of lunacy in Liverpool was soon joined by a ferocious rhythm and Liam's pleading vocal.

It still gives me tingles when I hear it now. The B-side,

'Take me Away', was a homage to Johnny Bramwell, Noel's earliest influence, and is as beautiful a record as Noel has ever written to this day.

13 APRIL 1994. THE LOMAX, LIVERPOOL

'Supersonic' had just been released, had been received well by the music press and was selling well. We were ecstatic. We made our way back to Liverpool, where we had recorded the song less than 12 months earlier. We were playing The Lomax, which had been recommended to us by The Real People. As ever in Scouse, the crowd were appreciative and we responded by playing a blinder. Each gig was seeing a more and more confident Liam, which in turn made the rest of the band more confident. We were met backstage by the Realies and another Liverpudlian genius, Pete Wylie. Once again it was gin and tonic and Stella until The Man who Can arrived with the goodtime. There was an air of exuberance in the dressing room until the group chatter suddenly died. I looked over to the door to see if I could spot the cause of the silence. Standing there, looking like a bunch of comedy villains, were The Farm. We'd always ripped The Farm among ourselves, but recently Noel had taken to doing it in the press. As a truce, they had brought a signed photograph along with them to hand to us. Noel made his way over and Peter Hooton, the lead singer, handed over the photograph and offered his hand in peace. Noel ignored the hand, looked at the photo, then immediately dropped it in a bin. The Farm looked for a moment as if they were going to boot off but instead left without saying another word. It was a bit harsh I thought, and I guess The Farm must have thought the same, for as we attempted to leave later we found that someone had let down all the tyres of both our transit vans.

We stayed back at the Realies' studio in Bootle. It was a good place to go back to. Good memories. The building itself was a mishmash of rooms. One was a dedicated party area. Then we had the kitchen. Well, sort of a kitchen. There was even a room full of beds for those late-night recording sessions. I worked my way through these rooms, by now well under the influence. There was a small recreational room at the end of one of the corridors, with a tattered old pool table and a battered television. I guess it was there to provide recreation. Not for me, though. Instead, I was more interested in the chubby blonde girl playing with her hair in the corner. I looked her up and down. She was your typical Scouser. Overmade and underdressed. She was also extremely heavy set. If she fell down the stairs you'd think you'd just heard *EastEnders* finishing. Sorry if I sound a touch stereotypical, but that's how it was.

'Ja wanna watch a zee vee zee wid me?' she asked. This translated into English as 'Do you want to watch a DVD with me?'

'Not really, kid. Any chance of a fuck?' I replied.

I'd always believed in the direct approach. I couldn't be mithered with a conversation if one obviously wasn't required. We shuffled off to the overnight room. She was definitely more playdough than *Playboy*, but as I said I was well gone by this stage. As we settled down and I began my exploratory mission, I suddenly became aware of a doughnut magically floating in the air to the side of me. Upon further investigation, I realised this was no conjuror's trick, for the doughnut was attached to the penis of The Real People's drummer, who had stealthily entered the room. Like a zoo keeper enticing an elephant with a bun, he was intent on luring her away. My sexual cravings came a sorry second to hers for sugar, so I made a sharp exit and later told Noel about it. He was good to speak to for advice, as he had been on the road for a couple of years. I asked him about the groupie thing. He laughed and told me not to worry too much about it, as I wouldn't have to.

29 APRIL 1994. THE ADELPHI CLUB, HULL

We headed to the fisherman's Vegas, Kingston upon Hull, and the Adelphi Club. The new executive tour bus had arrived, looking very similar to the standard transit van we had been touring in for the previous two years. 'Hit the big time have we?' muttered Bonehead as we threw ourselves into the van. Our disappointment was soon overcome, though, by the excitement of a new tour.

30 APRIL 1994. COVENTRY UNIVERSITY, COVENTRY

Liam was not happy. He had just spotted the rack of shirts that a roadie was pushing towards the hotel for Noel. There must have been 15 designer numbers hanging there, all of them pressed and ironed. The rest of us had the clothes we were stood in and a spare pair of gruds. Fortunately, we still had the three boxes of trainers in the van. After gigs, we would open the back and have a quick car boot sale, which would raise enough cash to keep us going. Noel would still demand his cut, though.

1 MAY 1994. LEVENSHULME, MANCHESTER

We'd got a couple of days off. I'd sometimes taken to staying at BigUn's on Kettering Road when I was back in Levenshulme. Liam had been lodging there as well, but you had to be careful. It was always an adventure around BigUn. When we returned that morning, we found a new house guest. Alex 'Hurricane' Higgins, the emotional Irish snooker player, had found his way into my bedroom. In the kitchen, BigUn stood over a frying pan of bacon and told me that Alex would only be here a night or two and then I could have my bed back. It seemed that the snooker star had fallen on hard times and BigUn was playing Samaritan. Liam was laughing, as he has his bed secured. Suddenly, the Hurricane appeared at the door to the kitchen, looking extremely unkempt. It seemed he had slept in his clothes and already there was a cigarette hanging out the side of his mouth. His eyes were glassy and the cigarette moved up and down as he mumbled that he was hungry. We were introduced and then I watched as he wolfed down the breakfast that BigUn had knocked up for us. Liam and Mr Higgins got on famously and it was not long before we shelved our plans to rest for the day and decided to head down to The Church pub instead. In no time at all, the Hurricane was hustling at the pool table. He took small bets and was as entertaining and charming a fellow as I had ever met. In the space of an hour's drinking, though, he was betting against the meanest and most vicious hard men that the pub could offer. Enormous sums of cash, which we knew he didn't have. He had also taken to ridiculing any fan that might approach him. It seemed that whisky had the same effect on Mr Higgins as water had on a gremlin. Things went downhill fast. At one point, he sat down, bladdered, on a chair offered up to him by a middle-aged female snooker fan. He promptly told her she was a right fatty and that the standing up would do her good. Charming. There was a general unrest in the boozer about his behaviour, so before he got strung up we moved him to a quieter hostelry and continued our session there.

We headed home and as we were playing a gig the next day, Alex kindly let me sleep in my own bed. The sleep was not uninterrupted, though. During the early hours, I awoke in a panic. My senses had given off an alarm. The acrid smell of smoke had filtered into the room. I bolted upright to find BigUn stood at my bedroom door in nothing but a pair of underpants, shouting, 'Fire! Fire!' I wasn't sure what scared me most, the prospect of a fire or the sight of BigUn in his undies. He moved off to wake the rest of the inhabitants and we burst down the stairs to escape. When we reached the bottom, we opened the door to the downstairs room. The smoke was billowing from the cooker. The state of severe shock I was in notched up a level when BigUn whipped off his undies. He covered his mouth and nose with them and then crawled naked across the floor to the cooker and turned the gas off. The smoke began to subside. To speed the process, I opened the front door and as the vacuum cleared the smoke two things were revealed. Firstly, there was an unconscious Alex Higgins lying on the sofa. Whether unconscious through the beer or the smoke, we did not know. Secondly, we discovered the source of the smoke cloud: a Fray Bentos pie sat, still encased in its metal packaging, in the middle of the frying pan. It was blackened and still emitting heat. We managed to rouse Alex by means of cold water and shouting loudly. When he finally became aware of his surroundings, a smoke-damaged room and a naked BigUn, it seemed the only thing he wanted to do was eat his pie.

The next morning, completely knackered, we were picked up and headed for Portsmouth. It seemed we weren't the only ones. Bonehead was not happy at all. He had returned home in a lubricated state and had been awoken by a wrenching sound. It was two-thirty in the morning and his girlfriend Kate slept soundly beside him. He rolled out of bed and like an angry bear he pulled back his front curtain and looked out onto the rain-soaked street outside. He spotted a group of students removing his front-door knocker. In his normal muddled state, he grabbed two things: a baseball bat and his missus's dress. He stumbled down the steps at his front door, swinging the bat around in the pouring rain, dressed like a woman. He then chased the students up the street. He was beside himself with shame.

2 MAY 1994. THE WEDGEWOOD ROOMS, PORTSMOUTH

We arrived, very tired – for different reasons – in Portsmouth. Not the most attractive of places at the best of times, never mind a dark, wet and windy Monday afternoon. We checked into the hotel and noticed the swimming pool located immediately next to the bar. I thought that this was a disaster waiting to happen and the smile across Bonehead's face suggested he was thinking the same. We dropped our gear off in the hotel rooms. Bonehead and me were together, as was the norm, with Guigs and Liam sharing, while Noel had a room to himself. We scooted around the seafront, where the sea air blasted all and sundry. Our gig at The Wedgewood Rooms that evening was a sell-out. It seemed all our shows had turned into sell-outs. How times change, I thought. Less than six months previously, we had entertained an empty room in Leeds. That evening, we delivered yet another polished performance and the crowd lapped it up. Not only had the size of the audiences changed, the intensity and fervour had increased to match. There seemed to be a mild hysteria wherever we went, with most of it being directed at young Liam. After we finished, we headed off to find some goodtime at a party we had been invited to. Having located the house, and then the drugs, we all left and headed back to the hotel and the safety of the residents' bar. When we arrived, we noticed it was unusually busy for a Monday night. That was when I spotted a group of lads who had overdone it with the 'street' look. Their oversized jeans were tucked into chunky-heeled beige boots and were in direct proportion to their oversized overcoats. They all wore hats of various styles, even though we were indoors. It was then that I recognised them as East 17. They had played the Guildhall in Portsmouth earlier that night.

I realised I was staring when one of them asked me, 'Are you in Blur?'

Liam overheard this and immediately asked, 'Are you Take fuckin' That?' This led to a barrage of insults thrown at each other. The barrage from our side intensified.

'You silly cockney cunts. What's that hat on yer head, you twat?' Even Noel was having a pop. In Brian Harvey, he'd finally found someone his own size. The smiles on East 17's faces quickly faded when they saw our party shuffling together as if to make our attack physical, and so the mood changed. We had the usual mob with us and they were keen to sort it out there and then. Fortunately for them, East 17 backed off towards the lifts and the safety of their own rooms. It wasn't to end there, though.

In due course, Brian Harvey and his girl reappeared at a balcony, looking down on the hotel foyer. After a few minutes, during which Harvey simply stared down at us, Liam had taken enough and shouted up, 'What the fuck are you looking at, dickhead?'

Harvey gave back straight away, as if he had been waiting for it. 'You what? You fuckin' what?' As he shouted away, his girl stepped back... and opened her dressing gown so we could all see her ample breasts. She put a finger to her mouth and tried to look coy as she paraded. Priceless. We all enjoyed the show as Harvey ranted on. Finally, Liam told him that his girl was showing us her breasts. He whipped his head round as she pulled her gown shut, her face the picture of innocence. As he turned back to Liam, the gown opened once more and the show went on. Again Liam pointed them out and again Harvey turned to see his re-clothed girl wearing an innocent look on her face. After a minute or so of this hilarious routine, we have had enough and headed back to the bar, leaving an angry man in a funny bobble hat frothing at the balcony.

3 MAY 1994. TJ'S, NEWPORT

I liked TJ's. It is rumoured that this was where Kurt Cobain proposed to Courtney Love, so I reckoned the alcohol must be dangerously fuckin' potent. We arrived to yet another packed-out house. The Welsh crowds were always that little bit less stable than elsewhere in the United Kingdom. There was always an edge.

4 MAY 1994, THE WHEREHOUSE, DERBY

Another packed performance. We stood and stared at each other in disbelief.

5 MAY 1994

Day off.

6 MAY 1994. THE PRINCESS CHARLOTTE, LEICESTER

We always had an entourage with us. It had been the same for the last two years. And it was always a noisy and boisterous one. The attitude that we gave off on stage ran right though the group, so it was always adventurous, to say the least. The mentality was that of a Manchester City 'away day', which would inevitably lead to a right load of mither. Noel had started to lay down laws concerning behavioural requirements, which mainly fell upon deaf ears. 'Stop fucking thieving, will you?' he would demand of the group, but to no avail. With Noel, though, that meant most of the entourage were living on borrowed time.

We were stood on stage at the Princess Charlotte in Leicester, setting up for our soundcheck, when Noel noticed that BigUn was already leaving. We had arrived earlier than the rest and had already left our belongings in the dressing room. BigUn had only been here two minutes and he was already heading back to the van. Noel ordered him to stop. Through the microphone, his voice boomed around the large and empty room. BigUn turned to face us with a look on his face that screamed, 'Shit I've been caught.' He also looked pregnant, due to the fact he had obviously stuffed some ill-gotten prize under his shirt. We hadn't even soundchecked and he was already grafting. Noel was not going to be happy.

'What the fuck have you got under your jumper?' Noel asked the sheepish-looking BigUn. In response, he pulled out a couple of dodgy silk shirts that Noel had brought down to change into after the gig. I presumed that BigUn had not been listening when Noel had told everyone to calm down – and not only that, he had actually grafted two of Noel's own shirts. Things couldn't get any worse for him.

But they could and they did.

In a vain attempt at a defence, BigUn now raised the two shirts in front of him and said, 'Look Noel, it's only two girl's blouses. They're shite, but our Kelly could wear them to college.'

Our ring of laughter was drowned out by Noel ordering him out of the venue over the microphone. This act of BigUn's signalled the end for the majority of the Entourage, though – ironically – not for BigUn himself.

7 MAY 1994. THE OLD TROUT, WINDSOR

We now had a new team member. Paul Slattery was a photographer who Mark Coyle had known from his time as the sound engineer for The Stone Roses. Slatts followed us around for the next year or so and would become an entertaining member of our set-up. We were quite insular as a group, but Slatts's personality and humorous outlook on life had crowbarred him in. After a gig that left him well impressed, we all headed back to the hotel. Bonehead was head on and knocking them back. When he spotted the Jacuzzi across the far side of the lobby, he was off, leaving the hotel and returning 10 minutes later. After a toilet break or two, we sat and drank while the receptionist glared over, keen for us to retire. It was 4am. Suddenly, I noticed a large tidal wave of suds erupting from the Jacuzzi. When Bonehead had nipped out, he had bought a litre of bubble bath, which he had dropped it in the bubbling pool. He sat with his eyes wide and roared his head off like a child. Reception declared it an emergency situation and began to evacuate. Only Bonehead.

9 MAY 1994

Day off.

11 MAY 1994. THE BOAT RACE, CAMBRIDGE

The meat of the whole rock 'n' roll image that the band had become famous for lay firmly at the feet of Bonehead. I know this, for it was normally me who sat there and handed him the furniture. We were sat in a hotel room in Cambridge.

'I love the sound of lightbulbs smashing. Pass me that lamp.'

I passed him the lamp.

'That's a least two hundred quid so far, Bone,' I informed him. I was keeping a running account for him.

'Just another fifty quids' worth and I'm done,' he replied, wearing an insane grin. I just had to laugh as the lamp left the hotel room via the window.

12 MAY 1994

Day off.

13 MAY 1994. THE VENUE, NEW CROSS, LONDON

After another barnstormer we were met in the dressing room by a pack of music journalists. Few people could have had any doubts about who the hottest act in town was. There was now a real intensity surrounding the band. Each gig was more and more frenzied. From clamouring fans to admiring journalists, we all understood that something had definitely changed. We towelled down and The Man who Can arranged for us to be whisked across to Browns, the nightclub. I was thinking that that was not a good idea, as Browns represented everything we were not – the club was suited more to the likes of Spandau Ballet and Rod Stewart – but nevertheless, off we headed. When we arrived, we settled down and order drinks. Within minutes, Noel stood up and ordered everyone to move. The bar had told him we were sitting in Prince's area and sure enough, the wee fella – who was dressed in a colour that was similar to the colour of my helmet – duly arrived. We started protesting, but Noel glared at us and we had to move off. I laughed as Liam pointed out that Prince was actually taller than Noel.

14 MAY 1994. THE LEADMILL, SHEFFIELD

Outside the Leadmill stood a doppelganger. It's me good self, but a foot taller. Curly hair, Burberry shirt, desert boots. He was just missing a set of drumsticks.

'Hiya mate, my name is Tony McCarroll,' he said to me, hand outstretched. 'How you doing?' he asked, following his introduction with a number of tales concerning the fucks, drugs, free rides and drink he had managed to blag over the previous few months. I laughed and asked him if he could possibly help me find some.

We played a solid gig. Afterwards, as I was winding down the staircase at the Leadmill in Sheffield, he was busying himself in some girl's mouth. As I passed behind them she opened her eyes; the look of passion soon turned to disbelief as she recognised me. She pushed him away and made a beeline for me. I rushed out the doors, to the sound of my impostor's laughter ringing through the stairwell.

4 JUNE 1994. THE ROYAL ALBERT HALL, LONDON

'We've really made it,' said Noel, with a laugh.

He was excited about the prospect of his own first solo performance. Not sure why he said 'we'. The band were at The Royal Albert Hall for a Creation 'Undrugged' night. Liam refused to sing acoustically and so handed the baton to Noel, who took it with both hands. We moved out front and sat in the crowd. Noel and Bonehead completed an admirable job.

Liam watched them performing on the same stage as the great Arthur Lee and then looked around The Royal Albert Hall, which was filled to capacity. He was overcome by it all. We had only just released our first single but we all already knew our destiny. Or so I thought.

'I can't believe this. It's too much,' he whispered to me, as he used his sleeve to dry his eyes. One of the few nights I saw Liam so openly emotional.

20 JUNE 1994. 'SHAKERMAKER' RELEASED. REACHED NO.11 IN THE SINGLES CHARTS.

And so our second single hit the shops. We were working at releasing a single every three months, just as The Smiths had. As Johnny Marr had advised, 'They can't ignore you if you keep releasing records.'

'Shakermaker' owed a lot to the song 'I'd Like to Teach the World to Sing'. It was done in such an obvious way, though, it became immaterial. I'd loved the lazy feel of the song when I'd first heard it and to me there's still something special about it to this very day. *NME* applauded it:

> *Predictable, maybe, but even in a fantastic week for singles, inevitable. Which just goes to show that, as starts go, Oasis has been pure Ben Johnson at the 1988 Olympics. Fortunately there are no urine tests in pop, so this almighty second single will undoubtedly grant the brothers Gallagher access to mass adoration. They deserve it, too: for in much the same way that my entire life has been a tawdry dress rehearsal for 'doing' the NME singles, one suspects that Oasis' entire existence has been leading up to this moment. By rights, 'Shaker-maker' should lack the colossal impact of 'Supersonic', but from the second they unapologetically strike up a crunching, gob smacking twelve bar boogie, you know this is going to be one unspeakably cool record. And, by the time Liam's vocals loll out of the speaker with 'I'd like to teach the world to sing', you know you're dealing with greatness. The three other tracks are more formulaic (especially the hey let's write a B*

side 'D'yer wanna Be a Spaceman?') but sod it, it's A sides that matter. Even minus 'that' line, this is a Coca Cola classic of a record.
Mark Sutherland

21 JULY, 1994. WETLANDS, NEW YORK

We were suddenly halted in our tracks and told of a change of plan. We were to fly to America for a showcase for Sony at New York's Wetlands.

'Right, here are your tickets.' A very studious-looking lady called Maggie Mouzakitis was standing in front of us. Bonehead had been relieved of his duties organising our tours and Marcus had installed Maggie instead. She was a beautiful girl, young yet very driven and a sisterly figure to us all. It had taken Liam some time to warm to Maggie, but then again it took Liam a while to warm to anyone. She was originally from Greece and had soft Mediterranean looks that disguised an American soul as tough as old cowboy boots. When she first arrived, we thought it a mad decision to employ her as our tour manager. She looked about 12 with her American accent, baseball cap and ponytail. But Marcus had been right. A sisterly touch would be just the thing to keep control of five young men.

She took a deep breath and then told us that we didn't have working visas. There was no reaction from us, because we didn't know what this meant. She then informed us that this meant we had to enter the country illegally. And if we got caught trying to enter the country illegally, we would be sent to an Illegal Detention Centre. Sounded like a right laugh.

We were all given an instrument to carry and told that,

if quizzed, we were to state that music-making was our hobby, not our living. I had been given an item from Noel's prized guitar collection to carry, and he stared at me with a look that could kill. 'Do not fuckin' leave a mark,' he said, just as I pretended to drop it. Although this tickled Liam, who was standing next to me, it didn't seem to amuse Noel.

Guigs asked Maggie if we would be kept in solitary confinement in an Illegal Detention Centre, or would we have to mingle with the rest of the inmates. I didn't think 'mingle' was the appropriate word, and I told him. He gave me the dictionary definition to prove his choice of word was correct. I suspected that if he took that attitude into prison, the only thing that would be mingling around the prison block would be his battered arse.

The flight went without incident and we all entered America illegally. I was surprised that our record company, always in search of a story, hadn't already rung the authorities to let them know what we were doing. It would have made a great headline. I headed for the gig in a yellow taxi with Bonehead and Slatts. I liked New York: the constant blur of traffic and people; the city orchestra playing taxi horn and whistles. Slatts was clicking and whirring away, capturing time on celluloid for posterity. We arrived at a dressing room that had been staged to look like an old dusty storeroom full of empty beer crates and cardboard boxes. There was one beer box that was not empty, however, and instead housed 36 ice-chilled bottles of lager. We greedily sucked away, as the warm, thick evening air had everyone looking flushed. Then again, maybe it was the bugle that The Man who Can was throwing around.

We played a storming gig which, was well received by the

'Americans' – though the crowd must had been 90 per cent British. It was a fantastic night and, on a high, the band started the aftershow. Liam asked if I wanted to come to some apartment. I looked over to see a girl we had met earlier that evening. We called her Mary Poppins, due to her high-class English accent. She was a model from Britain who had decamped to New York. She was also an addict. Drugs, fame, alcohol, money, sex and danger. These were a few of her favourite things. She lived in an old converted warehouse in Manhattan, which – like her – had been around the New York scene since the mid-eighties. That night, she only had eyes for Liam, who for once actually seemed captivated by a woman. We duly headed to her loft apartment and Liam vanished into the bedroom for a few minutes, where he sewed his rock 'n' roll seeds and then re-entered the main room, looking flustered and agitated.

'Fuckin' weirdo wanted me condom. She tried to stick a fuckin' label on it.'

The girl herself had also returned from the bedroom and was now sitting down and talking about spiritual things. Warning bells started to ring and Liam and me looked at each other. The large industrial door to the apartment suddenly swung open and the room started to fill with various model types, each looking more withdrawn than the next. I was half expecting Andy fuckin' Warhol to come waltzing in. Mary Poppins next set about lighting a great many candles, and I stood transfixed at the church-like appearance of the high-roofed apartment. With the echo of some unknown underground post-punk band reverberating through the open space, Mary moved towards an alcove that was burning candle bright. She slowly unlocked a steel cabinet in the corner, which looked like a small fridge. From inside, she removed a number of items and held them up in the light. It took a moment, but I finally realised what they were. She was waving a handful of used condoms with white labels attached. I suddenly realised Mary Poppins' plan and started to roar with laughter. This agitated Liam even more, who was now beginning to panic. He looked at me, wide eyed, so I decided to take the bull by the horns.

'What's on the labels?' I asked Mary.

'Previous donors,' came the reply.

Each rubber had been labelled with the date and time of donation, as well as the origin of the man fat. The small fridge was actually keeping the juice loose, so to speak, and I guessed Mary was planning to artificially create her own supergroup. The two labels I caught read 'Kurt Cobain' and 'Nikki Sixx'. I found this fuckin' hilarious, though it didn't have the same effect on Liam. By now he was yanking at various locks on the enormous front door in order to escape into the New York night. He seemed to be heaving them open and then, in a drug-induced panic, locking them again. The longer this went on, the crazier he seemed to be getting and the more I laughed. After I calmed him down, we made off back to the safety of the group's hotel. I told Liam he should be proud of being held in such high company. He told me to fuck off.

The next morning, I awoke in the Big Apple. The hotel window framed a Lego-like skyline; it reminded me of one enormous film set. I walked to the window and looked west, half expecting to see King Kong hanging from the Empire State Building as he swatted biplanes. The hotel phone rang. It was BigUn.

'All right, fella' I said brightly, eager to relay last night's hilarious events.

'Have you seen the news?' he replied, in a serious voice.

I explained that I was in New York and that the events in little old Manchester, England, were of little importance to them American boys. BigUn then told me about the events of the previous evening. The Policeman had been driving his car through the outskirts of Stockport after visiting an off-licence for a bottle of wine and had stopped at a set of traffic lights. As he sat waiting for the change, a white Ford Granada had pulled up next to him. Slowly, the passenger window of the Granada was lowered and a shotgun barrel emerged. The Policeman looked casually to his right and spotted the gun. He stamped his foot violently on the accelerator of the powerful car, which shot off at a ferocious speed, but not quite quickly enough. The gun was discharged and the Policeman took the full extent of the blast to the right side of his head. He and his black Mercedes 500 SLE headed off towards a local pub. By the time the car smashed through the pub's brick wall, he had already well and truly left this life.

Although I guess I had always expected the Policeman to come to a tragic end, it still shocked me. I remembered back all those years to when he first cuffed me round my head and gave us all a stern warning. I suppose when I thought back on my youthful attempts to pull myself away from the streets I realised that joining a band is actually a serious way out, and promised myself to enjoy every single moment of the trip. But even so, my first performance in America had been overshadowed by the events from back home.

26 JUNE 1994. GLASTONBURY FESTIVAL, SOMERSET

We were back in the UK after our whirlwind visit to the States. It was our first Glastonbury. We rolled up to security in our minibus. The security looked at the five band members and driver and gave a knowing look: our reputation preceded us once more. They would have shown more concern if they had taken more time and discovered the six or seven people who were lying on the floor of the minibus with enough to keep us going for a week. We marched out onto the stage to a welcoming applause. Everyone was in a boisterous mood, and the carnival atmosphere had gotten to the band. We played a rousing set and left to a thunderous appreciation. It was a good moment, but very quickly turned sour. When we headed back to the minibus we passed Paul Gallagher, who was living it up with the Inspiral Carpets outside their tour bus.

'Cunt Balloon,' hissed Noel from the side of his mouth, and stopped. It was as if we had spotted the bad guy in a cowboy movie. I half expected Noel to spit after he said it. He and Clint stared off in the afternoon sun. After an uncomfortable moment, I pushed Noel off and we moved on, laughing. Although Noel had avoided the confrontation, he would not let it go. When Paul Gallagher returned to us, Noel let rip.

'What the fuck are you talking to them for?' was his first question. Paul said nothing and shuffled away, recognising that to argue could lead to problems with his getting in to any future gigs. We then headed out into the crowd. After much consumption, we arrived at Johnny Cash's performance. It was the first time I'd seen him live and I sat and watched in awe. Life just could not get any better. Then, we passed through the fairgrounds and saw the trapeze artists. It was all hot dogs and dreadlocks as our revelling group headed back to the minibus.

When we arrived, we were greeted by The Man who Can. He then introduced us to a tall wiry chap called the Cat in the Hat. The Man who Can told us that if he were ever absent, the Cat would look after all our needs. The Cat in the Hat then bid farewell to the Man who Can, who vanished like a dog in the fog. People are just too kind sometimes.

29 JUNE 1994. ELSTREE, LONDON. TOP OF THE POPS

We were at *Top of the Pops* to perform 'Shakermaker'. The stage manager was running through the stage layout for that day's recording and showed us the plan. There were three separate stages. Liam and Noel on the highest stage, but right at the back. Bonehead and Guigsy slightly below, on the middle stage. And on his own on the front stage, right at the front, Tony the Drummer. Fuckin' brilliant. 'About time they put the looks up front,' I told the rest of the band, to hoots of derision and playful punches thrown. 'Maybe this will boost the number of female fans,' I added, only to be attacked again.

Afterwards, as I searched for a toilet, I was stopped by a runner who told me I was required in make-up immediately. I made my way there and spent a good 30 minutes in the chair, being made to look orange and waxy by a gorgeous-looking girl. I asked her if she'd be doing the make-up for the rest of the band, to which she replied that the rest of them had refused to come down due to their, quote, 'masculinity'. I looked at myself in that mirror surrounded by lightbulbs and thought, Fuckin' hell, I'm gonna get ripped to shreds. I looked like Dale Winton. After returning, to a bout of howling and piss-taking, I sat proudly at the front, blemish free.

* * *

We were standing at a cash point on Piccadilly Gardens in Manchester city centre on a wet and cold summer's evening. The Lemonheads' Evan Dando stood shuffling in the queue for the cash machine, his sheepskin coat pulled over his head to protect him from the Mancunian drizzle. Evan had become an honorary member of the band, upon his own insistence.

He suddenly swivelled around and yelled at the top of his voice, 'Hey guys, how much money shall I get out?' The American accent alerted all possible scoundrels that it might be feeding time. Like meerkats, certain cagoule-clad individuals in the queue suddenly become upright and alert.

'Five hundred will do us for now,' said Liam, with a laugh. 'And hurry the fuck up.'

The meerkats were now aware that the American had local back-up and their necks retracted, although a couple seemed to be weighing us up as well.

'Are you sure that's enough?' asked the oblivious Dando.

'Well if it ain't, we can come back after midnight,' I reassured him, as Liam stared down anyone who might still appear interested.

Although we had released our first two singles and were by now regarded as the saviours of British rock music, neither Liam nor me had the proverbial pot to piss in. So with Evan Dando's wedge of notes, it was party time. Liam made the phone call and we waited outside Hurley's Sports shop on Piccadilly. Fifteen minutes later, a Honda Civic pulled over and the drugs were delivered. We immediately headed for Corbiere's, a club basement bar that housed what must have been the most comprehensive jukebox in the North-West.

Dando began to rattle on about how he and Courtney Love were very close and I advised him to step back and take a good, long look. Never understood that Courtney Love thing. He then told us that she had given him Kurt Cobain's coat, which he was wearing. It was a scruffy old chequered trench coat. We headed back to his hotel room, where we watched as Dando proved how tough the hotel windows were by running towards them and then leaping at them. We were on the 10th floor. My heart stopped every time he connected, as I was sure the window would shatter and Dando would fall to his death. I diagnosed it as Extreme Attention Seeking Syndrome.

'Evan Helpus', as we had taken to calling him, suffered terribly from this debilitating syndrome. At the Buckley Tivoli, he had invaded the stage when we began 'Live Forever'. He had brought a girl with him, with whom he waltzed round the stage. We all looked at each other as if to say, What the fuck? He had also 'written' a song with Noel one night, which he labelled 'Purple Parallelogram'. Not too sure how much of this songwriting Noel remembered, though.

We had gone out in Manchester to celebrate the impending release of 'Live Forever', which we knew was a fantastic record. It turned into a hazy evening of low-quality drugs and alcohol. I was told later that Dando then returned to his hotel, near Manchester Airport. Apparently, he wound up totally destroying his room, which woke up the rest of the floor. When the hotel management visited to remove him, he barricaded himself in. The police were duly called, and identified him as a potential lunatic. Finally, six experienced police officers armed with machine guns broke his resistance and arrested him. I never saw him again.

8 AUGUST 1994. 'LIVE FOREVER' RELEASED. REACHED NO.10 IN THE SINGLES CHART

Our third single was a stormer and my personal favourite. Our first Top Ten hit. I suppose if anything reminded me of the fantastic time we had in Liverpool, it was this song. Noel was furious, though, after reading an *NME* review that alluded to the same:

> *Two ungainly slabs of thug-boogie down the line, and I had this lot marked down less as the Beatle-browed saviours of rock n roll and more as The Real People for 94. Remember the Real People? Scally bruisers with a heavier take on baggy, a taste for scrapes and an inevitable obsession with the Fab Four... See? 'Live Forever' though, is much, much better. With predictable bravado Noel classes it alongside 'Wild Horses' and 'Cortez the Killer', but really it's more like the Las 'There She Goes'. It totally gives off the impression that the Gallaghers believe they can make the world dance around their little fingers – which they can nowadays, more or less. And it even succeeds at being extremely pretty, a quality you'd hardly expect from such svelte sophisticates. Basically what thus far looked like Mancunian lad arrogance, looks like sheer effortlessness. A terrific record.*
> John Mulvey

The fact that John Mulvey had alluded to the influence of The Real People had upset Noel's equilibrium. To throw petrol on the fire, I asked if they would get their production credits on 'Supersonic'. Noel seemed less than amused. But neither was I.

9 AUGUST 1994. THE RIVERSIDE, NEWCASTLE

We were playing to another hall that was packed to the rafters. It was a particularly wild one; I watched a full can of lager fly over the crowd, soaking those under its flight path. Radio One were broadcasting the concert live and Jo Wiley was watching us from the crowd. Jo always enthused about us as a band and we all really liked her. There was something grounded and normal about her. Liam was receiving the usual heckles and stood glowering into the crowd.

We had just started 'Bring It on Down' when I first noticed him. He was stary-eyed and his face was pulled tight in anger. Then he was off, jumping the barrier and running towards us. Before I could move, he had jumped onto the stage. His arm retracted quickly and then he punched Noel square in the eye. Noel howled and sank to the floor. I pushed my kit over and with Liam, set about the assailant, who was about to complete a follow-up blow on Noel. Liam caught him on the jaw as I threw a flying kick. The roadies and security then jumped on him, which upset the crowd, who now viewed the invader as the underdog. He was dragged off stage and it was announced that the gig was cancelled. This news did not go down very well at all. To add fuel to the already raging fire, Noel then picked up a microphone stand and raised it above his head. He moved to the front of the stage, where he shook it victoriously. I watched as balls of phlegm were launched in his direction and became aware that the hostility of the crowd had boiled over. Bonehead and Guigs stood motionless, with their instruments still strapped on, through the whole commotion.

'C'mon, let's go,' said Liam and we quickly headed off stage. After being told to leave our belongings in the dressing room, as they would be collected later, we were fired out the fire exit to the entry behind the concert hall and into our minibus. Our bus had seats that could spin 360 and the windows were blacked out. The only problem we had was that there was a car parked immediately in front of us, which blocked our escape. As we sat and pondered our next move, the crowd erupted out of a door further down and quickly spotted the van. The mob soon surrounded us, and were intent on our blood.

'Just push the car out of the way,' I screamed at the driver as the first brick left a spider web on the strengthened window next to me. He put the bus into gear and slowly, at first, started to push the car. All the band were now in their seats, with their heads between their knees. Bricks and bottles rained down on the bus. Somebody was attacking the back door windows with a steel pipe and I was thinking that it was gonna come through any minute and then we would be in trouble. The bus driver, though, suddenly created enough space to swing his vehicle around the car and we pulled off. I heard screams as we ran over somebody's limb and watched as those still clinging to the bus were thrown to one side.

30 AUGUST 1994. *DEFINITELY MAYBE* RELEASED. REACHED NO.1 IN THE ALBUM CHART

We released our first album to huge critical acclaim. *Definitely Maybe* became the fastest-selling debut of all time and would eventually shift over 7.5 million copies. It hit No.1 on the first week of release and stayed there for three weeks, while also topping the charts in over 30 other countries. Since then, it has been voted both the best debut album and the best album ever released. I guess when I sit my grandchildren down and try to define my life, I will have to point to this record. It had really meant something to me to be working with the boys I had grown up with, the boys who had known just how harsh times could be in Manchester. We took on the world with our band of merry Mancunian men and no one could stop us. And then we made this album. With the magic of Owen Morris sprinkled all over it, it was a rock 'n' roll debut to be extremely proud of. And I was.

5 SEPTEMBER 1994. HACIENDA, MANCHESTER

We played the Hacienda which was always going to be a hectic night. The house security weren't the sort to let you think you were different because you were the band. And they weren't the sort you would argue with either.

Shaun Ryder was backstage before the gig. He wanted to watch the performance from the side of the stage but Noel wasn't wearing it. Our security man told Shaun 'it's not going to happen' which led to a barrage of unveiled threats from a pissed off Shaun. I noticed that Noel had made himself scarce.

It was a solid performance at the Hacienda and it was good to see so many familiar faces. The after-gig dressing room was in a jubilant mood and the gin and tonics were flowing. Unfortunately, events were brought to a premature end as we were ejected by the house security in a very no-nonsense manner. Nobody argued. Not even our own security. We just drank up and left. Shaun Ryder was stood amongst the security and gave us a little wave and a smile as we did.

CHAPTER 6

OASIS ADULATION AND THE BASSIST REVELATION

JAPAN TOUR

PERSONNEL LIST

BAND
Liam Gallagher, vocals
Noel Gallagher, guitar
Paul Arthurs, guitar
Paul McGuigan, bass guitar
Tony McCarroll, drums

CREW
Margaret Mouzakitis, tour manager
Ian Robertson, assistant tour manager/security
Jason Rhodes, production manager
Mark Coyle, sound engineer
Roger Nowell backline technician
Melissa Linsalato, merchandise/promotion

Quattro, Tokyo (Japan) – 13 September
Quattro, Tokyo (Japan) – 14 September
Quattro, Toyko (Japan) – 15 September
Quattro, Toyko (Japan) – 16 September
Quattro, Osaka (Japan) – 18 September
Quattro, Nagoya (Japan) – 19 September

11 SEPTEMBER 1994. RINGWAY AIRPORT, MANCHESTER

We were off to the Land of the Rising Sun for the first time. I couldn't fucking wait. I'd been interested in Japanese culture ever since I'd watched Monkey blowing on his finger to summon his cloud car on BBC2.

We were sitting in the airport lounge, waiting for the shuttle to London, when Noel told everyone that, for whatever reason, they were not to put The Real People on any future guest lists. This came as a shock to everyone.

Liam told him to fuck right off. 'I'll put on whoever I want,' he said angrily. 'And then I'll take them off,' came the reply from Noel. He would soon take to checking the guest lists and removing people he didn't want. This would cause constant problems for the rest of us.

The recordings from the studio in Bootle, and also the recording we released as 'Supersonic', had original production credits to the Claggies. This is what Noel would call the two Scousers as a joke and was part of the deal we struck when we had arrived at their door with a desperate look and three songs. I had noticed no production credits on the album's version for them, though.

We were on a 12-hour flight and already into the complimentaries. Noel had sat himself away from the group after the fracas in the lounge. To amuse ourselves, I suggested we decide which Monkey character each band member should be. We all nominated ourselves for Monkey himself, but Liam insisted that it has to be him as he was the lead singer. I wasn't sure about the logic on that one, but we moved on. Guigsy was put forward for Pigsy, mainly because of the fact that one name rhymed with the other, but also due to his eating habits. Bonehead's haircut was similar to the cut sported by Sandy the Fishface, so that was him sorted, which left me as Horse. When asked by a stewardess why I was called Horse, I explained it was due to my large genitalia. Seemed to be a distinct lack of service from there on in.

Somebody asked, 'What are we going to do for the next eleven hours?' It was a good question. Liam thrust his hand in his pocket and pulled out a bag of capsules.

'Tomazees!' shouted Guigs, and quickly threw two down his neck. Rather untypically, he had being getting amorous with one of the stewardesses, so hopefully the tablets would calm him on two fronts.

Myself and Liam followed suit and within the space of 15 minutes, it seemed, we had crossed two continents, slipped through a wormhole and were ready to land at Ota, the main airport for Tokyo.

12 SEPTEMBER 1994. TOKYO

The large jumbo had hit the tarmac with a shudder and a squeal. We gathered our belongings and shuffled off the plane. Nobody really knew what to expect in Japan. We would soon find out.

Everything in Japan seemed to be neon-lit. Even the

airport looked more like a casino. As we made our way through the bright corridors, we heard a commotion ahead. Rounding a corner, we found ourselves faced with hordes of people – mainly young and female, and mainly crying and hysterical – waving posters and banners. They were being controlled by policemen. The cameras flashed in a white explosion. When we were able to refocus, we realised the posters depicted ourselves and the banners proclaimed 'Oasis'. Fucking hell. We were immediately set upon. Photographs were taken and autographs were given. Then came the gifts. Walkmans, Game Boys, jewellery, clothes, Beatles memorabilia, underwear, DVDs, instruments, photographs, CDs. As these gifts were bestowed upon us, I decided there would be no need for Christmas shopping this year. Liam looked over at me. He had at least thirty girls pulling at him – his clothes, his hair, his ears. But he was laughing as he tried to extract himself from their grasp. We managed to regroup and fought our way out of the airport to the waiting vehicles. As we did so, the clawing crowd moved with us. To be honest, that crowd would move with us for the next five days or so. Oasismania!

The waiting vehicles sped off into Tokyo centre. Along the way, we passed buildings that reached far into the night sky. The neon lights attached to these buildings gave off a fluorescent glow that lit the night, making everything luminous and magic. It was extremely impressive, but I wouldn't like to see the 'leccy bills.

We arrived at our hotel, which was already a staging point for another two to three hundred fans. They stood outside, in eager anticipation of our arrival. The group seemed to be a carbon copy of the airport crowd, who would also be heading this way shortly, hot on our tails. This was the first time the band had received such adulation and, to be honest, we were all a bit thrown by it, in particular Liam. More flesh was grabbed at, clothes torn and presents received.

Paul Slattery had also joined the tour. Liam had insisted he travel to Japan with us to document our Far Eastern adventure. He was clicking and flashing away to his heart's content.

We booked into the Roppongi Hotel and were informed that our room had three single beds. So there were three single beds and only me and Bonehead to fill them. There was a fella from Levenshulme called Fatboy who had also accepted Liam's invite to come along, but had had to pay his own way. He overheard our room arrangements and asked if we minded him bedding down. We were unsure at first, as Fatboy was in his forties and the nightlife could get a bit hectic. Last thing we needed was a 40-year-old sat there when we returned. Things were weird enough already. But Fatboy was one of us, so we offered him the third bed in our room. Always looked after our own. Loyalty and trust counted.

Me, Bonehead and Fatboy headed to our sterile hotel room. Plastic, white and spotlessly clean. No television or mini-bar, which suggested that our reputation had preceded us. And the fact that we had been placed on the 15th floor meant that anything thrown from a window really would be deadly. I made this point to Bonehead. We immediately threw our bags under the bed and headed back out towards the adulation, leaving Fatboy behind. He had some knowledge of Tokyo and had promised to take the band to the finest noodle bar in town. Judging by the size of him he probably had excellent knowledge of most types of restaurants. We were not due to play until the following night, so like excited children me and Bonehead were off into the noisy and frantic Tokyo streets.

We had two hours before we met the rest of the crew for some food, so we decided to go for a drink. Bonehead located a bar or, 'izakaya', and made to enter. He was stopped and asked to remove his footwear. This request was met with some hostility. 'Yer can fuck off if yer think I'm taking me shoes off. I've got big fuck-off holes in me socks,' Bonehead told them.

The door staff were adamant, though, and it was not long before me and Bonehead were sat on a slightly raised cushioned platform, facing each other with legs crossed. Bonehead's big toe peeked out from the end of his sock. It was hairier than his head. He was shouting for wine, wine, wine. The bartender came over, poured out some local sake and explained in English that is wine made from rice.

'Rice?' replied Bonehead, incredulously 'Wine is made from fucking grapes, mate, not rice.'

'They don't have mass use of grapes in Japan,' I said, trying to help Bonehead cross that great cultural divide.

'What, not even in the supermarkets?' Bonehead slurred back.

I shook my head. He had not even started proper drinking yet. We both raised our glasses and saluted each other. We then threw the sweet-tasting liquid down our throats. Bonehead paused for a moment and then his eyes lit up; he ordered two more. Within an hour, he was completely decimated and I was glad I had restrained myself. He wound up telling me he was going to try and 'ferment a box of Uncle Ben's' when he returned to England. We were late, so I told him the rest of the band would be waiting for us and we needed to head back to the hotel. But, yeah, good idea with the Uncle Ben's.

Bonehead tucked his feet under his ankles and laughed, but then lost his balance and rolled off the platform onto the marble below. He was floundering on the polished floor of the bar, lying on his side but still in a lotus position. He looked at me helplessly, unable to free his legs. The rest of the bar looked on in disgust. I laughed and decided I'd better get him back to the hotel and into a cold shower, so I untangled him and we left.

When we returned to the hotel room, we were met by Fatboy's duvet rising up and down at a furious speed. I guessed that, like most people who had got on the Oasis bus, he had been intoxicated by the hype and furore surrounding the band. We were impressed by his speed of conquest, though, it had to be said. After all, he was in his forties, balding and shaped like a dough ball. But then again, considering the circumstances, I suppose it wasn't that hard. Bonehead set about trying to shower while mullered, as the duvet continued to rise up and down and muffled grunts and groans were emitted. Bonehead shouted encouragement from the bathroom as he showered and then reappeared.

'I need to iron my gear,' he slurred.

The shower hadn't done him much good, by the look of it.

'You look great,' I lied. We left, with Bonehead looking proper chuffed with his crumpled rock star look.

We headed back down to the bar to find the rest of the group as arranged, using the stairs so as to bypass the groupies. Noel, Liam and Guigs were sat waiting for us. They all looked deliriously happy. At the bar stood Fatboy, who was mouthing 'Do you want a drink?' at us.

Me and Bonehead looked at each other in confusion. If

Fatboy is here, then who the fuck is writhing around in our room? Fatboy later admitted to giving his key to one of the road crew, who had told him he needed a shower. I told Fatboy that the shower in question might not be the one he had imagined.

We headed off for a night of noodles and JD. Not the greatest of bedfellows, those two. It seemed that the mob of fans had disappeared until Liam pointed out of the noodle bar window.

'Fuckin' hell, check this out,' he said.

There must have been three hundred girls headed down the street towards us. Cars had ground to a halt in the melee, horns blaring. As the pack got nearer, the sound of girls screaming gradually increased. One girl floated from nowhere in front of the window and simply pointed at Liam, her mouth agape. The noodle bar owner, who at first had stood watching in some perplexity, suddenly realised that we were the attraction and the hordes were heading his way. He barked some orders and the door was locked and the waiters sent out to guard the steps to the entrance. This absolute fucking bedlam would surround us until we left, five days later. We were eventually ushered out the back and advised to return to the hotel; we would see more kitchens than foyers on that trip.

The Japanese were very musically aware and really knew how to enjoy themselves. They immersed themselves in the experience. Without wanting to sound chauvinistic, that evening I eyed up a pretty little thing who kept fluttering her eyes at me. She had an innocent look and seemed quiet. After I got her alone, all that changed. I had a right talker. I wasn't interested in talking, though. As she rattled away at me, I was mentally planning how to get her back to my room. I went for the direct approach once more, but she insisted we sit and drink and talk first. Or rather, she talked. I drank, frustrated by her talking. We finally headed back to my room where, after some more talking, I finally got her to the point of no return. She headed off to the bathroom to defrock. There was now nothing between me and a night of oriental passion. When she returned, she was stood in front of me wearing a bra and an impenetrable pair of hard plastic knickers. There was a key-shaped hole on the side panel where these 'knickers' could be unlocked. I stared at her, not knowing what to say.

'You ain't got a key for them, have you?' I finally asked her, forlornly.

She shook her head.

'I didn't think so.'

Time for sleep.

The following morning, the band were up early and communicating only by room phone. The corridors were still awash with girls trying to locate where we were. I spoke to Guigs, who wasn't himself. Guigs had never been one for the ladies. I'd tried to explain to him that cricket statistics or the correct direction for shaving facial hair would not interest them, but he remained shy around women. This was the worst possible place for him to be. No weed and a hundred women wanting to talk to him.

For the rest of us, though, it was open season. We were young and full of trouble and we were worshipped for it. We had a No.1 album and we were the biggest band in the UK. We didn't think in terms of words such as 'consequence', 'responsibility', 'morality' and 'self-control', as they didn't apply to us.

That night we played our first of four consecutive nights at the Quattro club in Tokyo. The final two nights, we were to head off for Nagoya and Osaka. All nights had sold out. The crowds were jubilant and really knew how to enjoy themselves. Their energy rubbed off on us and we began what would be a set of six supersonic performances. Liam was playing football with the crowd and they hung on his every move, silent at every utterance. He was as happy as I'd ever seen him.

The Japanese elders had a very clean-cut image of how a rock 'n' roll gig should be arranged. For all the intense fanaticism and rock 'n' roll debauchery that occurred before during and after the show, we would have to be finished each gig by eight o'clock at night. Also, the clubs where we played would have no bars. The only intoxicant was the music. This seemed a happy compromise. The seniors had their self-righteousness serviced, while the younger generation partied away afterwards. The whole culture was built on respect. We would greet people by bowing our heads and joining our hands together as in prayer.

As each gig would be finished by eight in the evening, it left us the rest of the night to fill. And we did some filling. We were at one small club when a Beatle tribute band scrambled on to the stage. It seemed that the city revolved around bands and musical influences. We all swayed in rhythm, with the help of the sixties sound and more sake.

Suddenly, Noel said, 'Fuck this' and promptly jumped up on the stage with the band. He soon had a guitar strapped on and was happily playing away, to the enjoyment of the band and the crowd. We moved on to the next club, which was a bit more disco. Me and Liam watched as the floor in the middle of the club lit up with frenetic strobe lighting. Suddenly, a couple appeared at the far side of the dance floor.

At first I thought that perhaps a new dance craze had stormed Japan. It seemed to involve the man dragging the woman by her hair across the floor and then, with some force, twisting away while she followed behind. It became apparent it wasn't a dance when he slapped her. Liam was over in a flash and I followed.

'What you doing, dickhead? Let her be,' Liam shouted.

He then tried to wrestle the woman from the man's grasp. The man shouted back furiously in Japanese as he held onto her tightly. I reflected that Japanese is a great language to use when you're angry, as whatever he was saying sounded fucking terrifying.

Liam didn't flinch or shout back, though. He was a good foot taller than his opponent and shot out a sharp left instead. Crack. The man's eyes opened wide as he realised he'd been socked. In that moment, Liam finally wrestled the woman from his grasp and pulled her to safety. Liam would always step in if he believed an injustice was being carried out and I admired him for that. Socked and shocked, the man made his exit.

We headed back to the hotel and sat in the lobby, drinking. It was just the five of us and we talked about how mind-blowing Japan had been. We had all consumed a lot of drink and Guigs was firing from too much Jack Daniel's and sake. His usual stoned silent observer role was gone. He hadn't stopped jabbering for an hour. Noel and Liam started on their childhood and how difficult it had been. That was unusual in itself. They didn't often talk about their upbringing. It was almost as if they had learnt to repeat what the papers had been writing. I'm not belittling Noel's issues, but their upbringing was virtually the same as everyone else's in the band. It was the seventies in Manchester. That's how it was.

I headed for the toilets. These were a very simple affair. It was as if someone had cut a circle in the middle of a pallet and then placed the pallet over a hole. As I weighed the situation up, Guigs arrived.

'Fuckin' hell, I can't believe how bad Noel had it,' he said.

His eyes were rolling from the drink. I argued that it was the same for a lot of people, which Guigs immediately took to mean something else.

'You don't care? You don't care?' He was sneering at me..

'I didn't say that,' I said in my defence.

'Yes you did,' he snarled and walked out of the door, announcing loudly towards the rest of the group that 'Tony said he doesn't care about your childhood, Noel.' What the fuck is wrong with him, I thought. It would become apparent a couple of days later.

When I left the toilet, Noel was standing there, waiting for me. I told him, 'I didn't say that.' He said nothing. Just stared at me. Then headed to his room.

14 SEPTEMBER 1994. NAGOYA

I was in Liam's room. Liam had almost completed his intense education around all things Beatle, and in particular John Lennon, that he had started in the States. The book pile was reducing. I could see how Liam would relate to Lennon and thought he made a good role model: that fighting Scouse spirit that had helped us back with the Realies, and a sense of social injustice to boot. All underpinned with a proclamation of world peace. I explained to him that Guigs had twisted my words the previous evening. I didn't have to, though, as Liam knew me and told me not to worry. Noel was not as understanding.

The final gig was at Club Quattro, Nagoya. Nagoya was yet another neon lit, obsessed fan-filled city. We travelled there during the day on board a silver bullet train. All the adulation had had a euphoric effect on us and we were in severe party mode. The paddy fields whirred by as we passed through the lush and wet Japanese countryside.

'What are they called?' asked Guigs, as he pointed out the train window.

'Paddy fields,' replied Noel.

'I went to school with a kid called Paddy Fields,' slurred Bonehead, who had now adopted the title Captain Sake.

We arrived late at a futuristic-looking train station, to be met once more by a mass of screaming and pawing. The performance that night went down as one of the best performances I ever took part in. Even Liam was smiling out front. We did an encore, our first. It was 'Rock 'n' Roll Star'. I had thrown my sticks into the crowd at the end of the show, so had to go back out and retrieve them. I then later returned them to the same fan. Bonehead had been drinking sake and, that evening, the emotion of the event had overtaken him. As we finished the encore, he grabbed for the microphone. We all stood by, bemused. He made his way to the front of the stage, where he struggled as he sat down. When he finally settled, he put his hand over his mouth to stifle a small cry. He looked at the crowd with his doleful eyes, shiny with tears.

'I just want to say…' he sobbed only for the crowd to go wild at the sound of his words. Thank fuck for that, I thought. The rest of the band pissed themselves.

The final aftershow was a wild one. I remember jumping up to dance and coming across Liam on the dance floor. As we passed each other, 'Supersonic' kicked in and we danced along to it together, singing loudly; as we quickly realised we were making right twats of ourselves, we headed to our seats. Our performance did not go unnoticed, though, as we had been spotted by the rest of the band. They pointed over at us and wet themselves. Everyone in the band took something different from Japan. It was our first taste of stardom and already strange people were jumping on board.

'John Lennon is searing through my veins.' said Liam, as we were sitting in the bar. I thought that he needed to stop reading them books now. Then I noticed one of our financial team enter the lobby. He came over and brought out a piece of paper that highlighted certain aspects of the contract we had signed way back in October the previous year. He said he wanted to confirm these aspects of the contract with us.

Although I was unsure what was going on, I knew that you didn't fly to another continent 'just to confirm' something. It seemed there was more to this than met the eye. The band looked at each other as if to support ourselves.

'I ain't signing fuck all. If it's no different than the first contract, our signatures on that should be good enough. So you can fuck right off back to Blighty,' instructed Liam, before he even had time to detail the document. I could see no reason to sign as I simply didn't think it was necessary.

Liam was extremely wary of the businessmen that surrounded the band at this time. After five years of our own sweat and toil, as soon as the first sniff of success wafted their way they had descended like vultures. Noel had the opposite view, though, and he stared at Liam, annoyed at our refusal to sign the document.

Later that evening, Guigs told me that, although he had

looked at the document, he had already known what it had outlined. Wouldn't tell me what that was, though. At least, not yet.

* * *

'This is fate.' Liam said to her.

This was the band's communal chat-up line. Not the most original, I know, but it would send the right girl all silly. Sitting next to him was a quite stunning Japanese girl who had approached him earlier on. She was dressed immaculately and sat holding Liam's hand. As far as Liam was concerned, he had met his own personal Yoko, only better looking. She was taller than the average Japanese girl and could only speak a handful of English words. They sat there for the rest of the evening simply staring at each other and exchanging the little language they could. Liam was fixated. There was no other way to describe it. Just the fact he was quiet told me that. There was something definitely alluring about her. She looked beautiful, but dangerous too. Liam later flew her over to England. He remarked afterwards that it had been a mistake, because he couldn't understand her. Could have figured that one out in Japan, I suppose.

Me and Noel were left in the bar.

'Can't go to my room. There's too many women in there. Never thought I'd have a complaint like that,' he said, with a laugh. Security were already heading to his room to remove the groupies as Noel ordered a final round. It had been a fucking kicking tour and it was sad to see it end. Noel sat down.

'Who was that with Liam?' he enquired. I told him about Yoko and Noel chuckled.

'You enjoyed it?' he asked.

I smiled and said, 'I'll always enjoy it.'

We clinked beers and I finally felt that everything was going to be all right. I suppose that times like these made my struggle with Noel even more frustrating. The flashes of the old Noel were seldom, though; most of the time, the cocaine-charged Commander-in-Chief was around.

I would love to finish the Japan story here, where it should end. Instead, the following morning there was trouble brewing. Due to the shortage of drugs on the tour, the dynamic of the group had changed. Scandinavian tours were also particularly difficult for this reason. The shortage of one vice led to an overindulgence in another.

That evening, we made our way through the enormous Japanese hotel lobby towards a fleet of taxis that awaited us. Guigs stepped in front of me. He had been ignoring me for the last day or so, which was fine by me considering what had happened in the toilets. He turned to me with an angry look on his face.

'Noel added a three-month notice period to the record contract you signed. If he wants to sack you, he can. That's you fucked. See you later.'

He turned and started to walk away. This was the first time anyone had mentioned a change in the contract. If what Guigs was saying was true, that explained his behaviour in the toilets. I felt he was clearly siding with Noel. Nice one, Guigs. I teetered on the edge. With the unavailability of any herb and the influence of only alcohol, Guigs could turn unpredictable. But this was different. We had crossed a line. We were never to return.

'Fuck off, Guigs. I'd rather go down fighting than giving out blowjobs like you. Get a fucking backbone, you soft cunt. Stand up to him. You didn't even get to record on the album,' I shouted after him. That was a low blow, but I was tired of it all. I wasn't sure if this 'three-month period' statement was true. If it was, we were all in serious trouble. Noel's masterplan was exactly that. Noel's.

Noel had wiped all of Guigs's recordings from *Definitely Maybe* and had re-recorded them himself. Guigs himself had told me that. This was down to Guigs's style of playing, which worked live but could throw a recording. I had learnt to adapt to his playing over time. We all had our little areas we needed to work on, but it seemed to me that Guigs couldn't take that next step.

I knew that I had to develop as a drummer and not everything I'd recorded was beat perfect. All musicians will point out flaws in their recorded material. That's the nature of the beast.

As if to strengthen his relationship with Noel, he had now also started to berate me, as Noel did. Again, I wasn't having any of it. Is this the same man that I had defended when Liam had tried to have him removed to make way for Noel? Was this the man I had defended like a brother and lent a helping hand to all those years ago?

Guigs did not take my reference to his absence on *Definitely Maybe* too well. 'You stupid Mick cunt,' he spat back viciously, even though his own blood was Irish.

'Shut it, Mr Milli Vanilli,' I shot back, laughing.

That remark sent him over the edge. His face went purple. McGuigan looked to his right. Through the 60ft-high lobby window, he saw the whole group watching from their taxis outside. Seeing this audience had spurred him on, and now he moved towards me – like an angry slug. He moved directly up to me and placed his sloping forehead against mine. It felt like I was getting amorous with Mr Potato Head.

That was the only time I had seen McGuigan actually front someone. And it was me! It was obvious he was trying to save face in front of the ever-growing crowd on the other side of the window. I was gutted that it had come to this. Aggravated by his history of manipulating conversations to his own advantage, I decided I had better do something. With everyone outside unable to hear, I decided that a game of charades was in order. Like a possessed Lionel Blair, I started to point at my chin and then hung it out right in front of McGuigan.

'There you go, Paul,' I said, still pointing to my chin. 'If you want to be a hard man, hit me. But I promise you this, as soon as you do I will take you apart piece by piece.'

With that I turned my head away and smiled at the crowd outside. I was praying that Guigs didn't slap me, as I was wide open. He didn't, so I straightened up and shook my head. I said nothing, but I was proper fucked off. I would have flattened him there and then, and that was a strange and new feeling for me. Me and Guigs went back a long way. We had been through the mill, but I had always stood next to him. I had simply had enough now. It was bad enough being disrespected by Noel, but by Guigs? Someone who I had stood up for and looked after for the last 10 years? It seemed to me that Guigs had rammed his head that far up Noel's arse that Noel had to brush two sets of teeth in the morning. During that tour, the dynamic in the band really changed. I still had Liam and Bonehead onside, and would do right up until my departure. But Guigs seemed to have decided that he was gonna be the main cheerleader for Team Noel. For the next eight months, anything that Noel threw at me would be repeated by the echo chamber known as Guigs.

After this altercation, and having considered his remark

about the contract, I decided to front Noel. I spoke to him later: 'Guigs has just told me that I'm on three months' notice. What the fuck is all that about?' I said.

'Have I told you that?' he shot back, looking furious. I wasn't sure if he was furious that Guigs had threatened me or furious that I had been told.

'No,' I replied.

'Well, don't fuckin' worry about it, then.'

Don't fuckin' worry? Noel seemed to be displaying some signs of a good man gone bad. He would not tell me I was going to be sacked even if I was. And he certainly wouldn't tell me if he'd changed the contract. I felt I had tried everything to smooth over this situation, but to no avail. Noel had become a different man.

CHAPTER 7

MAKE SURE YOU HOOVER BEFORE YOU REACH VANCOUVER

US TOUR

PERSONNEL LIST

BAND
Liam Gallagher, vocals
Noel Gallagher, guitar
Paul Arthurs, guitar
Paul McGuigan, bass guitar
Tony McCarroll, drums

CREW
Margaret Mouzakitis, tour manager
Jason Rhodes, production manager
Mark Coyle, sound engineer
Phil Smith, backline technician
Melissa Linsalato, merchandise/promotion
Doug Sheffler, bus driver

20 SEPTEMBER 1994. SEATTLE

We were in the air again. United Airlines Flight 828, from Tokyo to Seattle. We'd just left Japan and the greatest week ever behind us as we took the Oasis bandwagon on its first major overseas tour. To paraphrase the great Neil Diamond, 'We're going to America.'

We arrived at Seattle Sea-Tac Airport, eager to see what craziness awaited here. Japan had seriously blown our minds. The whole group exited the arrival lounge... to be greeted by fuck all. Not a solitary fan. Just your normal array of middle-aged drivers holding up card boards with names on them. No Japanese-style adulation. We made our way outside, to be greeted by a bright yellow minibus with 'West Coast Bellevue Motel' blazed across the bonnet. We hopped on and were soon delivered to a motel. The skies and our hearts darkened in unison. Japan had been such an intense ride that this was a severe comedown.

We booked in and hit the bar. Guigs was in a good mood, as he had an opportunity to finally find himself some weed and was itching to go.

'Let's go into town. C'mon, drink up,' he rushed me. I'd thought he seemed intent on making up for the scene in the hotel lobby. I noticed, though, he waited until no one else was around before he tried to right the situation. Then I realised he was not trying to make up at all. It was just that no one else would go with him on a search for drugs.

We were soon in a taxi heading for the city centre. Five months earlier, Kurt Cobain had decided to end it all in Seattle. As I looked out the window, I could understand why. And I thought Manchester was gloomy and depressing.

When we arrived in the city centre, we started Operation Narcotic. The taxi driver was the first person to be fronted.

He had no local drug knowledge whatsoever and looked relieved when we jumped out into the hustle and bustle of the city. Our Mancunian front could easily be misunderstood.

After two hours of fruitlessly questioning the unsuspecting Seattle public, we decided that enough was enough and headed back to the hotel. I could see the disappointment in Guigs's face as he realised he wasn't going to score. When we returned, we headed our separate ways. I was off to the bar with Jason Rhodes, our guitar tech. After an hour or so with Mr Jack Daniel's, we were feeling suitably relaxed. We'd started a conversation with an unassuming guest who was sitting in the corner of the bar, reading a newspaper. He asked our business, so I told him. He was excited by the musician part and recalled the old days, when he would follow Neil Young around the country. He then asked if I had any pot. I laughed and explained our dire situation. With that he made a phone call and told me he was going to put me in touch with someone. He then gave me a phone number on a crumpled piece of paper. I rang and placed an order for delivery.

'Go heavy on the topping,' I joked. The dealer remained silent, which made me feel like a right twat. I mooched down to Guigs's room and told him the news. As agreed, the weed was hand delivered by a huge black man, resplendent in cheap gold. All was good in the world again.

21 SEPTEMBER 1994. SEATTLE

The following day, Noel asked who I had got the weed off. Noel didn't smoke the herb and wanted to locate some bugle instead. I gave him the story and the phone number and he wandered to the other side of the hotel lobby to make his call. Fifty dollars each was the buy-in and with delivery service not available Noel himself was going to fetch it.

'Be careful,' I warned him, as no matter how confident you were any transaction involving cash and drugs could quite easily get dangerous.

'Listen I've been there, done it, got the sweatshirt, cap and key ring. No need to fuckin' worry about me,' replied Noel.

'We're coming with you,' said Liam, and looked at me for support.

'Yeah, I know what the guy looks like,' I added.

Noel considered this and then reluctantly said, 'Right you fuckin' pair of clowns, come on, then.' I didn't think Noel was happy about the arrangement. We jumped in a taxi and headed once more for the centre of Seattle.

When we arrived, Noel pushed past me and Liam and headed out the taxi to conclude the deal; we had given him every last cent of our 'per day' money for the drugs. We watched as he made his way towards the bus stop. It had a large waiting room, the inside of which was hidden by thick plastic glass that had criss-cross wire mesh running through it. As Noelly Montana approached, a very large black man stepped into his path. It was the same man who had delivered to us the previous day.

'You with the kid from yesterday?' he asked Noel.

'Yes,' said Noel.

From behind you could see that Noel's leg was shaking slightly. He had suddenly become very nervous. I imagine it was even more apparent from the front. The dealer immediately took control of the situation and took the money from Noel. Didn't give Noel the drugs, though. Basic drug purchasing mistake, I thought. I didn't like where this was going. The dealer pointed inside the bus shelter and then slid off with a wink and a smile. Noel darted into the shelter and a few moments later returned with a bag. It might turn out OK after all, I thought to myself. He jumped in the back of the taxi and behind the cover of the passenger seat he dipped two fingers in the white powder and placed it on his tongue to test for quality. He quickly dipped again for another sample and then turned to us and said, 'I think it's flour. Self-raising flour.'

Like we gave a fuck what type of flour it was. All that we gave a fuck about was the fact it was not cocaine. We looked at Noel, expecting some kind of apology for his fuck-up. As usual, it was not forthcoming. Although he would readily ridicule anyone else's misdemeanours, I seldom heard him apologise for his own.

23 SEPTEMBER 1994. SEATTLE

We were up early and itching to go. Japan had been barnstorming, performance wise, and it had been nearly a week since we had performed. Suitably recharged, we headed for Moe's tavern on 10th Street in Seattle. It was a good gig, but somehow the heights of the Japanese trip seemed to have raised our expectations and even the first night of the tour had an air of drudgery about it. Afterwards, we travelled down through Castle Rock and into Portland, Oregon. Although the herb corner was content, those of our party fuelled by a more galvanising stimulant were suffering, due to the 'flour incident' in Seattle. They took to their beds early. Slept away their cravings.

24 SEPTEMBER 1994. PORTLAND

As we arrived in the early morning, we decided to take a walk around Portland. We walked the city, happy to be free from the confines of the bus and lazily strolled down Lovejoy Street as the sun bounced off the Willamette River towards Mount St Helens, which rose to the east of the city. It was a beautiful place and a beautiful day. The mood was light hearted. It was twelve noon when we arrived at the Satyricon, where we were playing that evening.

We introduced ourselves, to be offered a free round on the house. I was just beginning to get used to that American hospitality thing, and I liked it. Guess I don't have to spell out what happened next. We had a right old day playing cards and just being us again. The rest of the bar had warmed to us; songs were sung, jokes were told and there was not an insult in sight. A welcome break for us all. Particularly me. By 6pm, Noel was as ratted as the rest of us. We were ordered back to the bus to refresh ourselves. On our return, we played a blistering set, mainly to the patrons we had been drinking with during the day, and then we were back on the coach. We were given a crate of Bud and a few bottles of Jack on the way out as a gift; we had a whole night and over 600 miles in which to demolish them.

'This Guy's in Love with You' by Burt Bacharach had been played constantly on the bus, courtesy of Coyley. I had pointed out the drum shuffle to Noel, as this type of drumming would sit well with some of the more acoustic songs he was developing. Noel listened, with his head cocked to one side. He said nothing and moved off. You took silence from Noel as approval, so I continued to work on this idea.

25 SEPTEMBER 1994. SAN FRANCISCO

The streets of San Francisco were melting, even in September. The cars shimmered as they approached us from the distance. The highway was filled with commuters and tourists. We were staying at the Abigail on McAllister Street.

There was a direct correlation between our ever-growing popularity and the number of 'celebrities' that had begun attending our shows. Someone had mentioned that Patsy Kensit was planning to be at tonight's gig. I told everyone that I reckoned I was in with a shot, which started them howling. 'Just watch,' I replied.

During the gig, I spotted her. She was stood at the side of the stage. It seemed that every man that passed her became instantly nervous. 'How ya doing, kid?' I said to her with a smile, when we came off stage.

'All right. What's a girl got to do to get a drink round here?' she asked.

Better not tell her that, I thought, and then instead offered, 'Why don't you meet us on the tour bus? It's quiet there, we won't get interrupted.'

'Interrupted?' she asked.

My mind was three steps ahead of the situation. It was the fact that it was Patsy Kensit that had made me lose all control. I had never succumbed to being star-struck and honestly believed that confidence would get me anything. Only almost anything, it seemed.

I hurried her onto the bus trying to ignore the last statement. She wore a Lycra stretch top, which was matched with a short black mini skirt. She had not come dressed for winter and looked absolutely stunning. I just couldn't get the image of her and Mel Gibson in *Lethal Weapon* 2, writhing around in a caravan on a white beach, out of my head. I smiled as I pictured her bouncing up and down on Gibbo just prior to him being attacked by yet another group of revenge-driven terrorists.

'What you smiling about,' she asked.

'Nothing,' I replied, with a laugh.

I just wished I could have been in Mel's position. (By that I mean getting laid, not getting petrol-bombed by terrorists.) We linked arms and made our way to the tour bus. Already present were the rest of the band. I walked on, trying to pretend that me and Patsy had made a connection. The rest of the bus started to roar with laughter, seeing straight through my charade. This left Miss Kensit a touch confused. She took a seat in the middle of all of us. I wasn't fucking happy. Already her eyes were off me and were firmly fixed on Noel. It was funny the way he attracted women. He was not exactly Hollywood handsome, yet he still seemed to get plenty of attention. Then again, I suppose even Shane MacGowan's got a woman.

She sat in front of us all, facing towards us. Now, this was not a woman short on confidence. We sat mesmerised, as we couldn't think of anything decent to say. With an innocent laugh, she then said to Noel, 'Right then, you northern hooligan. Shall we see who is capable of partying harder? I don't believe there is a man here that can drink or smoke more!'

Jesus. This was the innocent and delectable lady known as Patsy Kensit, sat with a mouth like a Liverpool dockworker. Who'd have thought? Her challenge was accepted by everyone.

Here was an actress whose poster adorned most men's bedroom walls in Manchester during that period. And before too long there she was, drinking and flirtatious. As I looked at her, I realised that I'd a snowball's chance of it being me, as she seemed in complete awe of Noel. Funnily enough, it was about as quiet I'd ever heard Liam. Who'd have thought his future wife was sat here trying to get his brother's attentions?

I think it's important that I take this opportunity to point out that the normal jealousies and insecurities that are part of most average groups of people did not apply to us as a band. It is not for me to take the moral high ground, and I know that in retrospect it was a very promiscuous and irresponsible attitude, but we were young and on the crest of worldwide musical domination. Just ask Alan McGee.

* * *

We had the day to ourselves and top of the agenda was to hunt down some bugle. If we couldn't score in Frisco we couldn't score anywhere, it seemed. The days of selling trainers from the van had come to an end and instead we had to front Maggie for our daily allowance early. This was always left to yours truly, the others implying that Maggie had a soft spot for me. Whether she did or not I didn't know, but I certainly had one for her. She was a straight-talking-from-the hip kinda lady and her self-assurance impressed me. She was also completely unflappable in every frantic or critical situation – and we put her through enough to know.

I spent an evening with Maggie and a couple of bottles of red on one occasion. She looked at me with a worried face and then said, 'You know that Noel will kick you out of the band if you continue.' I asked her what I was supposed to do. I had tried to approach him, but he would have none of it. So fuck it. Nothing I could do.

'You should stop arguing with him,' she insisted. I told her that what she called arguing, I called defending yourself. I told her how we all grew up together and had in some shape or form been together for previous 10 years. She was amazed by this and told me she hadn't realised. I laughed and went on to tell her stories about Jimmy the Butt and Trampy Spike. She was a great girl and a trusting confidant on what would be a rocky tour.

26 SEPTEMBER 1994. BOTTOM OF THE HILL, SAN FRANCISCO

Frisco was freakin' fantastic, as one of the locals informed us. That Monday, we were at the Live 105 radio station. We sat in the green room, which was painted bright yellow, and awaited instructions. Suddenly the door opened and Damon Albarn popped his head round. He clocked Noel first, but ignored him.

Then he spotted Liam and offered, 'All right, geezer?'

I liked Damon Albarn. He was a genuinely nice fella and we all – bar Noel – held him in high regard, musically. We never told him this, though.

'Fuck off,' said Liam.

Damon didn't look too impressed. The rest of Blur followed up behind Damon and laughed off Liam's insult as a joke. It wasn't. Nor was he an act. It was just typical Liam.

We played at Bottom of the Hill, a very aptly named bar. It's an old converted wooden house that looks like it might collapse in a heavy shower. I suppose it had survived numerous earthquakes, though, so it couldn't have been all that unstable. We rocked the foundations that evening and all of us were happy; Blur stood at the back, tapping their feet and nodding their heads. I've always thought them a good set of lads, even the strange one who makes cheese.

We headed off back to the Abigail for a heat-induced drinking session followed by a sweaty evening's sleep.

27 SEPTEMBER 1994. MELARKY'S, SACRAMENTO

We hit Route 80 the very next morning and made the short trip to Sacramento. Once again, the heat made the air con on the bus an essential. We played Melarkys' on Broadway and after the gig we drove overnight to Los Angeles, some 392 miles away. There seemed to be a general excitement surrounding LA, or the Lunatic Asylum as we tended to refer to it. Another man that Mr McGee introduced us to was Jeremy Pearce, who was the Chief Executive of Sony. Jeremy was a good bloke and a very shrewd operator. Although he was a most effective businessman, he wasn't your run-of-the-mill chief executive. He actually understood music and was popular with all the band – partly due to his musical knowledge and, of course, partly due to his limitless company credit card. 'Do you know, I've never realised what an important part of this band you are,' he told me.

Bullshit or not, 'Did you hear that Noel?' I shouted, chuffed by the comment. A compliment at that stage was as rare as an honest politician. There was no reply from Noel. Just that look. Lately, his insults had become particularly cutting. The rest of the group picked up on this, and we were all treading on eggshells.

28 SEPTEMBER 1994. LOS ANGELES

I woke in a cool and dark hotel room in the Hyatt on Sunset Boulevard. From Levenshulme to Los Angeles. Bonehead was still sound asleep in his bed next to mine. I was itching to get out and discover a bit of Los Angeles, though, so I dressed quietly and slipped out the door. The hotel had been dubbed 'the Riot House', due to the large number of touring bands that had stayed there. I made a mental note to let Bonehead and Liam know this. Got to keep our end up. I could see the attraction for bands, though. Nightclubs such as The Roxy, The Rainbow and The Viper Room, were just around the corner. Also nearby were The Wiltern Theater, Universal Amphitheatre, The Hollywood Bowl and Hollywood Boulevard. The Whisky a Go Go, where we were due to perform the following evening, was local too. I headed out into the crisp morning sunshine.

When I returned, Bonehead was proper excited. Later that day, he was meeting Martin, his brother, who had moved to Los Angeles. As it was also a day off, he was planning a heavy drinking session. Liam and Noel were visiting radio station KROQ for yet another interview. We tuned in to listen. One fan asked Noel if he had ever considered a penis extension. Noel replied that the band already had one on the drums. The hotel group laughed and pointed at me with some attempting a pile-on, which I fought off. Even I had to laugh at Noel that time.

I told Noel later how ironic it was that he was making jokes about penis extensions when he had the smallest penis in the band. He didn't find this funny.

We all headed out in good spirits. We first dropped in on a couple of the local bars, where I began to notice people in our troupe whispering together; like schoolboys holding their very first pack of cigarettes, they were passing something among them. Liam barged in and grabbed it. 'What the fuck's this, then?' He held a small, clear square aloft and then looked through it as if it was a monocle. 'It's crystal meth,' came the reply. Liam removed it quickly from his face. Crystal meth was not the wisest road for us to choose that evening, but as usual we all tried to outdo one another.

After Guigs stared at the present, he recounted the various issues that were associated with it: 'Hyperactivity, dry mouth, headaches, diarrheic, blurred vision, convulsions, coma, heart attack and death.' He had saved the best for last.

'Do you want some?' we asked.

'Yeah, go on then,' he replied.

We head to The Viper Room which was owned by the actor Johnny Depp. The previous year, a fellow actor, River Phoenix, had overdosed and died on the pavement outside, which had given the club a certain notoriety. Wasn't sure if I really wanted to go.

We made our way there, with me and Liam leading the way while the rest of the band were a couple of minutes behind us. The two of us entered the club and waited just inside for the rest.

Pap. Pap, pap. Gunfire rang from outside the door. Everyone in the club foyer dived for cover. Liam looked at me with panic in his eyes.

'They've shot our Noel,' he yelled, as he turned a 360, unsure what to do. I immediately ran to the front doors, to find that some unfortunate stranger had been gunned down just before the arrival of our group. Guigs was crying, hands to his face, some thirty yards up Sunset Boulevard. He had always been easily alarmed and he took this incident harder than most.

29 SEPTEMBER 1994. THE WHISKY A GO GO, LOS ANGELES

Five am. This was not good. The gun incident and the dose of crystal meth had left everyone wide awake all evening. Everyone was wired and most seemed still out of control. We had a gig that night, for fuck's sake. I headed to my room, fully aware that if I didn't grab a few hours' sleep I simply would not be able to perform that evening. I left the rest as they start to drop E to negate the effects of the crystal meth. For fuck's sake. The drugs in America were simply too strong for the band as a unit. Not the normal washing powder-diluted narcotic we would ride on back home.

That night I turned up for the gig feeling terrible. The rest of the band were a fucking mess too. We plugged in and began the show. We had to start 'Rock 'n' Roll Star' twice because no one knew what the fuck was going on. Liam was barely audible, Noel's backing vocals were out of tune (he even squealed at one point) and he forgot to start the intro. He and Bonehead then played the wrong chords on the bridge and then Liam sang lyrics from a completely different song. Finally, Guigs's amp blew. Top fucking class. It seemed that everybody had different set lists, so there was up to three different songs going on at the same time. A major fuck-up. Everybody was still methed out of their heads. To make matters worse, Ringo Starr was watching from the crowd. We'd done it again. Noel was looking round at everyone, obviously unhappy. We were not doing much to raise his bad mood. I raised my arms outwards, as if to say 'What?' I had kept in time and drummed the right song, yet most of Noel's glares were heading my way. Nothing new there. Bonehead's reaction to the breakdown was to start taking photographs using a disposable somebody had thrown on stage. He roared out laughing, with his thumbs

Above: Glastonbury 1994. Rock 'n' roll shades are by now standard issue as we wait to enter the arena. Even though we were playing our biggest gig to date, there was an air of nonchalance about it. Some called it arrogance, we called it confidence.

© Paul Slattery

Below: Staring out over the sea of people as we perform at Glastonbury. It still remains one of the highlights of my time in the band. A wonderful day that was capped by an electric performance by Johnny Cash in the evening.

© Paul Slattery

Above: Naumberg Bandshell, Central Park, New York, 1994. Liam was enjoying himself as the crowd gathered to watch. He demanded we play a set to please them. I think by the looks of the crowd, though, they were probably more interested in stealing our belongings than listening to our music. Noel rightly told Liam it was a crazy idea and the inevitable arguments ensued. *© Paul Slattery*

Below: USA, 1994. Who's the man who can shift his own bodyweight in sweat? I was always exhausted after a performance but it felt good. *© Paul Slattery*

'Live Forever' video shoot. When the director asked for someone to be buried, all hands remained firmly by sides. I decided to do my bit. On the shoot, I had to tell Guigs to slow down: he was shovelling a bit too eagerly for my liking.

Above: Big Yellow Taxi, New York, 1994. Bonehead was fantastic company and has left me with more memories than any other band member. Some of those memories keep coming back even though I've had therapy to try and block them out. A superb musician and an integral cog in the Oasis music machine. *© Paul Slattery*

Below: On the train to Osaka from Tokyo, Japan, 1994. A brief but welcome break before we reached the next frenzied mob of Japanese fans. Liam had enjoyed playing football with the crowd in Tokyo so much that we had brought our own ball along. *© Paul Slattery*

When things turned sour in Japan ... Me and Guigs are standing at opposite ends of the band. The tension is evident, even in this photograph. This was the beginning of the end.

Above: The Met Café, Providence, USA, 1994. Liam marched into every venue like this, ready to take on the world. This venue had waiters carrying plates laden with steak and ribs, who would pass through the band while we performed. How rude!

© Paul Slattery

Below: Elstree, London, 1994. We enjoy the moment prior to performing 'Whatever' on *Top of the Pops*. A happy and relaxed band before we break for Christmas. Even Noel is laughing along.

© Paul Slattery

Above: The Academy, New York, 1995. Liam shows his appreciation of the crowd. © Paul Slattery

Below: Sheffield Arena, April 1995. My final concert as the drummer for Oasis. A packed house and a storming performance to boot. © Paul Slattery

Paul Ashbee, otherwise known as BigUn. BigUn has taken to travelling on a Lambretta Series 1, the largest scooter they ever manufactured. It would have to be. It has a top speed of 60 mph until BigUn actually gets on it. Then it's lucky to touch 30.

up to the crowd. He didn't notice Noel's icy cold stare from the opposite end of the stage. The gig went from bad to worse. Liam had a parcel of powder that he had put down behind my bass drum. In between songs he was literally taking handfuls and troughing down, hidden behind my kit. The excess was blown over my kit. With a wipe of his face and a wink to me, Liam turned back to face the not-unsuspecting crowd. He screamed and contorted his face like he was in a wind tunnel. We muddled through a shambolic set until we reached 'I am the Walrus'. With the gobbledegook Lennon lyrics, I guessed it didn't matter how fucked Liam was and he sailed through it. Noel cut his final guitar section, though, and simply marched off the stage, leaving the rest of the band staring at each other in bewilderment.

Afterwards, Noel was as angry as I'd ever seen him. He dragged Liam into the dressing room, where Marcus was already waiting, and slammed the door shut, leaving me, Guigs and Bonehead outside.

Bonehead slurred, 'Fuck this, I'm going for a drink.'

Like that was needed. Me and Guigs waited nearly an hour and amused ourselves by signing autographs on records, clothes and breasts. Guigs moaned, 'The whole band should be behind that door. It's about all of us.' I shook my head in disbelief and replied, 'Open your eyes, Guigs. It is about them and you know it. Tell them you're unhappy when they come out,' I teased.

When Noel and Liam finally exited the dressing room, Guigs gave it. 'Everything all right, Chief?' The question wasn't even acknowledged. Noel simply made an exit. We wouldn't see him again for a week.

Liam was looking apologetic, to a degree. He sidled over and whispered, 'Let's get the fuck out of here.' We found out which bar Bonehead had been directed to and made our way there. Liam told me he had been dressed down in the dressing-up room. His drinking and drug consumption was seriously affecting the band, he had been told. Liam had agreed with this diagnosis, in an attempt to get out of the room so he could party on. I laughed, until Liam told me that Noel wanted to see all of us the next morning.

We arrived at the Rainbow Bar and Grill on Sunset Boulevard. Bonehead was hurrying towards us from the opposite end of the bar. Towering behind him was one of the largest ladies I'd ever set eyes on. I was sitting with Liam as Bonehead rocked up.

I looked at the girl stood next to Bone. She was a fucking mountain. Don't get me wrong. She was not fat. There was not an ounce of fat on her body. It was all sheer muscle; I was wondering whether she took steroids. Then she introduced herself, though I've not used her or her sister's real names, for obvious reasons.

'My name is Hilda,' she sang, in a Scandinavian accent. Hilda the fucking bodybuilder I thought. Brilliant. 'And this is my sister, Tove.'

A delicious brunette had appeared at her side. Slender and petite, she was the polar opposite of her well-endowed sister. Me and Liam looked at each other. It was now a race to see who could impress her first. The Drummer didn't fancy his chances against the Lead Singer. After a quick question-and-answer session between the two, though, it became apparent that Liam was maybe a touch too young for Tove. This left the door open for me. Get in. It soon became apparent, though, that maybe I was a touch too unattractive for her. Can't win them all.

After an hour or so we headed back to their apartment,

which was situated in Santa Monica, in a small complex of Spanish-style villas. Bonehead immediately opened another bottle of red and we moved to the balcony, where we watched the peculiar and eccentric Californian public, rollerskating or jogging beside the Pacific Ocean. It was eleven at night and they were still at it. I was in the country that never slept.

It transpired that Hilda had something of a reputation among the bands of Los Angeles. Her sister now informed us that she had a thing for extremely rough sex and had left a number of men hospitalised. We all looked at each other with eyes wide and started to laugh.

Eventually, we headed back to the Hyatt, to be confronted by Marcus, who for once actually looked like he was flapping. 'Noel's gone,' he told us.

'What do you fucking mean?' asked Liam.

Rather angrily, Marcus replied, 'I mean he's not here, he's moved on, disappeared. What the fuck do you think I mean?'

Liam was visibly shocked, as Marcus had never even raised his voice before, never mind sworn. He then told us the story. After the lockdown in the dressing room, Noel had told him he'd simply had enough; he had relieved Maggie of all the tour money and fucked off to LAX. Liam's immediate concern wasn't the mental state of his brother, but rather why the fuck Maggie had let him take all the money. Marcus simply shook his head at that question and, as if he had all the world's problems on his shoulders, sighed and made his way to bed.

30 SEPTEMBER 1994. LOS ANGELES

The next day, the general topic of conversation surrounded Noel's disappearance and state of mind. Bonehead laughed it off: 'He'll be back today,' he assured us.

Although the performance at the Whisky had been shambolic, to say the least, it wasn't as if it had been the first time we'd fucked up.

We were due to play the Casbah in San Diego that evening, but without our songwriter, backing vocalist and lead guitarist, we might find this difficult. We were told to hang loose around the hotel and not to get into any trouble. Marcus was still unhappy and it looked like the whole tour might be cancelled. Gigs in Arizona and Salt Lake City were pulled. We hung loose around the hotel.

1 OCTOBER 1994–6 OCTOBER 1994. LOS ANGELES

We were still in LA, with Liam conducting a few interviews. Asked why he felt the tour was not going as planned, he replied, 'Americans want grungy people stabbing themselves in the head on stage. They get a bright bunch like us with deodorant on, they don't get it.'

Bright? Deodorant? We all fell about laughing. As usual, the mood lifted when Noel was absent. It was six long days lying round the pool mashed on a mixture of cocktails and drugs.

When Noel did finally return, we all sat down for a clear-the-air meeting. It had been agreed that Bonehead should be our spokesperson and explain that the rest of us understood why he had been upset. When he started, though, Noel cut him short and said that he didn't ever want the event to be discussed again. He then started up a tirade that he must have stored up inside him since walking off the stage at the Whisky. We all sat and listened, as we had said we would.

He was back.

Me and Noel were sitting in the bar later. I was arguing my case for the drumming fraternity, but Noel was having none it. One of the main problems was that Noel considered himself to be a better drummer than Ringo Starr.

'Ringo is very underrated as a drummer,' I told Noel. If you listen to The Beatles, you can hear how musical he was and how the songs would not have been the same without him. Little things count, like a certain skip in just the right place. You can hear his embellishments and great timing all through the music. There are plenty of people that can tear it up on a drum set, technically speaking, and yet still not contribute anything useful to a band's music. There is more than one way to be good. Most good sticksmen, and I've known a few, would tell you that Ringo is a very good drummer and essential to The Beatles' sound.

Noel argued his case. 'But nowhere near as good as Mitch Mitchell. He can fill gaps with drumrolls and more drumrolls'. Mitch Mitchell was the drummer with The Jimi Hendrix Experience

I told him his argument fell down because, 'It's a little like saying Johnny Marr is not a great guitar player because he can't play as fast as Jimi Hendrix, but Jimi could not play with the wonderful fire that only Johnny Marr seemed to have.' He agreed, which left me shocked. I had made an opinion and it hadn't been decimated in front of me. Maybe things were changing. Maybe, just maybe, Old Noel was making a return. This warm feeling of hope lasted about a day.

7 OCTOBER 1994. THE CONGRESS HOUSE STUDIO, AUSTIN

The name implied a purpose-built recording studio. The reality was a spooky old weathered wooden frame house that would have looked more at home in an episode of *Scooby-Doo*. A mishmash of recording kit had been accumulated there over the years, starting in the early forties by the looks of it.

'How are the boys doing?' An accent as deep as the Welsh valleys themselves suddenly boomed out. Owen Morris had been flown in to take control of the recording. Everyone was happy knowing the music was in his capable hands. I gave him a bear hug and was genuinely pleased to see him. A new face on tour, even if only for a few days.

I arranged to go out with him. You were always guaranteed a heavy night out: although he looked unassuming, Owen could still out-drink us all. He was a genuinely good man, though, in an otherwise dirty business. We headed out and we soon had the fire burning in the belly. As usual, he was lively company, and had all the locals going.

At one point, he pulled me to one side. 'Noel keeps having a go at your drumming, but I keep tellin' him he wants to be looking at the bass, not the drums. He doesn't want to listen, though, if you know what I mean.' I knew what he meant. Them was the breaks, I guess.

Owen then told me that it was my drumming that gave the first album its kick. I respected him and that opinion meant a lot to me. Noel's recent harassment had been directed at my drumming skills – he had decided to leave my hair, clothes, shoes, toothpaste, girlfriend and 'Irishness' alone for the moment. It seemed when he only focused on one subject he became even more hostile. Brilliant.

While we were in Austin, Noel told us he had a new song

and, sitting down with his guitar, he played us 'Half the World Away'. I laughed. I had suggested adapting the drum shuffle from Burt Bacharach's 'This Guy's in Love With You'. Instead, Noel seemed to have adapted the whole song and renamed it 'Half the World Away'. I pointed this out to him, and suggested that the original drum pattern be used.

'You wouldn't be able to play it,' he replied, coldly.

It was a simple as pattern as they come, so I played it in front of him and everyone else. I had been practising since we spoke about it. Owen sang along, smiling. Noel pulled the sticks from my hands and told me to stop. It was time for a break.

The break lasted an hour and by the time I had returned Noel had recorded the drum track himself. Jesus. He had only to ask rather than going through the charade. There lay the problem, though. He had to ask and he doesn't like asking. Doesn't really like giving, either. As I left, I got a thumbs-up and a knowing wink from Owen. The big Welshman is Spartan all over.

We released our fourth single from the album. It was the song that Bonehead had at first refused to play. 'Cigarettes & Alcohol' was a great song, our biggest hit yet at No.7 on the UK charts and an anthem for the nineties. But it didn't half cause us some problems. Look at *NME*:

> *Take a look at Oasis on the cover of 'Cigarettes & Alcohol'. There they are, slumped round a four-poster in an immaculately untidy hotel room. They've got the beer, the champagne, the girls, They've even got a pitiful hanger-on to sit at the front, cockiness incarnate, arms aloft in triumph. It's a vile image, arrogance turned fetid and corrupted,*

and the best illustration yet why Oasis' laddishness is, ultimately, so useless. The witless and emotionally impotent hide in gangs. They sublimate character and feeling to banalities and clichés borne of boy's-own dreams. They never dare reveal their true selves in case their friends laugh at them. Pathetic.

Oasis are by no means alone in British pop of course. The utterly obnoxious Cult of the Lad had taken a nasty grip in 1994, thanks to the likes of Primal Scream, Shed Seven, These Animal Men, the worst bits of wannabe lads Blur and practically every poxy nouveau mod bunch of chancers loitering, clannishly, in the darkest corners of Camden. Certain magazines even shape themselves around this post PC world of 'football and tits' where no real man's allowed to show a humane gentle, likeable side... Not us, mate.

Oasis are the worst culprits by a mile, though. Scared they'll be ridiculed for exposing actual emotions, what do they fill their allegedly classic songs with? Lyrics about their friend's passion for Lasagne. Cheers. I'm moved. Some of the best songs have had simple lyrics but 'I'm feeling supersonic/give me gin and tonic'? COME ON!

God forbid that there should ever be hard and fast rules about what rock bands should and shouldn't do. But, for the most part, I want one of two things: bands who sing imaginatively, emotively and truthfully, who are brave enough to look foolish and vulnerable in the eyes of their audience and – this is the really tough bit – in the eyes of their mates; or bands who are freaky, challenging, just out there. I want Suede, and REM, more people like Kurt Cobain – the sort lads sneer at as 'whining losers'.

I don't want any more bands that look like the snarling thugs that have to use their fists to make a point, who'd try to beat anyone who's just a bit feminine, or different, or – perish the thought – weak. And, no, I don't want any more bands like Oasis, clubbing together to cover up the inadequacies that, if they had any sense, they'd flaunt.

Maybe Huggy Bear's war on boy rock wasn't such a bad idea after all...

John Mulvey

14 OCTOBER 1994. THE UPTOWN BAR, MINNEAPOLIS

Finally, we restarted the tour. We arrived in Minneapolis and crossed the Mississippi River. I told Noel about the famous quote from Mark Twain: 'I would like to live in Manchester, England. The transition between Manchester and death would be unnoticeable.' I laughed after telling him.

Noel looked at me like I was mad.

'Mark Twain didn't fuckin' say that, you knob. Mark Twain wrote *Huckleberry Finn*.' I fought my corner, but Noel told Guigs and they took the piss in unison until we reached the hotel, another Holiday Inn. That night we were booked to perform at The Uptown Bar in Minneapolis. The large green neon letters spelled 'Uptown' high into the night sky. After an uneventful gig, we boarded our silver bus and headed down another godforsaken route towards another godforsaken city.

15 OCTOBER 1994. THE METRO, CHICAGO

We arrived in Chicago to stay at Days Inn on West Diversey. In some cities we had day rooms only, due to the fact we would travel overnight. This was one of them. And I was fucking ecstatic. Sleeping while in motion didn't seem to be as refreshing as sleeping in a normal bed, it seemed.

I retired to my day room with Guigs still rattling on about Mark Twain. 'Give it a rest, Guigs, and go and read a book about Mark Twain,' I told him. 'You may even learn something that way.'

I'd stopped reacting to Guigs's pokes and insults since the incident in the hotel foyer in Japan. I was disappointed that he had jumped on Noel's bandwagon, but hardly surprised. One of the reasons for the friction between me and Noel was the fact that I would sometimes disagree with his views or actions and would say so. That was how I was raised: defend yourself and express your views, whatever the circumstances. Guigs, on the other hand, was a follower not a leader.

That evening, we played the Metro on Clarke Street. Afterwards, we were sat at yet another meet-and-greet. A suit from the record company stood at the head of the table. His round face was positively glowing with a mixture of red wine and enjoyment. His dinner suit and those around him clashed with the street wear that the band was wearing. On occasions such as these, we agreed to a forced compromise: we didn't wear trainers. It was desert boots all round.

'Well, it's a pleasure to have our English friends here with us this evening. A potential superband that we will endeavour to support and drive throughout the American continent. I'm sure when you have a moment in their time later you will find, like me, they are a truly determined and dedicated group and it's a pleasure to have them as my friends.'

Who the fuck was this clown? I looked at Noel and started laughing. Noel frowned back at me – which left him with no eyeballs, owing to his eyebrows. My laugh wasn't loud enough to be overheard, but still Noel hissed. 'Shut it, dickhead.'

This fucked me right off. The balloon in the suit at the top of the table claiming to be our mate was typical of the back-slapping, corporate bullshit that we had slagged off earlier. 'What, so he's your best fuckin' mate, is he?' I fired back, angrily.

'Well as it happens, yeah, I have met him and he's fucking sound. Now shut the fuck up.' The argument was starting to get the attention of the room, so I shut up as Noel sat glowering at me. Here we go again, I thought.

The MD continued. 'And now it gives me the greatest pleasure to introduce you to the musical genius that is Norton Gallagher.' I nearly choked on my drink as I tried to contain my laughter. I looked at Noel, who was staring at me with enough hatred to melt a holy candle. Liam was sitting next to Noel and his face lit up with laughter. The suit cum stand-up comedian carried on with his shtick. 'With his trusty sidekick and younger brother, Leland.' The amusement had vanished from Liam's face. The man's gotta be fucking joking, I thought. Even Guigs started to laugh. Noel had now gone crimson and I guessed it was me who was gonna get it again. But fuck it. It was worth it.

That evening, we trundled very slowly along Route 94, connecting Chicago to Detroit. The mood was sour.

16 OCTOBER 1994. ST ANDREW'S HALL, DETROIT

Our coach pulled into Detroit, home of Motown and the highest crime rate in the States. The skies had opened and the constant patter rattled the bus like a tin can. We stared out the window and the resemblance to Manchester was plain for all to see. Crime, music, sport and industry all play a major part in the histories of both cities. Detroit also seemed to possess that dark shade of greyness that hung over Manchester most days. That evening we were to play St Andrew's Hall and first thing, I needed to see if I could get my clothes cleaned at the hotel.

'Is there a laundrette around here?' I asked at reception, receiving only the vaguest of directions. After leaving the commercial sector, I soon found myself in a more neglected part of the city. I spotted a faded sign that read 'Spin City Laundrette'. The Laundromat had originally been painted white, but had yellowed with age. The front was heavily fortified in a makeshift kind of way – corrugated panelling and strengthened mesh. I opened the door and immediately wished that I hadn't. Inside, all heads turned and looked at the young white Englishman standing in the doorway. I decided to make my way to the nearest machine, hoping I would be ignored. Not so. Within seconds, I had a dangerous-looking black man sat next to me. He caught my eye and then pulled a blade out of his pocket and began to clean it against his trousers. What looked like old bloodstains were ingrained up and down the blade.

He was silent for a while. Just sat there. And then: 'You scared, boy?'

Not until you just fucking asked me, I thought. Now, I needed to make sure I got the balance right with this answer. I wasn't going to say yes, for that would surely end in him taking control, so I had to say no but not in a way that would challenge or antagonise him.

'No. Should I be? I asked, innocently, with a childlike voice and widened eyes.

The man chuckled and put his knife on the bench next to me.

'Yes you should be, boy. This here's a bad part of town.'

America. You can't even clean your gruds without it becoming life-threatening. I pulled out my cigarettes and offered him one. He took it and after taking a deep pull gave me a wide smile. Seemed like I would survive to live another day.

We played St Andrew's Hall that evening. Halfway through the performance, Noel laid down his guitar and simply walked off the stage. Worried, we looked at each other.

'He's just gone for a piss,' Liam said, laughing, when he saw our concern.

Upstairs after the Detroit show, in what passed for the hospitality room, rumours were rife of a special delivery by a dodgy-looking Mexican. He arrived with the words 'Creeestal! Creeestal!'

'Get him out now,' ordered Noel, and for once we all agreed.

Afterwards, we were approached by a suit and Liam decided it was time to be telling them straight. Corporate time was over. The pristine-looking man was wearing a large smile, which displayed his American white teeth.

'Wassup?' he said, grinning at Liam.

'Fuck all's up with me. What the fuck's up with you, dickhead?' came the growled reply.

The grin disappeared quickly. We finished the evening and, with all due respect to Detroit, I was happy to be moving on.

17 OCTOBER 1994. CLEVELAND HEIGHTS

We were on Route 75, heading out of Detroit and on our way to Cleveland Heights, Ohio. A day off was planned, and so we arrived fresh at the Holiday Inn, Lakeside. Liam was unhappy with Noel. Again. We were trying to placate him, as any offensive strike at Noel would surely mean the tour was over.

'It's not fucking on,' he shouted. He was angry about the lack of finances. We had lost a lot of our tour money through bad drug deals and Noel's escape away. Noel, on the other hand, was having his shirts reeled behind him on a rack while enjoying all the local luxuries.

18 OCTOBER 1994. THE GROG SHOP, CLEVELAND HEIGHTS

We spent the early part of the day wandering around Cleveland Heights looking for places of interest. There weren't any. We headed back to the hotel and tried to stay out of any bars. Everybody had promised to be responsible and adult. The Temperance Movement would not have their grip on us for long, though. After a very long day, we made our way to The Grog Shop. Bonehead thought the name of the gaff was the business and was talking about opening his own pub in Levenshulme and calling it such.

After another stunning display, we packed up and headed for Toronto. It was three in the morning when the bus pulled into a brightly lit service station, desolate at that hour. Margaret appeared at the front of the bus with Noel by her side. She was holding a vacuum cleaner, which had us all intrigued. She then explained just how detailed a search the Canadian authorities would undertake when we reached the border, explaining that if they found a grain of cocaine or a seed of weed they would not only refuse us entry but would also alert the American authorities, who would probably have us deported. Or put in jail.

'Where we might get raped,' Noel added. No one laughed. Tumbleweed time.

As if to break the silence he had created, Noel asked us to watch him as he vacuumed – like we needed a lesson in hoovering. We all told him to fuck off, but were drowned out by the noise of the Hoover as Noel switched it on and swept it backwards and forwards. The scene was made even more surreal by the fact that Noel had taken to wearing a smoking jacket and cravat on the tour bus. Prepping for that knighthood, I suppose. It was all too much. But funny.

Liam shouted, 'I'm a professional, me,' referring back to his valeting days, and jumped up to take control. The inevitable argument ensued.

We stashed all available goodtime together and rolled it in a ball of cling film. This ball was then stuffed in a couple of plastic bags. I spotted a hoarding advertising some fizzy drink or other and decided it was as good a place as any to hide the drugs. Unlit and no pedestrian traffic. Heading over, I stashed it under the large wooden foot of the hoarding.

Nearly three hours later and we were finished. Maggie inspected the coach, which looked like new. After the all-clear, we approached the border control between the States and Canada and after another three hours, during which they dismantled musical equipment and rooted through my bag of underpants, we were let through. Must remember to let BigUn know his valeting training had been put to good use.

19 OCTOBER 1994. LEE'S PALACE, TORONTO

We checked into the Primrose, on Carlton Street in downtown Toronto. Facing the hotel is the Maple Leaf Gardens, and Guigs was heading that way to see if he could score any weed. It was only a day before we were back in America. I tried to tell him, but to no avail. His Mancunian arse disappeared into the park.

After a day spent in bed trying to catch up with the sleep I had lost over the previous fortnight, we headed off to Lee's Palace on Bloor Street. The venue was in the heart of Chinatown and was quite large considering the bar and grills we had been playing in America. At least there wouldn't be any plates of ribs passing my head as I played. It was our first Canadian appearance, which Liam was made fully aware of. In a diplomatic gesture to unite the countries of England and Canada, onstage Liam told the crowd that someone had better get their arse over to England and retrieve that pock-faced twat Bryan Adams. He was then all smiles as the crowd threw food and empty plastic beer pots at him.

After the gig we drove a mind-numbing 600 miles to Boston. We remembered to stop along the way and retrieve our stashed bag of goodtime. I couldn't seem to get Guigs or Noel off my back. At every opportunity they were at me. I was beginning to think that something else was going on.

20 OCTOBER 1994. BOSTON

We arrived at the Days Inn at Soldier's field in Boston. This was a day off, so me, Bonehead and Liam decided to head into the city to shop. When we returned, we hit the sack.

21 OCTOBER 1994. LOCAL 186, ALLSTON

We played Local 186 in Allston, then returned to the hotel in Boston. It was a good gig, but I could still feel the tension. That night, I decided to try to speak to Noel again. I knocked on his room and entered.

'It's getting a bit fuckin' much,' I told him.

'Don't take it personally,' Noel replied.

'It's difficult not to take remarks such as "Yer a fuckin' dick" personally,' I countered.

'They're only getting you at it,' he said, with a laugh.

22 OCTOBER 1994. THE MET CAFE, PROVIDENCE

It was a short 44-mile hop to Providence in the morning. We played the Met Cafe that evening on Providence Street and then drove through the night to Philadelphia.

23 OCTOBER 1994. PHILADELPHIA

Bonehead kept telling everyone that Tom Hanks was born in Philly. I thought he may have been a touch confused. I told him Tom Hanks had been in the film *Philadelphia*.

'DJ Jazzy Jeff and the Fresh Prince are from here,' piped up Liam. We all roared laughing and launched into the intro from *The Fresh Prince*. Liam had done his best to forget his days breakdancing outside Kwik Save in Burnage, but we were not about to let that happen.

Bonehead laughed, 'Oh yeah I forgot about your hip hop connections' and imitated a DJ scratching a record. As usual, Bonehead went a step too far. He attempted a windmill. This left him in agony and the surrounding area in turmoil.

30 OCTOBER 1994

We were lying in the hotel room, bugged out on the previous night's mushrooms, when Liam looked at me. It was the kind of look that said 'I've had enough.' The cracks had started to appear. Liam would often struggle with the notion that he was an idol for others. In truth, he himself seemed to be on some sort of pilgrimage, which was most definitely a solitary trip. The fact that other people were more than happy to join in seemed to ruin it for him. It was almost as if success brought about a feeling of failure. It was a good time for a break and we all headed happily home to Manchester.

Naturally enough, we had a heavy night out as soon as we were home. We even dared to go out in Levenshulme, which was strictly against the rules. The next morning, we woke and made our way to a café on Stockport Road. It had been pretty intense the previous evening. Everywhere we'd gone there were people offering congratulations and having their photographs taken with us. These well-wishers would invariably want a private party, which was easily arranged by simply offering us drugs. Private audience in cubicle number three. It had got a bit messy and I hazily recollected a number of arguments and insults thrown. Mainly by Liam. The whole circus that surrounded the band had become almost non-stop. Because of the image that Oasis put over, it also meant that we had become fair game for a confrontation or two. I guess if you go round telling everyone how tough you are, someone will eventually challenge you. We were getting challenged on a daily basis, Liam in particular. I could see it was beginning to wear him down.

As we sat in the café, Liam had his head down, suffering

from a hangover and also trying to keep a low profile. Suddenly there was a beat as one of the customers at an opposing table tapped the sugar holder with his spoon. He started to sing 'Live Forever'.

'Mebeee, a don't rilly wanna know.'

He must have been fuckin' 60. The rest of the café soon joined in and I looked at Liam. He pulled his hood over his head and curled further into the corner. The price you pay.

18 DECEMBER 1994. 'WHATEVER' RELEASED. REACHED NO.3 IN THE SINGLES CHARTS.

The little ditty that Tony Griffiths composed is running around my head. We had released the whole version of it that week. It was our fourth single and would surely cement us as the No.1 band in Britain. *NME* liked it:

> *You waited five fucking years to be disappointed by 'Love Spreads' and 'Second Coming' but you waited just over five months to fall head over heels in love with this record. I won't pretend I was there at the beginning and was blinded by the brilliance of Oasis right away. It was probably at Glastonbury, the second time I saw them, that I thought fuck me, I better try and see this lot when I'm straight. Comparisons with the Roses are unnecessary, pointless and shouldn't be allowed, but you can't help yourself, really. OK, a band have their whole lives to make a debut album and normally about a year to make their second. If they are on an understanding label. And who knows? Maybe Oasis will be gone in a flash. Oasis*

shrewdly do not promise you the Earth as the Roses did. There's none of this 'We only want to play free gigs in underground car parks in Sarajevo for our fan club' bullshit about Oasis. Sure, they're arrogant bastards, but they are a better live band than the Roses were. Maybe the only way they couldn't top the Roses is that they never had a song that soared. One that slipped the surly bonds of Earth and touched the face of God. Sure the songs were good, bloody good in fact, but they hadn't quite written one that was great. That's great with a capital G. As in 'When a Man Loves a Woman', 'All the Young Dudes' or 'Alone Again'. Until now. 'Whatever' basically pisses over everything else. A song to die for with a descending scale and a fucking string section: from 'Love Me Do' to 'All You Need is Love' in under a year. The fact that it sounds like any number of other songs is a mark of the confidence that Oasis have in their song writing. Amateurs borrow, pros steal and look you straight in the eye, unashamed.

Definitions of great are hard to come up with. But there is one simple way to look at it. A great song is one that makes you feel better, happier, more optimistic. More comfortable about yourself and the world than you did before you listened to it that maybe there's something more and greater than the mundane, excremental, day to day, slog. These are the songs for the days we'll be nostalgic for in the next millennium.

Tommy Udo

I guess Tommy Udo knew his shit. I guess Tony and Chris Griffiths did as well.

29 DECEMBER 1994. BRIGHTON CENTRE (EAST WING), BRIGHTON

We played to another rapturous full house. To spend every night in a room full of people simply screaming at you was fucking insane. I'd taken to screaming back until Noel told me to shut the fuck up. At the aftershow we were warned of Paula Yates's arrival. There were lots of panic-faced people hurrying around with wide eyes mouthing 'she's here'. It started to make me nervous. We had already met Paula at the recording of *The Word* and right from the start she and Liam had hit it off.

Paula first encountered myself and Bonehead as we entered the party venue downstairs from the main stage. There was only one person who Paula wanted to talk to, though. 'Where's that gorgeous man?' she asked scouring the bar.

I laughed at her confidence, and because I knew how Liam would react. Paula was Liam's type of woman. 'If you grab him in the right places he'll be yours for the night,' I replied. She giggled as only she could, grabbed my hand and Bonehead's and marched us straight across the middle of the dance floor. We passed through the younger members of the *EastEnders* cast and straight to the bar. Liam was slouched there, looking paralytic. I laughed as Liam looked her deep in the eyes. She was one of 'them famous birds off the box', so was right up Liam's street. He was also wired from 48 hours of continual and finding it hard to focus.

'What's yer name again, kid?' he drawled. Liam had already met Paula, but was in no state to conjure up that memory.

'How about we cause a scandal?' suggested Paula Yates.

Liam laughed and he and Paula got to know each other all over again. He then gave me one of his wicked grins and ushered Paula outside behind the tour bus. Ian, our security man, turned up looking for Liam, who soon emerged from behind the bus wild eyed and delirious. The night continued as if nothing had ever happened but, hey, that's why they call it rock 'n' roll.'

28 JANUARY 1995. DV8, SEATTLE

Hey you, up in the sky. We were at 10,000 feet again, on our way back to Seattle to start another US tour. Spirits were high, though we'd been told there had been an amendment to the tour. We were to return to England a week or so later to attend the Brit Awards. Sounded good to me. Must have won something if they're flying us back, I thought. We had been warned about our consumption on this tour, so it began with a 10-hour champagne-and-whisky session. Yankee Doodle Dandy.

We arrived and immediately boarded our tour bus and headed to Seattle's DV8 club to soundcheck. All of us were a little bit nervous before the gig, as Liam had recently slated Kurt Cobain in the UK press and it had been picked up Stateside, causing some outrage. We waited on the bus as the crowds arrived. Before we were due on, I looked out at the full house under strobe lighting. It was a flickbook of writhing bodies and hysteria. As we marched on stage the lights came up and the whole place erupted in a deafening noise. We quickly assembled and I first looked at Noel, who gave me the nod, then a confirmation wink from Bonehead that he was ready, followed by another nod from Guigs. Liam stood out front, with his back to me. One arm on the mic stand, the other with fist clenched behind his back. He was already staring the crowd down. I banged the intro to 'Rock 'n' Roll Star' and as Noel hit his first riff of the night the crowd turned the noise up even further. So much for a hostile crowd – that night went down as one of the best gigs we'd ever performed. Afterwards, we left the stage to be ushered by a mob of baseball-capped suits towards the customary meet-and-greet. As a band, we had decided that on this tour we would not be dragged into the endless rotation of these faceless corporate affairs. We weren't meeting the fans; we were meeting the Director of Northern Territories for distribution and his wife or girlfriend. They would rattle on about margins and productivity and we would all nod. They weren't there for the music; they were there as a display of their power and privilege. Fuck that. They should be thanking us for giving them the music, rather than the other way around. We had Robbo section off the room with advertising boards and we created a VIP area where the only VIPs were the band. Robbo stood guard as we hid.

It was straight back on the bus after the gig and on to Canada. There was no need to hoover before Vancouver any more. We're all getting that little bit wiser when touring and the coach had been carefully maintained over the previous 24 hours. We arrived in Toronto to play at the Commodore Ballroom on Granville Street. After the show, we faced another room full of suits waiting to meet-and-greet. We schmoozed for 15 minutes or so and then decided to slip out a side exit into the Canadian night. We found ourselves in the heart of red-light Toronto. It felt good to be surrounded by a more honest and upfront set of people.

Later that evening, we headed back to the States. It had

been a fantastic start to the tour and we were looking for a hat-trick in Portland.

30 JANUARY 1995. THE ROSELAND THEATRE, PORTLAND

The tension that had been growing on the coach was lost on stage and as I drummed I hoped things might be on the up again. It went downhill rapidly, though. Liam opened his mouth and released a sound that didn't sound human. The timing wasn't good. The tension rose in the room as the crowd realised it was not gonna happen. We were getting accustomed to tense crowds and now, under the military command of General Robertson, we were hurried onto the coach. It was not long before we were encircled by an angry mob intent on displaying their displeasure. We took it all in our stride and were already racking them out as we pulled away. No more ramming cars in a transit for us.

1 FEBRUARY 1995. THE FILLMORE, SAN FRANCISCO

We arrived in freakin' fantastic Frisco, where we were set to play the Fillmore theatre. First, though, was a photo shoot with Jill Furmanovsky. With Alcatraz and the Golden Gate Bridge as the perfect backdrop, we posed as the camera whirred and clicked away. After playing the Filly that night, once again the band played hide and seek with the meeters and greeters.

We were on a slow one, as we had to return to England the following day... for the Brit Awards, where we were up for Best Newcomer. We flew into Heathrow and were ferried to a nearby hotel. In each of our rooms we found a brown suit individually tailored. They looked kinda retro, with a definite Beatle thing going on.

Noel had recently met a new girl called Meg and she was waiting in the lobby of the hotel. With her was another girl, Kadamba. Liam had taken an instant shine to Kadamba, which was understandable. There was something alluring about her. They had become an item, although I thought that their fiery personalities would be too much.

'Everywhere you go people just stop and stare at her,' he had complained. He didn't like the competition, I thought to myself. I watched as, before we set off for the Brits, Liam made his way up the marble corridor towards me. Between us lay four sets of large glass doors, which Liam threw open and then let swing shut violently behind him. Kadamba was running behind, finding it difficult to negotiate the wildly flapping doors.

As he reached me he exploded with, 'Enough is enough and she's more than enough.'

Then he was gone, to be then replaced by Kadamba, who skidded up the corridor and came to a halt in front of me. For some strange reason she was wearing a pair of studded football boots. A fashion statement. I guess that was Kadamba for you.

'Hiya, Tony,' she said and then screamed up the corridor after Liam, 'If I'm not on your guest list just say so and I will ring Madonna.' Liam didn't even look around, just strode out the front doors of the hotel and into the waiting car.

We were soon at the Alexandra Palace, where the awards were to be held, and were met by Sonya and Debbie from the group Echobelly. Sonya and me had become quite close. Sonya had a serenity about her that was unusual in the coke-fuelled narcissistic business we worked in and I found her company enjoyable.

That night, we did indeed receive that Best Newcomer award, which was presented by Ray Davies of The Kinks and DJ Chris Evans. Afterwards, we went to a party at Nellee Hooper's house. Nellee was an almighty successful producer and his house gave an indication of just what could become available to those who were successful in the music industry. The drink flowed freely and we duly took advantage. I was winding my way through pockets of people with a nod and a smile when I came face to face with Björk.

'Hellooo, wee Björk' I drawled, chang'd out of my face and a little taken aback by her appearance. My mind whirring as fast as my jaw I said to her, 'You look like a little Eskimo girl.' My mind was a blank white canvas and even this lame line had been a struggle. She said nothing and quite wisely moved off, looking slightly confused. Not as confused as me. We grabbed a taxi and returned to the hotel.

The next morning, a very sorry-looking bunch of musicians boarded a flight back to the States.

6 MARCH 1995. PHILADELPHIA

We arrived in Philly and stayed at the Warwick on 17th and Locust Street. The brothers had a girl apiece in Meg and Kadamba. Bonehead had Kate and Guigs was still in with the air stewardess from the flight to Japan. My girl was Elle, who I had met before Christmas at Philly nightclub JC Dobbs. Unfortunately, instead of my drumming, my new girlfriend was now the subject of Noel's new daily tirades.

'She ain't right man, she's not one of us.' Noel made this

statement as Elle stood next to me. He was surrounded by a bunch of his 'followers'. I was a bit put out.

'Show me anybody right here and now in this room who is one of us,' I retaliated.

Noel looked around, in hope of locating a Mancunian head. There wasn't one. We had started with so many. I took Elle by the hand and apologised for Noel's outburst. Elle was a Cuban air hostess, and I guess those three words said it all. She was a feisty and lovable girl who certainly enjoyed life to the full. I didn't mind Noel having a pop at me, as that had become almost a habit. But I wasn't going to wear him berating a girl in front of a group she doesn't really even know. Liam defended me, which made Noel even angrier. In terms of pissing Noel right off, I'd excelled myself this time.

Somebody passed me a copy of the *San Francisco Chronicle*. Our review was highlighted. I read it to myself and then aloud. 'The guitar play between Noel Gallagher, rhythm guitarist Paul Arthurs and bassist Paul McGuigan was sterling. But the most vital person was drummer Tony McCarroll who was more energetic than anyone else in the band.' I got told to fuck off by everyone present and laughed as they threw cushions and empty drink cartons. Noel had vanished with his big bag of white line and so the mood was more positive. It had been a good tour from a performance perspective, but that was beginning to become overshadowed by the rift between Noel and I.

8 MARCH 1995. THE ACADEMY, NEW YORK

I was at an aftershow party. John McEnroe was with me – and it seemed to me as if he had intentions on my new girl. This was a tough one.

'Hey, Elle, have you ever thought of moving to New York? You should, you know.'

'Why?' asked Elle, giving me a second glance, so as to make me realise she was only playing.

'I think you know why,' a mischievous McEnroe replied, with a grin.

I couldn't give a fuck if it was JP McEnroe. Something had to be said.

'What, am I not fucking stood here?' I blazed. 'Can you not see me? Show a bit of respect. How would you like it if I asked Tatum to move to Manchester, you cock?' I'd not lost my temper, but I'd never been one to stand around while someone rips the piss. JP smiled back, his head lolling to one side. He slowly focused on me.

'Wouldn't give a shoot, Tony, I'll give you her number. It's a deal.' McEnroe started asking those surrounding us if they had a pen. Fuck me. I wasn't to know that he had just got divorced. Did he really think that I'd done a swap with him? Elle for Tatum.

'You cannot be serious?' said Elle, and she wasn't even taken the piss. This was going horribly wrong. Once again my communication skills had proved impotent across the Atlantic. Mancunian sarcasm is very often misinterpreted – which the whole band had found out, to our cost. Finally, McEnroe came clean and explained he had been 'hoaxing' us and we all laughed it off for the joke that it was.

He then decided to play a few of his own songs on air guitar. No, really. He added the lyrics, 'It's fifteen love to me, baby, and yes I'm being serious, It's forty love and more, you know you're gonna score...' He finished with an imaginary Slash windmill. Jesus. A lifetime's admiration shot to pieces in minutes.

We were soon distracted from his performance by Bonehead shouting, 'Lob on. Lob On. Lob On.' I headed over, wondering why he was insulting someone with an eighties schoolyard term for a hard-on. It just didn't sound right in New York in the nineties. I arrived to find a not-very-amused looking Simon Le Bon standing next to Bonehead, who had his arm firmly clamped round his shoulder. Le Bon couldn't move an inch. Bonehead's face was reddened by wine as he spluttered, 'Look I've found Simon... Lob On. Ha, ha, ha, ha!' He started to roar again. If I'd been Mr Simon Le Bon, I would have cuffed him.

8 MARCH 1995. LATE SHOW WITH DAVID LETTERMAN, NEW YORK

We played the *Late Show* to an estimated 50 million people. From Granada Red Nose Day to Letterman in the space of three short years. Not bad going, really. We had to cut the set short to fit around the advertising break – very American. After performing 'Live Forever', we jumped back in our limousines to head to the aftershow. It was all a whirl.

After finishing the tour, we got the big iron bird back to Blighty.

CHAPTER 8

A FAREWELL TO ARMS

I was back in Manchester on a flying visit. We had a gig in Southend to do and then we were off to Paris. After Paris came the Sheffield Arena, which we had sold out. Then we were to start recording the second album. Life was beautiful.

I was in Manchester city centre with BigUn on a busy Saturday night; we were on our way to meet up with Liam and have a night out. As we passed the Hacienda, I heard a sudden outburst: 'Hey, dickhead!'

I looked around to see who was under attack. The words were actually being aimed at me. What the fuck? Then I realised who was offering up these pearls. It was Gilly, the drummer with the Inspiral Carpets, and I was in no mood for him.

At first I thought that the reason for his outburst might be because, at one time, he'd wanted to be in Oasis and had even asked Liam some months earlier if he could replace me. At the time, Liam had told him to fuck off and then waltzed back to the bus where I was sitting. 'That fuckin' clown Gilly has just asked if he can drum for us. Told him staright, T. Told him to get on his bicycle and head for the hills of Oldham.' That was Liam. For all his faults, he was an honest kid who understood how the Mancunian social standing system worked. You mind your own and they mind you.

Gilly's apparent anger turned to sorrow as the real reason for his beef became apparent. 'You tried to nick me tom-tom, you twat,' he sobbed. Gilly was referring to the time that Liam had decided he would take one of Gilly's tom-toms and flog it. It had been lying around The Boardwalk, and Liam had thought it was simply asking to be pawned. I had told him that no one bought second-hand tom-toms, as they were adapted and personal to a specific kit. I added that if he knew of any North American Indians, though, they might want to buy a tom-tom from him...

He told me to fuck off and cracked on with his madcap idea. Liam, unfortunately, had chosen to sell the tom-tom to Johnny Roadhouse Music. The owner of the shop was a good man who even had time for the (often-overlooked) drummers of this world; with a name like John Roadhouse, I guess he just had to open a music shop. Liam and I had entered the store and offered them to the guy behind the counter. After one look at the drum, he had asked Liam why he was selling Gilly's drums.

Liam replied, 'We're not. We're just getting an idea of how much one was worth.'

'Why, then, did you use the words "Do you want to buy this?"' came the quick reply. That question left Liam short of an answer, so we were on our toes back to replace the tom-tom. That was the long and short of it.

Gilly still didn't seem to realise that he could never be in Oasis. He had never been forgiven for making Noel sand down his drumsticks before each Inspiral Carpets show. To Noel, this request had served no purpose musically and he believed it was only done to irritate him. He swore that one day he would return the favour and was actually excited when he heard of Gilly's plea to join the band. The look of satisfaction that spread across his face when telling Gilly to fuck off was one I would see again in the very near future, though I did not know it at the time.

Maybe it was Gilly who kicked off Noel's dislike of drummers. Well, fuckin' nice one, Gilly.

17 APRIL 1995. CLIFFS PAVILION, SOUTHEND

Apparently, we were recording a DVD that night. Nobody had told me. Fortunately, it was an absolutely storming gig and a very exuberant crowd lapped it up. The resulting DVD captured perfectly just how tight we had become as a unit. I was loving it.

20 APRIL 1995. LE BATACLAN, PARIS

Noel was really not happy. It seemed that an argument between Elle and me the previous evening had kept him awake during the night. He was already in poisonous mode and I had been keeping my head down so far. On cobra alert. This argument had raised my head.

'You kept me awake last night. I don't like you or your bird. Don't make me sack you.' The constant digs had gone way over the line now and I'd had enough. Noel had threatened to sack everyone at some stage over the previous three years. I was probably in treble figures so, as you'd expect, the threat had lost its potency. But this time there was real intent in his voice. I had genuinely tried to sort our differences out, but the more I did the worse it seemed to get.

I soundchecked in darkness. Twenty yards in front of me sat a stool and a microphone. It was Noel's solo set layout, lit by a single spotlight. I banged away in the black until he arrived and filled the stool. Everything was sorted with my kit, so I made to leave. As I passed, he gave me one of his 'Don't even talk to me' looks and I thought, Fuck that. I moved in front of him before he could start his soundcheck.

He looked at me and said 'What the fuck do you want?' The look that came with the question was one of absolute dismissal. I moved within an inch of his face. I had finally lost it.

'If you ever talk to me like that again, Noel, I'll snap you in fucking two and throw you away. Do you understand?' I delivered this message in a flat and steady voice. I meant every word I said and Noel could see that I meant it. I stared at him without breaking eye contact. Silence. He looked back at me with his hooded cobra eyes cold. He then finally looked down at his fingertips and started to pick away. In the ensuing silence, I kicked the fire door open and strode out onto a cool Parisian boulevard.

Later that evening, we met to perform. Noel wouldn't acknowledge me. It was gonna be a rough ride. Better hold on tight. We played our set to a hot and swaying French crowd. They really appreciated the music, screaming, 'Encore! Encore!' through their noses, as only the French could.

Set completed, we headed off stage as usual. Oasis. We didn't do encores. As I arrived backstage, I found Noel lighting a Benson. 'We're doing an encore,' he told me. Bit fuckin' odd, I thought. It was a good night, but not worthy of an encore. We all had a quick cigarette and then Noel nodded me on. He had that look about him.

'"Supersonic",' he said. Armed with sticks in one hand, the other hand held upright, fist clenched, I reentered the stage. I was happy that Noel had chosen this track; he knew it was my favourite song to drum on. The crowd erupted, as surprised at me at the events. I started the intro and looked to the side stage. Noel stood tapping his foot to the beat. Three minutes is a long time in drumming. But that was the time I had before the band would eventually join me. It was my moment in the sun and would normally be a memory to cherish event. For me, it was to prove bittersweet. I hit every beat perfectly in those three minutes, but by the time the band joined in I realised that Noel was saying goodbye.

He led the rest of the band on stage, staring directly at me. He took a long last pull of his cigarette and then flicked it over towards me. I watched as the cigarette landed and its glowing embers scattered and died by my bass drum. His confidence stemmed from the fact that he knew he had the power to eject me from the band. From there on in, it seemed to me as if he had become a completely different person.

I had finally snapped after 17 months of insults and nastiness. That had been the tipping point.

22 APRIL 1995. SHEFFIELD ARENA, SHEFFIELD

I walked onto our tour bus and made for the lounge area. As I arrived, I found Noel sitting there with Guigs and Marcus. They were huddled round the table and looked up, shocked at my sudden arrival. The atmosphere was strange, to say the least. Their muffled hellos and sheepish looks gave a conspiratorial feel to it all. I took my seat upstairs and warmed myself for the biggest gig we had performed to date.

As I walked into the Arena later, its sheer size hit me; it

was fuckin' huge. We soundchecked and were then informed that we had sold out the place. We were now a stadium band.

All the mothers were ferried across the Snake Pass from Manchester to Sheffield. No small feat in a stretch limousine. As we came out onto the stage there was a surge as the huge crowd burst forwards. It was a hero's welcome for us, and we lapped it up.

It was a fantastic night, though Noel ignored me all evening. I was still worried that the 'Supersonic' encore in Paris had been a message. I was hoping I'd got it wrong.

17 APRIL 1994. THE WHITE ROOM, LONDON

I was in the studios of *The White Room* with Noel, Paul Weller and ace drummer Steve White (for more of whom, see Appendix 1, 'The Perfect Beat'). Weller introduced me to Steve and we immediately clicked. As Noel was deep in conversation with Weller, about deep meaningful things such as shoes and haircuts, me and Steve discussed the virtues of all things percussive. It was a real honour for me to meet him and I told him so. He laughed modestly. After an hour of banter about drums – although we also covered Charlton Athletic and John Bonham, and the peculiar differences between the north and south of the country – it was time to go. Steve told me that he thought *Definitely Maybe* was a sterling piece of work. He also told me that I was a good man and that if I needed anything in the future I was to ring him; he even gave me his number. In hindsight, I suppose he knew that his brother was being lined up to replace me. I did end up ringing him, though, and we remain friends to this day. A definite Spartan.

The shoot during the day didn't go as planned. The microphone that sat over my cymbal kept falling from its perch and halting the filming. Noel started to berate me as if I worked for Channel 4's sound department. I told him to ram it.

24 APRIL 1995. 'SOME MIGHT SAY' IS RELEASED. REACHED NO.1 IN THE SINGLES CHART

Our first No.1 single. We were virtually assured of it on the day of release, from pre-sales. I was still out in the cold with Noel and was wondering how he could say that the drumming was shite on a No.1 record?

NME applauded us:

> *OK so it's no 'Whatever' but what is? Anybody would have difficulty following a record like that, but don't let the recent brilliance of Oasis blind you to the charms of their new stuff. 'Some Might Say' is still one of the finest examples of pop music you'll hear this year. What's strangest about this song is that on the first couple of hearings you convince yourself there's no hook, nothing go on at all. Then, a few hours later, you find yourself humming a tune that you genuinely can't remember hearing before. It's certainly a deceptive little fucker. Noel Gallagher is back on the barmy lyrics again ('She can do the dishes / She's got little fishes on the brain'), and it's nice to hear Big Bro joining Little Liam on the neat call and response coda. Noel makes his presence felt strongly on the rest of the EP and gets to do his John Sebastian solo*

acoustic thing on 'Talk Tonight', as previewed at live shows late last year, while 'Acquiesce' is a song which could be read as a peace plan for the brothers Gallagher. 'We need each other / We believe in one another.' Meanwhile Liam sounds more like Lennon than ever before. We close with 'Headshrinker' a slight steal from The Faces' 'Stay With Me' and possibly the fastest song you'll hear by Oasis.

Terry Staunton

27 APRIL 1995. *TOP OF THE POPS*, ELSTREE, LONDON

'We've got a No.1 single. Add that to a No.1 album, a Brit Award, all-round critical acclaim and I suppose you could say we are doing all right,' said Noel.

We were sitting in the brightly lit dressing room before we were due to record. Noel was looking directly at me as he made this statement. I wondered why he was being so friendly and positive. Liam was surprisingly quiet and subdued, as were the rest of the band. We smashed out our first No.1 single for the cameras and then Liam and me returned to Manchester.

Liam sat in the back seat of the car. I looked directly over my right shoulder at him as he stared silently out the window. BigUn maintained a steady speed.

Suddenly, Liam said, 'Tony.'

'What?' I replied.

He stared at me, his eyes alight, and made to open his mouth. He paused, though, and the light quickly died. 'Nothing, it doesn't matter,' he mumbled and returned to focus on the English countryside flashing by. Something was definitely not right. I had a horrible feeling in my stomach.

* * *

On 30 April 1995, the phone rang in my mother's hallway. It was an old phone, one of the first mass-produced British Telecom models. Lipstick red, with the circular dial like a big shiny button on front. The whirr and click as the call connected to the local exchange. I answered.

'Hiya, Tony, it's Marcus,' in a soft Welsh accent.

'Hiya, Marcus,' I said, as dread started to fill me.

He continued. 'Look, it's not easy, this, but there is no other way to say it... You're out of the band.' They were the words I had been waiting for. I suppose I managed to contain my immediate reaction. Marcus went on, 'You know I tried to stop this. I tried to help. I'm sorry.'

Not as fuckin' sorry as me. It would have been easy to have blown off at Marcus, but he was merely the messenger. And he *had* tried to help. I suppose I never really expected it to come from Noel anyway. I thanked Marcus for his time and understanding and asked what would happen next. 'We'll meet to discuss how the future should work out for all of us,' he told me.

'OK. No worries. Take care. Bye. Bye.' I replied. There you go. It was that simple. Nice and clean, like we had agreed to meet for a pint and a sandwich. It had finally ended.

Returning to my room, I closed the door behind me. I stood and looked out of the window at the tarmac road outside. I read my name in the tarmac, still visible on the pavement. I remembered chasing that Boys' Brigade drummer all those years earlier and I smiled. My bags were still on the bed, unopened from the last tour. Rows of drumsticks lay scattered across the bed. Gold discs were stacked back to back in the far corner. I sat, head between my legs in another corner of the room. There was a knock on the door.

'Are you OK, Tony?' It was my mum. Slowly, she pushed the door open and cautiously entered the room. She sat on the bed and listened as I told her the whole story, the fights, the insults, Noel.

After a considered silence, she spoke and told me something I would never forget.

'I love you, Tony, for what you are and what you do. I was as proud of you that day in the nursery as I am of you in Oasis. In a while, you'll see that none of what has happened will really matter anyway.'

My mum was right.

I knew that Liam had been in touch with BigUn and we had arranged to meet next time he returned to Manchester. The only band member beside Liam who made a call was Bonehead. Considering how Noel and Guigs were, I suppose I didn't really expect them to phone.

The conversation with Bonehead took a familiar route. 'I didn't know, Tony. It's a shock to me. If there's anything I can do,' he stammered.

I thought back to Huts's departure all those years ago. Bonehead just didn't do confrontation. I couldn't dislike him, as he was a good fella. And to be honest, there were occasions when he had tried to guide me about how to handle Noel.

I wasn't surprised to be the first. I would always argue my corner if the line had been crossed. As much as I admired this trait in others, though, it seemed that Noel did not. Not that I was bull headed or ignorant. I made several gestures towards peace-making, usually to be met with a sneer or a putdown, so you learn to accept that in life you will meet people you simply do not get on with. Sadly, I had been able to get on with the old Noel; I just couldn't manage with the new one.

'I'm just hangin' on in there, Tony,' Bonehead told me. 'Don't like the atmosphere myself.' There was the sound of defeat in his voice. The headlong ferocity of the previous five years was beginning to show. He would never upset the applecart, though. Not his nature.

'Well, put your helmet on, Bonehead, and strap it fuckin' tight, my friend, because the flack will be heading for a new target.'

I knew Bonehead would be all right. Noel had respect for him, even after he had threatened to wipe the cobbles outside The Boardwalk with him – maybe *because* he had threatened to do it. The only target left was his side lieutenant Guigs. And true enough, within eight weeks of my departure I read that Guigs had pulled out of the band due to nervous exhaustion. I bet he was exhausted. The constant fighting can be cruelly tiring. I knew.

I was now officially an ex-member of Oasis. The papers initially reported that Liam and me had had a fight in Paris, with one writer going so far as to state that he had actually witnessed it. Never happened. Never would. I sat and waited, expecting them to contact me, as agreed. Nothing. Nada.

I rang Noel, but he didn't answer, and Liam had no phone. I spoke to BigUn, who Liam would ring frequently, to pass a message on to call me. (There was no point in talking to McGuigan, he was not a major player, and Bonehead was possibly on a binge.) On one occasion, BigUn told me that Noel was drinking in the Crown Pub in Heaton Moor and arranged to pick me up. We headed there, but there was no sign. A grumpy landlord told us he had left an hour previously.

The following evening, BigUn was at my door. It was the second time that day. It seemed he had been there earlier with Liam. 'He was genuinely upset, Tony. We called, but there was nobody here,' BigUn told me.

I suppose one of the most sorry things about the whole situation was the fact that our friendships had dissolved. The people I had grown up with and worked with had gone. I guess most bands have to accept that there comes a time to part – unless you're in Status Quo, of course. The initial thrill of the creative force as you meet and begin to understand each other's musical tastes and styles tends to wane over time. Personalities change, as do expectations and your perception of yourself.

I felt I knew the reason I had been expelled from the band. My three arguments with Noel had led to us not seeing eye-to-eye for the previous three months. Noel has stated that he had other reasons for sacking me – such as low regard of my talents as a musician – but I had my own opinion.

I waited for over a month and still had no contact from the band. The word was that I was not gonna receive a penny, that I had no legal standing.

I approached the Musicians' Union, who I was registered with, and explained my predicament. They put me in touch with a solicitor called Jens Hills. Ironically, he had previously represented Pete Best, so, as if in accordance with the masterplan itself, I headed off to London to meet him.

Jens is a large man with a trusting broad face. His jeans, loose shirt and sandals were not what I expected, but as I was to learn, Jens wasn't your stereotypical pin-striped brief. We met in the World's End pub in Stratford, taking our place amongst the city types forcing lunch down their throats. I told Jens my story and my thoughts. I wasn't angry any more. It was already sounding tedious to me. He sat and listened, occasionally making notes.

Jens finally had a copy of my contract. The contract I had signed that day was a hastily arranged document that essentially left me up the proverbial river. He spoke to their legal team and told them of the negative publicity that would accompany my claim. Jens then proposed a fair deal that would stop such hassle for everybody. It was the bog-standard average music industry offer. I would be paid for my work on all the recordings I completed. I really wasn't interested in going to court and the palaver that it would inevitably bring. I could pay for a house for my girl and I was happy.

* * *

Smaller were playing the Roadhouse. This was Digsy's band, which meant that The Real People's entourage would be in tow. I had arranged to meet Liam there.

Liam was with Robbie Williams. I had been told it was a low-key affair, as Liam was under doctor's instruction to lay off all goodtime as his throat was playing up.

Due to the volatile Mancunian weather, we ran from the taxi and into The Roadhouse. A few minutes later, a hooded figure entered The Roadhouse, dripping. He stood in the doorway, looking like a lollipop man in the rain. The whole room turned and to stare. The steam rose off him, looking like stage smoke in the dimly lit club. As he dropped his hood, the lollipop man slowly revealed himself to be...

Robbie Williams! The crowd all pointed and clapped as he posed. I was surprised there wasn't a spotlight trained on him as he waved and smiled and shouted, 'Who's buying?'

'He's really fuckin' low key, isn't he?' I said to Liam.

Liam laughed. 'He's like that wherever we go.'

We slipped in unobtrusively after Robbie's grand entrance and found a quiet corner. The place was hammered, though, and even the quiet corner wasn't quiet. Liam seemed genuinely sorry about what had happened and, to be honest, it played as I had expected it would. He looked well and had the glint back in his eye. He admitted that after our argument in Paris, Noel had told him he was going to get rid of me and he had shouted 'Whatever,' at Noel, thinking it would blow over. He read of my exit in the paper over breakfast. My departure had left a massive void in Noel's life, which he had to fill. So, unhindered by Liam, he launched an attack of the same magnitude that he had fired upon me. Liam felt that my departure had signalled the end, in a way. Not just for me, but for the band as he knew it. The bond that had once been between us had been slowly eroded away.

I told him that I played the drums on *Definitely Maybe*, which was as smart an achievement as any, considering the circumstances. He told me he liked my outlook. He was then back again as Liam Gallagher International Rock Star, and that manic grin spread across his face. 'They want the showman. They get the showman,' he said, with a giggle.

I stared at the man who had first introduced himself to me as a young boy, over 10 years before, in that park. Time and money had affected both his appearance and confidence, but the glint in his eye remained as youthful and infectious as ever. Although you might not think it, Liam had always struggled with the celebrity part of his life. He had made a decision, though, that now he would milk it for what it was worth. 'But if they want young northern upstart, then they can have that instead.' He leaned back in his chair and threw out two pink stiff ones, his face lit with laughter.

Liam asked me what my plans were. I told him that I couldn't seem to get the travelling bug from my bones. All that touring had become routine and I was itching to go somewhere new. I thought of maybe travelling through South-East Asia and then down into Australia.

The next morning, I decided that it was the States for me. The newspapers and televisions were frothing over with the Blur versus Oasis saga and it seemed the whole country was intrigued. I decided that staying in Manchester could leave me getting dangerously close to being inaugurated onto The List and I would soon be hanging round with Peter Hook for some solidarity. Noel was in the papers doing a hatchet job on me. 'Shite drummer. Shite hair. Shite trainers.' That kind of thing. I decided that a spell away would be refreshing and rewarding. I was quite enjoying not being in a band. No timetable to adhere to, no meet-and-greets, no daily assault from Laurel and Hardy. At the same time, though, I was kind of missing it as well, if truth be told.

It has always antagonised me that my musicianship was brought into question by Noel. I will not sit here and pretend to be the most intricate or competent drummer in the world. I have never claimed to be and I never will. But drumming had been my love. It was my passion. It became my livelihood. It was never, There's the clever kid, or, There's the kid who's great at gymnastics. It was always, There's Tony, He's a drummer. And I loved it.

I watched the greats in action and they inspired me. I

strived to improve myself. And then it was ended. And as if it wasn't bad enough that I'd been sacked, Noel was also telling anyone who would listen how shite I was at doing the thing that I cared about so much. As I said, I understood my limitations and areas in which I needed to improve, but I also know that as a band, overall, we would not be compared to, say, Crosby, Stills and Nash in terms of musicianship. It was a cheap and easy shot and one that still hangs over me. Just lucky I'm not a sensitive fucking soul.

Needing a break, I headed off to Florida to meet Elle. I sat inside one sweltering balmy afternoon in order to make full use of the state-of-the-art air conditioning. I was in legal hell with the band by now and just wanted it to end. It was time to move on. The warm breeze blew off the Gulf of Mexico and through the apartment. The humid conditions were as distant from the brittle and brisk cold air of Manchester as could be. Not everything was quite so far removed, though.

The afternoon radio was blaring away and my ears pricked up when I heard Noel's instantly recognisable voice. A song filled the room – it must have been a new Oasis song. I had a silent chuckle to myself as the chorus kicked in that claimed we were all part of a masterplan.

Brilliant. I pissed myself laughing. The video that later accompanied the song depicted the five of us walking the grimy industrials streets of Manchester. We trudged along depicted as Lowry figures; watching it made me laugh again. Begrudgingly, I had to admire the humour in his message. The Lowry argument and the masterplan. I cast my mind back to Liam singing 'Matchstalk Men' in the rehearsal room under The Boardwalk. 'They came down to London as Lowry matchstick men and turned into a Jeff Koons,' somebody once said of us. I don't think they knew just how telling their statement would turn out to be.

* * *

I was back in Manchester, preparing myself for the impending court case, which was now only a week away. The case had also affected my relationship with Elle. It was difficult to fix from over four thousand miles away.

I felt fit and healthy and it was another beautiful day. My exit from the band had also led me on a march away from the chemicals. I guess when you see such a habit as a core part of your job description, it's easy to justify and, therefore, you overlook the dangers you are putting yourself in, both mentally and physically. As I said, I took my fair share, but my recent time abroad had cleared my mind from the numbing fog and I was firing on all cylinders.

We were sitting in a pub on Stockport Road. It was a sun-drenched afternoon and we hid in the shade. The carpets wore a coat of chewing gum, stains and burns. The usual collection of misfits and the just-released flitted through the place. The landlady was having a pop at the regulars over a half-hearted charity effort. BigUn suggested that if she wanted to do a bit for charity she should contact the local Tourette's society and offer her pub as a halfway-house-type establishment. She called him a cunt and told him to sit down.

'See what I mean. Perfect,' said BigUn.

I was feeling the urge to get off. 'What we doing in this khazi? C'mon, we're going out. I need to visit a pal first and then I'm gonna get some... gonna get some...' BigUn stood up and was now dancing in the pub doorway, his huge frame blocking patrons and sunlight alike. He was laughing and roaring and his eyes had that dangerous twinkle. He had obvious intentions. Behind him lay the picnic table-strewn concrete car park, which, even at this early hour was littered with miscreants and charlatans all busy skinnin' up.

After considering the options, we left the pub and the inevitable bloody brawl that would occur later, and jumped in BigUn's motor. As he was still in contact with Liam and Noel, I made sure he promised not to discuss the impending court case.

'Just got to nip and fix a small problem in Alderley Edge. After that, the horizon is clear and it's lift-off. I fancy town, maybe Ked's place,' he said as he turned the keys. It wasn't long before we had left the city streets and were flashing through the Cheshire countryside. As we entered Alderley Edge, I remembered the times we had descended on this suburb in my youth. We would gather as many as possible, including rival factions. At times, there had been more than a hundred of us on the train, including Guigs, Noel and Liam. The train journey would be free – an Away Day; you just hoped it wouldn't be you as the statistic.

I'd be seeing them all again soon. The court case was fast approaching and I just wanted to put a finish to it all. We sped past boutiques and pavement bars. A shop-fronted statement of the wealth that lay behind either side of the short high street – in sharp contrast to the kebab shops and fuggy pubs that lined the high road we had just vacated. At the end of the high street we struck a left and landed in a small courtyard in front of a suitably impressive house.

'Be quick, BigUn. Don't be fuckin' about.'

That was one of BigUn's many traits. He fucked about. What any other individual would complete in minutes, BigUn would take hours to achieve. This was mainly due to his tea breaks, mobile phone conversations every two minutes, cigarette breaks and the like. He needed to be constantly hurried, which was a fuckin' bore.

'Stretch yer legs and stop mithering. This fella reckons the roof of his motor wasn't cleaned properly by Jacobs.'

Jacobs was one of BigUn's star employees, which didn't necessarily mean much as BigUn seemed to recruit at the exit door of Strangeways. BigUn figured he was the first step in their rehabilitation and spoke to them like an aggressive counsellor. He also knew that the job he offered sort of sat between being unemployed and actually having a proper job. In the far corner of the courtyard sat a jet-black convertible Ferrari Spider. It glistened in the afternoon sun. Privately plated and a whole lot of mullah. BigUn walked over and I followed.

'Fuck all wrong with that. What's he rattling on about?' BigUn had his sleeve over his wrist and was trying to rub away a solid line of shite that still ran the length of the roof. Guess that was what 'he' was rattling on about. The line was not shifting easily and as BigUn increased the tempo of his rubbing to a pace that would surely burn a hole in the canvas roof, the door to the house opened and out walked David Beckham. BigUn spun round.

'Orwite, BigUn,' said Beckham, with a grin.

'Hiya Becks, how they hanging? Can't believe the mess that's been left here. Real sorry. I've just fired the kid who cleaned it. Tony, just fetch us that bucket from over there while I sort this out, will you? There's a tap at the side of the house.'

I sloped off round the side of the house, wondering how the fuck I let myself get in these situations with BigUn. Our day out had turned into a valeting job. Becks gave a smile and went back to the house to ready himself for the afternoon. I reappeared, holding a hose pipe.

'Why don't you buy a car like this, To'?' BigUn said, laughing.

I couldn't. I had never told BigUn about the contract I had signed. I never told anyone. I aimed the pipe towards him and he squeezed himself into the driving space of the Ferrari for cover. The windscreen wipers were knocked on by his huge frame and like a monkey at the controls of the space shuttle, BigUn prodded buttons and flicked switches while I levelled the hosepipe at the roof of the car. Water shot powerfully from the hose and battered against the roof. The pipe was a proper fucking water cannon. I was loving it.

'What the fuck you doing?' shouted BigUn angrily over the noise of the water.

Before he could say another word, the roof mechanism kicked into gear and the hood started to retract. With eyes wide BigUn pushed frantically at switches and dials and buttons and ashtrays in a vain attempt to halt the sequence. Rather than moving the hose away from the vehicle, though, I continued to batter water against the roof as it tried to rise backwards. With a loud crank the roof suddenly froze, pointing to the glorious blue skies above.

BigUn was now out of the motor and wrestled the hose from my grasp as I fell about laughing. Fuck him, it was only a laugh. BigUn didn't see it that way, though. No matter how hard he tried to physically force the delicate roof back into place, it would not budge. No number of buttons pressed helped either. The car sat on the drive with what looked like a gigantic side-on tailfin stuck three feet into the air. BigUn sat in the driver's seat with his head on the leather steering wheel of the Ferrari in despair. Shit.

'You fuckin' numpty. That's a two hundred grand motor that you've just fucked. I ain't paying for it. You're gonna have to cough up the dough.'

At this point, Becks decided to reappear on the scene. Coiffured and lotioned, he stood looking dumbfounded and bemused at the sight of his motor. 'Is everything all right?' he squeaked. 'I wouldn't normally bother, BigUn, but I'm signing a new contract today, so it's a bit special.'

I was thinking he was gonna look proper special driving his newly modified sports car which couldn't be less aerodynamic.

'Yeah, slight hitch with the drive compartment in the roof, David. It's very common on these cars. The Mancunian rain plays havoc with the Italian sports car, as my friend Luigi keeps telling me. He's one of the chief mechanics for Ferrari, you know,' bullshitted BigUn. As the overwhelming stench of manure still hung in the air, he continued, 'I'll ring the garage in Wilmslow for you, David. Hold on.'

He wandered off down the drive. After a moment, he returned and announced, 'They say it shouldn't be a problem. They come across this type of problem regularly. I can run it down there for you now, but it's not going to be returned until Wednesday. I reckon yer need to get the Escalade out, Becks, and get yerself down to OT. Don't want to miss signing your contract.'

Beckham looked really sad.

'Sorry, Becks, it's the best I can do,' apologised BigUn.

After Becks had departed, BigUn returned to the car and began to fiddle with the metal frame of the hood. Then he went to the front of the car, pressed one button and hey presto, the roof lowered and clicked into place. With a wicked grin, he hopped out singing the chorus to a Beatles song, subtly altered to: 'BigUn, you can drive my car.' 'I rang the General,' he laughed. 'He's a mechanical genius. I'll drive my motor and you can jump in the Ferrari.'

After an afternoon testing the various performance capabilities of the car, we decided to head back towards the pub. It had now completely overflowed into the car park. An assortment of striped T-shirts and Rockports through a haze of marijuana smoke. After filling our usual seats, we sat and had a drink.

I finished my pint and headed off into the evening. As I left, I noticed that the car park was rammed, the warm night air clouded with smoke. The Ferrari was filled with youths who were posing in it while smoking weed and photographing themselves with their mobile phones – like monkeys who had finally made a breakthrough at the safari park. Hope they don't burn the upholstery, BigUn.

I had spoken to a school friend who had become a youth social worker and was interested in opening a recording studio to help local children. I told him to find the building, cost it and let me know the outcome. For the time being, I just wanted the court case over and for my life to move on to the next chapter. It wouldn't be a long wait.

My friend Roy was true to his word and after a six-month refurbishment, the recording studio opened its doors to the musical youth of Manchester. I ended up advising and tutoring many bands who passed through that studio. It was all voluntary, it felt good to be back in the music business again and it helped with the musical withdrawal from my life on the road with Oasis. I needed a complete break, though. Somewhere far away. Alone. I decided that after the court case, which was only a few days off, I was gonna get off come what may.

* * *

Finally, we were ready to go. We were due at the High Court to finally put this sorry affair to bed. Or so I thought. No matter what the outcome, I knew I was the loser. My time with the band was over.

Me, BigUn and my brother Adi arrived in London and booked in at The Savoy. That evening, we received a phone call from Jens telling us they had just agreed a settlement with the Oasis legal team. A wave of relief ran through me. This meant that I wouldn't be in court for the next two weeks, or meeting the band the next day. I was an extremely relieved man. Still, although it also meant that I would get some financial compensation, even with my near-worthless contract, it still felt wrong. It was never about the money.

The next day, we stumbled through early morning commuters as we marched along the road towards the court. In the distance, you could see a gathering of what I took to be a large Japanese tourist group. We still had to have a formal court hearing to sign the settlement agreement. That day, the court list read like the back of a *Now* compilation album. In Court 29 was Robbie Williams, who was having it out with a former manager. Spandau Ballet were just up the corridor and had been appearing regularly there for the last month or so. Me, BigUn and Adi would sit in Court 17, where Bruce Springsteen had just finished.

As we neared the courts, I realised that the large gathering was in fact not tourists but a herd of media and press. It seems that no one had informed them that neither Liam nor

Noel would be present. BigUn sent Adi in first as my decoy, as we have a close resemblance. The cameras and tape recorders immediately bit. They descended on a very welcoming and smiling Adi, who offered to answer any questions they might have. The lights flashed as a volley of questions were fired at him. He actually appeared in the papers that day and was on constant loop on all the 24-hour news channels; he was very impressed with himself. Not too sure his boss felt the same, though, as Adi had rung in sick at work in order to attend. We sneaked behind him and headed into the court.

The courtrooms were small and could bring fans within feet of their idols without the intervention of burly minders. And unlike rock stadiums, entrance was free. There was a large group of girls, all fans of Liam and Noel, sitting in the court. They stared me down and I laughed at their front. I didn't want this to be personal. As expected, there was no turnout from the rest of the band. The barristers cracked their wigged heads in one corner, then Jens quickly approached me.

'The band would buy you out of any future royalties and put this to bed,' he told me. He also said that considering the contract I had signed left me with virtually no entitlements whatsoever, it was in my interest to sign..

Although it was a good offer, £550,000, it hurt me to agree to it. It broke the previous five years into a financial figure. Black and white. On a page. After legal expenses and a visit from Her Majesty's tax man it would leave me with enough to buy land in Ireland. Just.

As we made to exit the court, I saw a large group of photographers some twenty yards back, under control of the police. There was no Robbie Williams that day. No Liam or

Noel. No Spandau Ballet. Just little old me in a dodgy-looking suit. As I left the court, I raised my hands aloft in relief that it was finally over. We tore it up for the rest of the day and returned to the hotel.

BigUn banged on my door at The Savoy early the next morning. That morning, the papers ran the story in their headlines. 'Is this the Stupidest Man in Pop?' cried the 'Bizarre' page in *The Sun*. Below was a large photo of my good self leaving court the previous day. Perhaps what the journalists hadn't realised that, because of the contract I had signed, I had no choice but to accept the settlement offered. I didn't know why Noel had been upset about my exit from the courtroom; I thought I played it down.

* * *

We were in London to catch a game. Charlton Athletic were playing Sunderland in a Wembley playoff final. I was sitting in the bar beforehand with Adi and Ray Winstone. I had met Ray previously and it was good to catch up.

'Do you get much mither at the games?' Adi asked him.

'Not really,' replied Ray. 'You'll always get some nugget who will roar, "Where's your fucking tool?" If I had a penny for every time I'd heard that I'd have over a tenner,' he said with a laugh.

BigUn entered the bar and scanned the room. He spotted us. I looked at him as his eyes lit up and knew exactly what was going to come out of that mouth.

'Oi! Where's your fuckin' tool?' Hollered so loud by BigUn that it even made Ray Winstone jump in his skin. Who the fuck had given BigUn drink?

After a thrilling game, we headed off into the London evening. BigUn had a brainwave. Why don't we go track

Liam down in Primrose Hill? He told the taxi where to go and thrust a fistful of money at him.

We arrived in Primrose Hill and BigUn was now full tilt. Not a pretty sight. He charged into an old corner boozer, doors flung wide and started to ask, very loudly, where Liam lived. This question was posed to the whole room; everyone had now stopped drinking and they stared apprehensively at the sight before them. Before BigUn could decide where to begin his individual interrogations, he spotted an old Lambretta parked outside a flat opposite the pub.

'Found the fucker. Let's do it,' he slurred, his eyes glazed.

He had to be fuckin' joking.

He wasn't.

BigUn had deduced that we were in Primrose Hill and the flat had a Lambretta outside, therefore we had discovered Liam. I asked him if there was a Parka coat hung on the gate and a John Lennon statue in the front garden. BigUn looked out the window again and then said 'Nope. Neither. But I still reckon it's him.' With that, he was off out the door.

Fuck me. I thought he had gone mental.

'Right, let's go now before he finds some student who's dressed like Liam,' said Adi.

We went outside. BigUn had hopped over the old iron railings guarding the flat he had spotted and had started to bang on the windows like a fuckin' lunatic.

'C'mon, you little bastard, let's have yer.'

I told Adi to just humour the fucker. He was cuckoo. BigUn being cuckoo was not great. In the 12 years I had known him I had seen him drink once and that had been enough. BigUn was one of those people who did not need any artificial stimulants to ride high on life. He had an unquenchable thirst for mullah that led him to front most everything and everyone he crossed paths with. Add to this the build of an All Star American Wrestler and he could come across as quite forceful. He also had the habit of imitating accents while conversing with people. I had tried explaining to the mad cunt that it didn't work, but he disagreed. His Asian, East European and Irish accents were all highly insulting to Asians, East Europeans and the Irish respectively, and I'd seen many people absolutely bewildered by him when he began mimicking one. But BigUn ploughed on through with a smile. And one thing you were guaranteed with BigUn was an adventure. You just had to keep it at the back of your mind that it could always go tits up at any possible time.

The day had drawn to a close, though the same could not be said of BigUn's frustration at not locating a Gallagher. 'Right, Noel's gaff can't be far,' were the words that started the journey that eventually led to his arrest.

An unlucky taxi driver braked to a halt. We left the drizzle behind and jumped in, onto a smooth, worn leather seat. 'Noel Gallagher's house, please, I believe it's called Supernova Heights.' BigUn was now using the voice of the Queen Mother. He called this his 'posh' voice and was intended to create the illusion of wealth and education. It didn't.

'Whose house?' the taxi driver replied, in a strong Dublin brogue.

Fuck me, here we go. I knew it made no difference which part of Ireland the driver was from – BigUn did not have a wardrobe to choose from when it came to accents. His Irish attempt would alternate between Ian Paisley or Frank Carson and it was always a full-blood-and-spittle affair.

'Noel Gallagher's house please, Michael,' he roared into the grated separator. It was Ian Paisley tonight. I watched as a solitary spittle drop sloped its way slowly down the mesh on the separator and the driver tried frantically to weigh the situation up.

'What the fuck are you calling me Michael for?' he spluttered, angrily.

'Bejesus, because you're Irish,' came the matter-of-fact reply.

I had already explained to BigUn that his Irish impersonation didn't offend everyone in Ireland. Just those that heard it. His eyes rolled wildly round his head, which made the taxi driver jolt back like a kid at a horror movie; Boris Karloff had met the Reverend Ian and the resulting vision was now foaming on the back seat of his cab. I watched as BigUn sat and stared at the double-cardigan-clad driver. He had reached a chemical tipping point and was struggling to make the transition from thought to speech, so I decided to take control. 'Don't worry about him, mate, he's not trying to be offensive, he's on a programme.'

'What? *When Mad Feckers Attack*?' the taxi driver muttered.

'No a different kind of programme, kinda mental health thing. Look, if you just take us back to Euston I'll make sure he keeps quiet. What's your name, fella?

'Michael,' came the reply.

Fuck. 'There you go. Who's the dickhead now?' he said, triumphantly. And then, 'Fuck going home. I want to see Noel and I ain't going anywhere until I have. Brezhnev owes me. Not money. An explanation. That's all I want from the nugget.'

The taxi driver put his foot to the floor in an attempt to reduce the time he would spend with BigUn. After finding Supernova Heights, BigUn went into overdrive. Fuck this, I thought. Someone is likely to die at this rate. Maybe Noel, if

BigUn managed to wrap his huge hands round his neck. Maybe BigUn, if he shovelled any more bugle into himself.

I stared across the road at Supernova Heights. I had nothing to say to Noel, so with a quick nod to BigUn I said, 'Do what you gotta do, BigUn. Not my style. We'll be in the park.'

Adi and I made our way towards a large park in Hampstead. As we left, I watched as BigUn stood transfixed in front of the house. Then suddenly he leapt the front gate like it was a seventies football turnstile and hopped up the steps fronting the Victorian property. As the tip of his nose touched the paint on the front door he raised his right arm and began to beat on it, not loudly, but surprisingly in time. An upstairs light flashed on and off. Then nothing. I imagined Noel in his underpants at the crack of the upstairs curtain. Probably his worst nightmare had come true. His own personal Begbie had come to pay him a visit. I quickened my step, to the sound of BigUn's shouts. 'Hey Robo Dwarf, get your childlike buttocks down here. You're wanted for crimes against Manchester and your friends and music and hairstyles and yer brothers and...'

BigUn had developed a whole dictionary of derogatory names for Noel over the last two years. I was sure most of them would be put to use until the police arrived. His shouting faded as we moved further off. Adi walked with his back to the wind, facing towards Supernova Heights. He laughed at the slowly shrinking scene.

'He's running up and down the steps trying kung-fu kicks on the front door. Now he's throwing stones and shit.'

I didn't even turn round. We needed to get the fuck out of there. I lowered my head, upped the collars of my jacket and with Adi providing a running commentary beside me, headed off. The autumn streets were a carpet of greens and browns as we shuffled along. We melted into the night and the relative safety of the park. The sirens were already singing their way towards us.

CHAPTER 9

ARISE SIR NOEL, THE LORD MAYOR OF LONELINESS

'I feel you have the right to know that the level of verbal and violent intimidation towards me, my family, friends and comrades has become intolerable. And the lack of support and understanding from my management and bandmates has left me with no other option than to get me cape and seek pastures new.'

This was Noel's official statement on the day Oasis finally called it a day.

He cites verbal intimidation as a factor in his decision to quit the band. He's gotta be joking. Noel's sardonic outbursts have been aimed at those around him for years. Perhaps Noel simply did not like the taste of his own medicine.

I guess Noel's life story just shows how you can have it all yet still not have enough. He's the singer and songwriter in one of the biggest rock groups the world has ever seen. He's adored by millions. He's got his Bentley and his mansion. His cleaners and his personal assistants. He has drinks with Elton and Russell 'Scissorhands' Brand. He has even built a replica of the five-a-side court we played on all those years ago in his back garden. To me, he still doesn't seem happy, though. He will probably show you his veneers and tell you he is, but I'm not so sure.

Over the years, Noel has reshaped the beginnings of Oasis. It started early, with the loss of the videotape of our first gig, and he has carefully handled all public revelations since. To this day he is insistent that he did it all alone; he goes out of his way to make the point. 'Everyone else was a monkey.' Not true. He had four friends with him all the way. He had the sound we had created in a basement of a hotel. We had our songs performed by a mesmerising and gifted frontman.

In Tony and Chris Griffiths, he also had a songwriting team who had a lasting effect on the way he composed his melodies. He had Louise, who gained us a national television and radio audience at a critical stage. He even had BigUn, who gave us work when work was scarce.

'I arrived at the first rehearsal wearing a badge that read "the Chief" with a bagful of songs I had already written.' He was welcomed quietly as a friend. The 'Chief' days did not arrive until the record contract was signed and he had the power to match his ego. His bag only contained three good songs when we arrived at that studio in Bootle. The rest came from a combination of Noel, rehearsals and the Realies. McGee thought that Noel had 50 songs written by the time he was 20. Noel had written none of the original *Definitely Maybe* compositions until after we had formed.

Then there's his claim that he and Liam often fought with each other. I lived, worked and played with them for over a decade. I never once saw them come to physical blows. Not once.

And his claim that we used to burgle houses? Bollocks. As in any circle of friends, there would be a dodgy character or two around us. But never did any of the band commit burglary. It's a working-class crime. You paid heavily.

The Beatles were our greatest influence? Not true. This Beatle connection first came from the work with the Realies. They had always been compared to The Beatles stylistically. After we played at King Tut's, Alan McGee spotted the musical similarity that we now had with the Fab Four. After openly declaring us to be the next Beatles, it was 'decided' that they would be our musical influence.

How about the line that we signed to Creation Records because we liked what they stood for? In fact, we never signed to Creation at all. We just said we did because it sounded much cooler than us signing with Sony.

'After Tony McCarroll left those songs haven't sounded quite the same. Tony had his own thing – anti-drumming if you like – and I don't think *Definitely Maybe* would have sounded so good without him. He was the right man for the job.'

Hold on. That's actually a truth. After my departure, Noel said that I had a fight with Liam in Paris, and that this contributed to my exit from the band. Not true. I never had any altercation at all with Liam. Never would. Noel knows exactly what happened in Paris.

And then, of course, he claimed that I simply wasn't a good enough drummer. As I see it, if musicianship had been an issue, then Noel would have sacked the whole band, including himself. Jesus, Guigs didn't even record on the album. Part of the reason I left the band was a bit more personal.

My demise came in stages.

Firstly and most importantly, came my clash with Noel

over the money fronted to us by Alan McGee and Creation. Not a good time for me to argue with Noel, who had already begun the change from Old to New. Plus, the contract that I had signed gave him the power to sack me.

And then there was my threat on a dark Parisian stage after months of arguments between us. That threat gave him one of the reasons to sack me.

Would I change the way I acted in these situations, with hindsight? It is now as it was then. Right is right, even if everyone is against it, and wrong is wrong, even if everyone is for it.

But do I regret the way it all ended? Of course. I had strived to achieve everything I had aimed for all those years ago, but I didn't get to enjoy it for long. It was a sorry situation that led to the end of friendships that should have lasted a lifetime. I had tried to appease Noel on numerous occasions, but it just didn't work.

Don't get me wrong. We all have flaws. What Noel also possesses, though, is an immense talent as a songwriter. The first two albums have left him with a legacy of beautifully crafted pop anthems that nearly everyone in the land can sing along to. His self-belief was always a major driving force in his life, and for that I give him credit.

I think what I found most tragic was the way McGuigan and Bonehead reacted. After Noel effectively took control of the band at the signing of the record contract, those who were aware of the situation seemed to change their behaviour. Bonehead would always stand up to Noel before this point. After the signing, if they did disagree, which didn't happen often, Bonehead always seemed to hold back on his reactions. He was wary.

If Noel had an issue with me, I got the impression that

McGuigan would jump on it too. Some of us are leaders, some are followers, I guess.

I also find it funny how Noel mocks Liam's unhinged behaviour; then I think it's tragic. That attitude was typical of the Liam that Noel had encouraged all those years ago. Noel knew the media were intoxicated with the snorting, aggressive, working-class hero that Liam was. Perhaps all Liam wanted was acknowledgement from Noel, to hear 'I couldn't have done it without you' just once. But with Noel, everybody has their time. Even his brother.

As for Liam, I truly believe the split from Noel will serve him well. Noel has played his part in shaping Liam, so it will be interesting to see what happens now he is out loose on his own. Five years, I reckon, and they'll be back together. I don't think they can help themselves. Liam still holds true to those values and beliefs he started with. For all his arrogance and attitude, he has a generosity and dignity that those around him truly appreciate. He's not perfect, but he's honest. And he's real.

When I was asked to write this book, I decided to read a couple of the authorised Oasis books already published. I had never read one before. I guess any uncertainty I had about completing my chronicles quickly vanished. The level of hate dished my way by Noel and McGuigan came as a real surprise. I thought they might have got over it all by now. Although Noel's take on things was amusing, I particularly enjoyed McGuigan's recollections of the days when he was the most popular guy around. An all-round sportsman. Tasty on the cobbles. Always a smile and a wink for the ladies. Not too sure whose days he was remembering, though. I was also rather saddened to see him threaten to 'stab me in the gut' in one book.

* * *

JUNE 2010. SLIEVE BLOOM MOUNTAINS, IRELAND

I'm sitting on a hill by the foot of the Slieve Bloom Mountains. It is my hill. In the field below, chasing the sheep, is my six-year-old son, Oliver. Oliver is my second and final child. Soon he will be old enough to go up the mountain to catch rabbits, as I did all those years before.

I feel I have found my final stop. My days travelling this big and beautiful world of ours are nearing an end. I suppose I have achieved what I had aimed for all those years ago: I lived my life in the city and I found my easy way out.

The sun bakes the fields below as a tractor slowly trundles along in the distance. Young Oliver is down to his underpants. The joys of youth, still simple and easily achievable.

That Old Manchester seems like another life today. A different time and a different place. I now live my life between here and modern Manchester. For the last seven years I have lived with, and loved, a little old hippie named Sue. She is a daily reminder for me to smile. My daughter is 21 years of age. I still live my life with the same values that my parents taught me, and with that I sit proud.

I have long put the anger and frustration about what really happened with the band behind me and I haven't spoken to Noel for a long time. BigUn tells me that he has recaptured some of his old spark since he stopped taking drugs. If that is the case, then I wish him luck. The old Noel was a genuinely good lad; maybe the new Noel had just been a cocaine-powered creation. If that is so, I guess it makes my time in the band even more unfortunate.

I have enjoyed my life immensely and I do hope my story shows that. The last three months of the band and my exit were the low points of my last 40 years, so it has been quite difficult to write about. But it has also been entertaining. I have squealed with laughter at some of the memories recollected, and I hope you have too.

I pick up young Oliver in my arms and hug him. He feels warm. I put him down and we walk hand in hand down the hill back towards the village. I squint in the afternoon sun and smile. We're off to the old cottage where I had spent part of my own childhood. As we near it, we stop and watch as the local villagers arrive with their fiddles and guitars. Behind the cottage there still sits a beaten and weathered caravan. And in that caravan, there still sits an old set of red drums.

Live Forever. Tony.

APPENDIX 1

THE PERFECT BEAT

This section is where I get one back for the drummer. The little man of the band. The bottom of the musical food chain. The easy way out for guitarists all over the world.

I have mentioned how, at an early age, I was transfixed by that drummer in the Boys' Brigade. He was the musician who first prompted me to pick up a set of sticks, but there were a host of other musicians whose influence inspired and drove me to continue. I'll tell you about my top three drummers shortly, but before I do I would like to mention a few of the greats who didn't make my final three.

Although it pains me, there is no room for Hal Blaine. If the only record Hal Blaine had ever played on was 'Be My Baby', that would be enough to regard him as a legend. Hal Blaine didn't just play on one great record, though; he played on over 30 No.1s, for starters. But as I say there is no room for Hal.

Another drummer who hasn't made my final three, but can't go unmentioned, is Reni from The Stone Roses. Years ago I had dozens of Roses bootlegs – many of them were redeemed purely by Reni's liquid pulse, which tied not just songs but whole sets together. His laconic style, typified by an off-beat shuffle and perfectly placed fills, and played on a minimal three-piece kit, was always funky, always soulful, and seldom egotistical. Capable of delivering backing vocals as accomplished as anyone, there has never been, in my humble opinion, a British 'indie' drummer who even approached to his skills.

The final two sticksmen I would like to mention before counting down to my three greatest are Larry Mullen, Jr and Ginger Baker. Mullen for his style, which is subtle: a balanced backdrop to Bono's broad histrionics. Larry Mullen once said 'simple is best', which is a statement I agree with wholeheartedly; it's the basis upon which U2 have built their varied career. His style moves seamlessly from post-punk to stadium rock with ease.

And then we have Peter 'Ginger' Baker, a red-haired Londoner and as a jazz drummer trapped inside the body of a blues rocker. He replaced Charlie Watts in Alexis Corner's Blues Inc. in 1962, and through the Graham Bond Organisation, Cream, and Blind Faith, made a habit of sneaking in jazzy flashes that rock audiences could understand into enormously powerful sets. His remarkable dexterity gave him a stamina and variety worthy of two ordinary drummers, and with 'Toad', he developed the first extended drum solo on a rock record. Not bad for a ginger.

And so to the three drummers who have been the biggest influence on me, in descending order:

NUMBER 3

Steve White

And coming in at number three we've got another Londoner, but no red hair this time. Steve is the older brother and inspiration to Alan White, who replaced me in the Oasis chair. He was born in Bermondsey, south London, and has lived south of the river all his life. Steve began to show an interest in drumming with a snare drum that was given to him by an uncle at the age of eight. Aged 10, Steve began to learn simple side-drums parts as a member of the drum corps of his local Boys' Brigade company. I wonder if he ever cracked an inquisitive kid round the head with his sticks?

He worked hard and progressed quickly, inspired by the skill and playing of drummers such as Buddy Rich and Gene Krupa. At the age of 12, and accompanied by his long-suffering and supportive dad, Steve saw his first truly great drummer play live on a Friday night at Ronnie Scott's club in Soho, London. The sticksman in question was jazz legend Louie Bellson who, among other notable achievements, is regarded as the first drummer to have used two bass drums. From that point Steve was totally hooked, practising and playing at every opportunity.

Dennis Monday of Polydor Records called to ask Steve if he was interested in going for a try-out with another band, whom he did not name at the time. Steve gave it a go and seemed to strike a chord with the band's singer songwriter Paul Weller. He was duly invited to come and play with The Style Council on a David 'Kid' Jensen show on Radio One.

A few weeks later, he found himself driving to Paris in a transit van to record the band's new record, the *A Paris*

EP, which contained the classics 'Long Hot Summer' and 'Paris Match'.

An almost constant stream of hits and worldwide touring followed, pretty much uninterrupted, until 1989. In 1985, Steve became the youngest performer to appear on stage at the legendary Live Aid Concert at Wembley.

Steve went on to play with such artists as Working Week, Galliano, The Young Disciples, The James Taylor Quartet and Ian Dury.

Steve also found himself filling in for younger brother Alan in the hot seat for Oasis on the band's American tour with The Black Crowes.

Steve has now launched a successful career as an educator, both as an in-demand personal teacher and motivator and as a drum set clinician.

NUMBER 2

John 'Bonzo' Bonham

John Bonham was born in Redditch, in the Midlands countryside of Worcestershire, on 31 May 1948. He got his first snare drum aged 10, a present from his mum. Six years later, in 1964, he joined his first semi-pro band, Terry Webb and the Spiders; a year later, he joined his second outfit, A Way of Life. That same year he met Pat Phillips at a dance near his home in Kidderminster. At the age of 17, they got hitched.

The band became inactive and Bonham, with a new wife to support, had to either make a go of drumming financially or quit. (I can relate to those circumstances.) He had met a young singer called Robert Plant a couple of years earlier, who now needed a drummer. Bonham fitted the bill

APPENDIX 1

I love the fact that Bonham was completely self-taught as a drummer. Despite this fact, or maybe because of it, his drumming, the power and the volume, rapidly became known around the Midlands. After finally forming Led Zeppellin with his friend Robert Plant and Jimmy Page he reall hit the big time.

Bonham's powerful, hard-hitting drumming soon became one of the band's signatures. He favoured Ludwig drums throughout his career and used 'trees', the longest and heaviest sticks available. He regularly performed Led Zeppelin solos with his bare hands too, to get a tone out of the drums that couldn't be achieved with sticks. I found him awe-inspiring. They broke the mould when they made him.

One thing that had always struck me about Bonham was his athleticism. He would lean back and gives those things a proper pounding. What a reaction I would have got from Noel if I'd started apeing John Bonham...

At a Nuremberg show on 27 June 1980, during a European tour, Bonham fell off his drum stool and collapsed after the third song, a warning, perhaps, of what was to come. On 5 September 1980, the band announced a US tour for October. Tickets sold like hot cakes and expectations were high. But it was not to be. Ten days after the announcement of the tour dates, the band members gathered at Jimmy Page's new mansion on the banks of the River Thames near Windsor for rehearsals. On 24 September, Bonzo was chauffeured to Page's. He had reportedly quit doing heroin, but was taking anti-despressants. En route, he stopped at a pub and downed four quadruple vodkas. During the rehearsal, his drinking continued, though this was not unusual for him. Around midnight, he passed out on a sofa and was helped to a bedroom. He was left lying on his side, propped up with pillows, with the lights turned out.

Bonzo still hadn't appeared by the next afternoon, so an assistant went in to wake him and found him dead. The ambulance was called, but John Bonham, aged 32, had died several hours earlier and was far beyond resuscitation.

Weeks later, at the coroner's inquest, it emerged that in the 24 hours before he died, Bonham had drunk 40 measures of vodka. The death was ruled as accidental. After a cremation, his remains were interred on 12 October 1980 at Rushock parish churchyard, near the Old Hyde farm.

On 4 December 1980, the band announced that 'The loss of our dear friend and the deep respect we have for his family, together with the sense of undivided harmony felt by ourselves and our manager, have led us to decide that we could not continue as we were.' Led Zeppelin ceased to be. I have nothing but pure, undiluted respect.

NUMBER 1

Gene Krupa

Years ago, I was watching an old film with my dad. It told the story of Glenn Miller, a popular band leader during World War II. The band in the movie had just performed a song called 'Basin Street Blues' and I sat transfixed by the drummer. His name was Gene Krupa.

Unless you are a drumming enthusiast you probably haven't heard of him. But that was not always the way. At one time, everyone knew Gene Krupa. He inspired both Steve White and John Bonham, as well as countless other great drummers. He changed the drum into an instrument rather than a counting device. Not a bad testament.

Gene Krupa was born in Chicago, Illinois, on 15 January 1909, the youngest of Bartlomiej and Anna Krupa's nine children. His father died when Gene was very young and his mother worked as a milliner to support the family. All of the children had to start working while young, and Gene did so aged 11. He started out playing sax in grade school but took up drums, also at the age of 11, since they were the cheapest item in the music store where he and his brother worked. He reflected in later years, 'I used to look in their wholesale catalogue for a musical instrument – piano, trombone, cornet – I didn't care what it was as long as it was an instrument. The cheapest item was the drums, 16 beans, I think, for a set of Japanese drums; a great high, wide bass drum, with a brass cymbal on it, a wood block and a snare drum.'

His parents were very religious and had groomed Gene for the priesthood. Gene's drive to drum was too strong, though, and he soon gave up the idea of becoming a priest.G e n e Krupa has often been considered to be the first drum soloist. Before him, drummers had usually been regarded purely as time-keepers or noise-makers, but Krupa interacted with the other musicians and introduced the extended drum solo into jazz. He is also considered the father of the modern drum set, since he convinced someone to make tuneable tom-toms; plus, he was called on to help with developing the modern hi-hat cymbals. And here's another milestone for you: Gene's first recording session, in December of 1927, saw him become the first drummer to record with a bass drum.

Gene moved to New York in 1929 and the partying began. It's always New York. He was recruited by Red Nichols and, along with Benny Goodman and Glenn Miller, performed in the pit bands. Gene had never learned to read music and 'faked' his parts during rehearsals. Glenn Miller assisted him by humming the drum parts until he got them down.

In the summer of 1943, Gene Krupa was arrested in San Francisco in a drug bust. He was charged with possession of marijuana and contributing to the delinquency of a minor. Gene's valet, who had been drafted, gave him marijuana cigarettes as a going-away present. Here is Gene's own account of the event: 'By then I was the glamour boy – 15 camel hair coats, three trunks around me all the time –and he couldn't think what to get me. Finally he thought, "Gee I'll get Gene some grass." At that time California was hot as a pistol, you could park your car for a bottle of beer and get arrested. So he had a rough time getting the stuff. He probably shot his mouth off a little – "I'm getting this for the greatest guy in the world, Gene Krupa." '

Gene decided to leave the marijuana at his hotel. Following a tip-off, the police began searching the theatre where Gene's band was playing:

> *I suddenly remembered the stuff's at the hotel where they're going next. So I call up my new valet and say, 'Send my laundry out. In one of my coats you'll find some cigarettes. Throw them down the toilet.' But the kid puts them in his pocket and the police nail him on the way out, so I get arrested... The ridiculous thing was that I was such a boozer I never thought about grass. I'd take grass, and it would put me to sleep. I was an out-and-out lush. Oh, sure, I was mad. But how long can you stay mad? So long you break out in rashes? Besides, the shock of the whole thing probably helped me. I might have gone to much worse things. It brought me back to religion.*

Gene was sentenced to 90 days, of which he served 84.

By the late fifties, Gene had to slow down, due to increasing back problems. He had a heart attack in 1960, which forced him into a retirement. After recuperating, his ever-changing Quartet continued to perform, record and regularly appeared at New York's Metropole. He retired in 1967, proclaiming that 'I feel too lousy to play and I know I must sound lousy.'

Sad to say, he died from leukaemia and a heart attack on 16 October 1973. He was laid to rest at the Holy Cross Cemetery in Calumet City, Illinois.

Gene Krupa will forever be known as the man who made drums a solo instrument. He inspired millions to become drummers and also demonstrated a level of showmanship that has rarely, if ever, been equalled. Buddy Rich once said that Gene was the 'beginning and the end of all jazz drummers'. And who am I to argue with Buddy Rich?

APPENDIX 2

AND SO TO THE SPARTANS

And so to the 300 Spartans. I have often used the word 'Spartan' during the course of the book. This was a Mancunian term used for someone who would stand next to you against all the odds. Someone who recognised the difference between what you have, or what you say, as opposed to what you are and what you do. Someone who knew that, divided, we fall. Someone you could trust. Throughout my life I have met many such Spartans and many of them have played an integral part in my story, as I have in theirs.

For all those who stood shoulder to shoulder, my gratitude. I – and the band – could not have achieved the glory without you.

NON-GRATITUDES
Non-Spartans

Noel Gallagher
After numerous albums and a spot of stage diving in Canada, Noel finally decided to call it a day with Oasis. He can be currently seen on *Soccer AM* every Saturday morning with his hair. His impending solo career should prove the final step in his search for that knighthood. Good Luck, Sir Noel, although I hope and pray it doesn't involve a cover of Paul McCartney's frog song.

Paul 'Guigs' McGuigan
After marrying the stewardess he had met on the flight to Japan, Paul retired to his back garden in north London.

GRATITUDES
The Spartans

Liam Gallagher
Liam is due to release his first material without Noel shortly, and I hope he puts his heart into it. If he does, we might just get the magic that I know he is capable of. He is also still regularly insulting all and sundry, as only he can.

Paul Benjamin 'Bonehead' Arthurs
Bonehead is currently touring with The Vortex after helping out in various other bands over the last 10 years. Last we spoke he was starring in a movie and loving the road again. A good man and a great drinker. Noel said, 'It wasn't as if it

was Paul McCartney leaving The Beatles' when Bonehead finally made the decision to quit. Bonehead said in return, 'Ain't Noel a nasty little twat.'

Vinny Collins, my football manager

Vinny followed Manchester City fervently, though with age he mellowed out somewhat. He remained loved and admired by all those around him. A couple of years ago, Vinny had an argument in a pub. A vengeful coward's act extinguished one of the brightest flames that had ever burnt in Manchester. May God rest your soul, Vinny.

Paul Gallagher

Paul has probably benefitted from Oasis even more than his brothers. Destined for a rain-sodden life on the roads of Manchester, he has spent the last 20 years travelling the globe as a DJ or an A&R man. He loves his music and people love him. What better occupation? A good friend and a knowing man. Keep the spirit.

The Policeman

The Policeman was buried in Stockport after a quiet, solemn funeral. No one was ever charged with his shooting.

Alan McGee

McGee just about squeezes in as a Spartan, I suppose, for the fact he makes no bones about his business – unlike Noel, who for fear of not being loved will wrap it up in some bollocks. McGee went through his detox and after Creation finished in 1999 he formed a new label, Poptones, the following year.

Trampy Spike

Spike never did return to his previous life. He was one of the last old-school tramps in Manchester. He finally died, as many feared he would. A house fire he had started finished him. A true gentleman of the road and as dedicated a man as I have met.

Huts (Chris Hutton)

Huts is still in Burnage. He released a book called *Don't Look Back in Anger*, which remains the only other really authentic recollection of what actually happened with the band.

BigUn (Paul Ashbee)

The mighty BigUn is still going strong and has been in contact with Noel over the last year or so. Things are still a bit frosty between them, however, and BigUn can't see a reconciliation. Too much water under the bridge. He is still as lively as ever, though, and can currently be seen assisting Carlos Tévez after his move from Manchester United to Manchester City.

The General (Jimmy Regan)

The General is still trying to avoid BigUn and his expensive cars at his garage in Tallyrand. A recent incident involving a footballing icon's Bentley has left the relationship between them at breaking point. Again.

Jimmy the Butt / Robot Head Cat Killer

Jimmy the Butt. My great friend and babysitter. An upright and solid man. Jimmy left us early in May 1990. He was only 23. His failing hearing was of no help as he crossed Stockport Road between two buses and then got hit head-on by a third. I guess it would take a bus to finally floor the big man.

'Right is right, even if everyone is against it; and wrong is wrong, even if everyone is for it.'

You tell 'em, Jimmy.

Chris and Tony Griffiths/The Real People/The Claggies

Sick of helping Oasis with songwriting and not getting the recognition or the mullah, they went on to write records for too many acts to mention. They had a worldwide smash with a song that Tony had written for Cher and still produce their own material, which seems to get better with age.

Marcus Russell

Marcus still manages both Liam and Noel's personal affairs, as far as I know. They've certainly kept him busy. Yet another Welsh Spartan.

Owen Morris

The Welsh mountain is still going strong in the industry and telling anyone who will listen about his box. This is the box he used to produce *Definitely Maybe*. Not gonna get technical with you, because I can't, but by all accounts this box makes the music louder. Bit like a volume control, I guess.

Mark Coyle

Coyley finally retired from the group shortly after I left. This wasn't down to him missing me, more the fact he was losing his hearing that rapidly he was in danger of going deaf. He went on to form a band called Tailgunner, in which Noel drummed. After hearing his drumming, I would just like to take this moment to give my own personal review. To be honest I'd be giving it too much credit if I marked it down as average. If I closed my eyes I could almost hear the same drum beat I was rattling out on *Playschool* in 1974. His timing was poor and the less said about the way he missed count the better. You weren't expecting a good review were you, Noel?

Maggie Mouzakitis
Maggie grew from a steely but inexperienced young lady into a well-respected and award-winning tour manager. She now manages such national events as the MTV Awards and the Brits. Always knew the girl would go far. God bless yer, Maggie.

Meg Matthews
Meg eventually married Noel and they had a baby daughter, Anais. After a few years, though, the marriage ended.

Kadamba
After splitting from Liam, Kadamba went on to appear in a number of music videos as well as films starring the likes of Julia Roberts. She had the world at her feet, but she was tragically murdered by a jealous ex-boyfriend. The world became a slightly less beautiful place when she passed.

Bridie and Tony (Mum and Dad)
Both my mother and father still live life to the full in little old Levenshulme. Respect and love always.

Adi
Adi has played in one band or another all his life. His love for music is matched only by his love for life. He is currently

fathering the little miracle he has named Hollie. Thanks for everything, Noddy.

Ged
As a band and session musician, Ged has toured the world for the last 12 years. He is a highly regarded guitarist and songwriter in his field but is still slightly less talented than his eldest brother. Ahem. A pillar and a rock, the truest of Spartans.

Gemma and Oliver
They both live with Paula in Cheshire. Gemma has grown to be a loving and generous young lady who is currently pursuing her education. A father could not ask for more. Oliver is still bringing light to my life on a daily basis. Love you both.

FUTURE SPARTANS

Jamie McCarroll. Hollie McCarroll.

LEVENSHULME SPARTANS

I was lucky enough to be raised in Levenshulme, Manchester. My time there was magical and was made so by the number of terrific people who lived there. Thank you all. Spartans unite.

Patrick Mannion. Stephen Dwyer. Noel Lonergan. Tony Dolan. Brendan McGlynn. Anthony Hogan. Quinny. Michael Hogan. Adrian Mulchrone. Andy Molloy. Roderick Mannion. Paul Croke. Kevin Deasy. Andrew Deeney. Colin Jones. Peter Deeney. Sean Molloy. Derek Williamson. Darren

Griffin. Michael Dolan. Michael Kane. Howsy. Darren Panda. Paul Kelly. Rod Tate. Curly Macca. Lee Tate. Ted Ackroyd. John O'Connor. Aki. Tony French. Steve Reilly. Anthony Molloy. Steve Slack. Phil Booth. Mark Dolan. Michael McCarrick. James Brennan. Steve French. Dessie Walls. Paul Burns. Dave Molloy. Wayne Scott. Chris Walls. Peter Hanlon. Terry Kavanagh. Mickey Dolan. Paul O'Hara. John Paul Dolan. Chris O'Hara. Troy Scott. Dave Shepherd. Simon 'Beanhead' Muirhead. Mark Abbott Cotterill. Jason 'Smurf' Dexter. Mark Curley. Alan 'Biff' Bailey. Peter Dagleish. Michael 'the Tash' Gallagher. Eddie Finlay. Ian Shufflebottom. Martin Birbeck. Dave Pickering. Laurence Dolan. Martin Brady. Sean Croke. Tony Leishman. Dave McGriskin Paul Leishman. Darren 'Tango' Lang. Mark Albiston. Lee Panter. Kev Walls. Richard Croke. Paul Kedian. Wayne Dowd. Anthony Veale. Vinny Davies. Gary 'Fudge' Fletcher. Neil Pollitt. Ken Reilly. Pat Berry. Terry Corless. Chris Kelly. Mick Durber. Dave Slack. Little Jacko. Vinny Davies. Sean Davies. Tony Lake. Steve Brookes. Steve Lake. Russell Lake. Colin Masters. John Feeney. Paul Feeney. Joey Dowd. Paul Toland. Martin Brady. Alan O'Hara. John Duffy. Mark Duffy. Noel Dempsey. Derek McCreery. Andy Sweeney. Trevor Francis. Rolo. Keith Lyons. Roger Baldwin. Darren Pointon. Paul Dowling. Brian Dowling. Leo McKenna. Phillip Ramsden. Gary Lawler. Gary Roe. Jason Scott. Lee Panter. Mickey McGoldrick. Ray Hogan. Ged Hogan. Gavin Oakes. Darren Smith. Josh. Dean Smith. Gary McHugh. Jason McHugh. Carl Barry. Kevin Barry. Tommy Walsh. Peter Walsh. Rob Jennings. Steve Jennings. Kev Lynch. Paul McGoughey. Michael McClean. Mike Capp. Steve Duffield. Dave Gregg. Barry Westwood. Lee Robinson. Gary Howard. Gary Robinson. Simon Lang. Michael Phipps. Mark McGinley. Ged Cosnett.

Dennis Dolan. Martin Dwyer. Michael Dwyer. Mike McCann. John Barrett. Tony Barrett. Liam Barrett. Heath Wilson. Martin Birbeck. Martin McVarnock. Mark Teehan. Sid. Colin McFadden. Sean Cannain. John Duffy. Dave Duffy. John Henry. Martin Henry. Tommy Cunny. 'Simple' Simon Graham. Finten Griffin. Tommy Colleran. Steve Colleran. Paul Muirhead. Damien Mulhall. Paul Nugent. Alfie Hanneman. Darren Brennan. Darren Towey. Gary Platt. Stuart Barber. John 'Monty' Monteith. Patsy Monteith. Kevin Monteith. Jason Pickering. Kieran Kavanagh. Simon Friggieri. Michael Brennan. Mike Billinge. Gary Seddon. Jason Seddon. Gary Breslin. Darren Robson.

SPARTAN CLANS

The McCarrolls and the O'Donnells. Thank you all.

REMEMBERED SPARTANS

Mark McCarroll. Willie O'Donnell. Paul Pointon. Declan Hockey. Paul 'Ed' Molloy. John Noble. Jimmy Ackroyd. Dave Smith. Joe Connolly. Jimmy Higgins. Vinnie Collins. Trampy Spike. Marrsy. Pat Muldoon. Martin Morrissey. Sean Walsh. John Roadhouse. Bernard 'Sonny' Lodge. Kevin Woodhead. Stiggy. Najib Daho. Terry Devlin. Gina Armitage. Rob Oliver. Brian Griffin. Dave Teehan. Geoffrey Newton. Dave Cotteril.

WEST POINT SPARTANS

Pat Morrin. Joe Morrin. Mike Morrin. John Morrin. Brian Griffiths. Mike Lester. Phil McClean. Jeff Bulcock. Mark

Shenton. Steve Shenton. Vernon Cookson. Dave Rayson. Dave Ellis. Brendan Murray. Rick Heffernan. Dave Heffernan. Scotty. Jonathan Scott. Michael Hegarty. Kevin Hegarty. Lee Mall. Robert Bates. Gary Slack. Andy Slack. Colin Woodhead. Jason Watson. John Reagan. Geoff Bulcock.

BURNAGE SPARTANS

Chris Johnson. Anthony Dolan. John Hodkinson. Vinny Young. Willie 'Jock' McNeilly. Ged Young. Brian Jackson. Dave Lee. Robert Jackson. Pete Jackson. Rick McNeilly. Darryl Gordon. Dave Coates. Mark 'Sid' Cox. Paul Hewitt. Anthony Timmins. Steve Lee. Kurt.

SALE SPARTANS

Matthew O'Driscoll. Simon Jacobs. Kirkwood. Simon Bunyan. Danny Bunyon. Phil Garthwaite. Nick Hutt. Daniel O'Driscoll. Carl Wood. Jordan McLoughlin. Chinny. Paul Mercer. Craig Groves. Geordie Carl. Phil Hegarty. Kenny Cooke. Danny Jackson. Andy Bradley. Jason Bradley. Mike Cribbins. Rob Heale. Richard Sebatta. Jacko. Ged Carps. Steve Carps. Dominic Stuk. Gary Edwards. Dave Lambert. Mark Clibbins. Johnny Arcadia, Ryan Roberts and the true leader of Sale, Mr Christopher Bradley, 'Coeur de Lion'. Nick Holmes.

BARNSLEY SPARTANS

Justin White. Martin Fox. Jamie Drumgoon. Ian Utley. Michael 'Love' Newton.

SALFORD SPARTANS

Anthony Green. Michael Milton. Richard Jackson. Kev Bailey. Jamie Horton. David Owen.

SCOUSE SPARTANS

Chris Griffiths. Tony Griffiths. Tony Elson. Digsy and Sean. Brian Lawler. Dougie Carney. Arthur Steve Darey. Andrew Jaundrill.

THE CARRIGAHOLT SPARTAN

Tom Flynn.

SPARTANS EVERYWHERE

Justin Moorhouse. Julian Dyson. Steve Rycroft. Stephen Patrick Morrissey. Marcus Bayley. Tommy O'Neill. Brian Gallagher. Paul Walsh. Shaun Ryder. Tony the Fitter. Brendan Shortall. Ian Brown. Tom Millward. Peter Reilly. Stephen Fretwell. John Saunders. Anton Chilton. John Courtney. Ken Hulston. Joe McKnight. Clint Boon. Craig Gill. Johnny Bramwell. Glen Thetap. Graham Massey. Steve White. Steve Hayes. Gary 'Mani' Mounfield. Robert Manock. Ben Mellor. Brendan Shortall. Eddie Fitzpatrick. Ryan Fitzpatrick. George Irving. Ian Malileau. Wags. Jay Tonge. Gerry Kenny. John Travis. Lee Whelan. Paul Recca. Dave Recca. Peter Heneghan. Darren Heneghan. Declan Heneghan. Carl Brown. Sean Cummins. Jimmy Doherty. Tony Doherty. Tom Loughrey. Tony McCormick. Steve McCormick. Steve Ballinger. John Booth. Dutch Tom. Catwalk. Billy Mulackey. Sean McNally. Greg McNally.

Ollie Mulloly. Andy Murphy. Joe Casserley. Georgi Kinkladze. Nicky Summerbee. Michael Brown. Mike Corbett. Stephen Ashbee. Jeff and Jim Whitley. Nigel Wilson.

FEMALE SPARTANS

Sue Taylor. Tracey Jordan. Elle Alvarez. Jane Dolan. Louise Jones. Mairead Keane. Sinead Robinson. Debbie Lucas. Kate Newton. Jill McCarroll. Catherine Manock. Lois Ashbee. Louise Seal. Clare Dolan. Clare Manock. Vicky Hutt. Sheila Monteith.

STUDIO SPARTANS

Dan Greenwood. Roy Mitchell. Gibbo. Dave Giggs. Dan Marland.

SCANDANAVIAN SPARTANS

Anders Larsen.

LEGAL SPARTANS

Jens Hills. David Spaine. Chris Woods. Chris Panayi. Garry Hunt. Tom Witley.

OASIS SPARTANS

Brian Cannon. Jason Rhodes. Roger Nowell. Tim Abbott. Chris Abbott. Phil Smith. Paul Slattery. Melissa Linsalato. Ian Robertson.

GIGOGRAPHY

All gigs are UK, unless otherwise stated.

1991

The Boardwalk, Manchester – 18 August

1992

The Boardwalk, Manchester – 15 January
Dartford Polytechnic, Dartford – 19 April
The Hippodrome, Oldham – 20 April
Club 57, Oldham – 5 May
The Boardwalk, Manchester – 14 July
The Boardwalk, Manchester – 19 August
In The City Festival, The Venue, Manchester – 13 September
The Boardwalk, Manchester – 22 November

1993

The Boardwalk, Manchester – 5 January
Le Bateau, Liverpool – 1 March
The Krazyhouse, Liverpool – 1 April
The Boardwalk, Manchester – 1 May
King Tut's Wah Wah Hut, Glasgow – 31 May
Manchester University, Manchester – 1 June
Le Bateau, Liverpool – 1 July
The Boardwalk, Manchester – 3 July
The Duchess, Leeds – 11 September
The Canal Bar, Manchester – 14 September
Manchester University, Manchester – 7 October
Manchester University, Manchester – 14 October
Keele University, Keele – 27 October
Sheffield University, Sheffield – 28 October
The Wherehouse, Derby – 1 November
Wulfrun Hall, Wolverhampton – 3 November
The Powerhaus, London – 4 November
Sheffield University, Sheffield – 28 November
The Institute, Birmingham – 1 December
The Plaza, Glasgow – 2 December
Warwick University, Warwick – 4 December
Wulfrun Hall, Wolverhampton – 8 December
Manchester University, Manchester – 9 December
The Cathouse, Glasgow – 10 December
The Mill, Preston – 11 December
The Riverside, Newcastle – 13 December
King's Hall, Bradford – 14 December
The Krazyhouse, Liverpool – 16 December

GIGOGRAPHY

1994

The Water Rats, London – 27 January
Gleneagles Golf Club, Perthshire,Scotland – 6 February
The Angel, Bedford – 23 March
The 100 Club, London – 24 March
The Forum, Tunbridge Wells – 26 March
Oxford Polytechnic, Oxford – 27 March
The Jug of Ale, Birmingham – 28 March
The Joiners, Southampton – 29 March
The Fleece & Firkin, Bristol – 30 March
Moles, Bath – 31 March
Lucifer's Mill, Dundee – 5 April
La Belle Angel, Edinburgh – 6 April
The Tramway, Glasgow – 7 April
Middlesbrough Arena, Middlesbrough – 8 April
The Wheatsheaf, Stoke – 11 April
The Duchess, Leeds – 12 April
The Lomax, Liverpool – 13 April
The Adelphi Club, Hull – 29 April
Coventry University, Coventry – 30 April
The Wedgewood Rooms, Portsmouth – 2 May
TJ's, Newport – 3 May
The Wherehouse, Derby – 4 May
The Princess Charlotte, Leicester – 6 May
The Old Trout, Windsor – 7 May
The Roadmenders, Northampton – 8 May
The Army and Navy, Chelmsford – 10 May
The Boat Race, Cambridge – 11 May
The Venue, London – 13 May
The Leadmill, Sheffield – 14 May
Edwards 8, Birmingham – 1 June
Cardiff University, Cardiff – 2 June

The Island, Ilford – 3 June
The Royal Albert Hall, London – 4 June
Norwich Arts Centre, Norwich – 6 June
The Marquee, Manchester – 8 June
Manchester University, Manchester – 9 June
The Avenham Park Festival, Preston – 11 June
The Cathouse, Glasgow – 12 June
The Cathouse, Glasgow – 13 June
Erotika, Paris (France) – 16 June
The Brighton Centre (East Wing), Brighton – 18 June
Glastonbury Festival, Somerset – 26 June
Wetlands, New York (USA) – 21 July
T In The Park Festival, Hamilton – 31 July
The Riverside, Newcastle – 9 August
The Irish Centre, Leeds – 10 August
Wulfrun Hall, Wolverhampton – 11 August
Hultsfreds Festival, Hultsfred (Sweden) – 13 August
Rock City, Nottingham – 15 August
Forum, London – 16 August
The Astoria, London – 18 August
Lowlands Festival (Netherlands) – 28 August
The Tivoli, Buckley – 31 August –
The Limelight, Belfast – 4 September
The Hacienda, Manchester – 5 September
The Logo, Hamburg (Germany) – 8 September
The Arena, Amsterdam (Netherlands) – 9 September
Quattro, Tokyo (Japan) – 13 September
Quattro, Tokyo (Japan) – 14 September
Quattro, Toyko (Japan) – 15 September
Quattro, Toyko (Japan) – 16 September
Quattro, Osaka (Japan) – 18 September
Quattro, Nagoya (Japan) – 19 September

GIGOGRAPHY

Moe's, Seattle, WA (USA) – 23 September
The Satyricon, Portland, OR (USA) – 24 September
Bottom of the Hill, San Francisco, CA (USA) – 26 September
Melarky's – Sacramento, CA (USA) – 27 September
The Whisky a Go Go, Los Angeles, CA (USA) – 29 September
The Uptown Bar, Minneapolis, MN (USA) – 14 October
The Metro, Chicago, IL (USA) – 15 October
St Andrew's Hall, Detroit, MI (USA) 16 October
The Grog Shop, Cleveland, OH (USA) – 18 October
Lee's Palace, Toronto (Canada) – 19 October
Local 186, Allston, MA (USA) – 21 October
The Met Café, Providence, RI (USA) – 22 October
JC Dobbs, Philadelphia (USA) – 23 October
9:30 Club, Washington, DC (USA) – 26 October
Maxwell's, Hoboken, NJ (USA) – 28 October
Wetlands, New York (USA) – 29 October
La Cigale, Paris (France) – 4 November
Transbordeur, Lyon (France) – 5 November
Theatre Du Moulin, Marseille (France) – 6 November
The Palladium, Stockholm (Sweden) – 16 November
The Cue Club, Gothenburg (Sweden) – 17 November
The Dairy, Lund (Sweden) – 18 November
The Loft, Berlin (Germany) – 20 November
Markthalle, Hamburg (Germany) – 21 November
Batchkapp, Frankfurt (Germany) – 23 November
Luxor, Cologne (Germany) – 24 November
Paradiso, Amsterdam (Netherlands) – 25 November
Zeche Carl, Essen (Germany) – 27 November
Botanieve, Brussels (Belgium) – 28 November
Southampton Guildhall, Southampton – 30 November
The Octagon, Sheffield – 1 December
The Corn Exchange, Cambridge – 4 December

Barrowlands, Glasgow – 7 December
Wolverhampton Civic Hall, Wolverhampton – 11 December
The Astoria, Cardiff – 12 December
The Hammersmith Palais, London – 13 December
The Royal Court, Liverpool – 17 December
Manchester Academy, Manchester – 18 December
Barrowlands, Glasgow – 27 December
The Brighton Centre (East Wing), Brighton – 29 December
Middlesbrough Town Hall, Middlesbrough – 30 December

1995

DV8, Seattle, WA (USA) – 28 January
The Commodore Ballroom, Vancouver (Canada) – 29 January
The Roseland Theatre, Portland, OR (USA) – 30 January
The Fillmore, San Francisco (USA) – 1 February
The Palace, Hollywood, CA (USA) – 3 February
SOMA Live, San Diego, CA (USA) – 4 February
The Nile Theatre, Mesa, AZ – 5 February
The Bar & Grill, Salt Lake City, UT (USA) – 7 February
The Bluebeard Theatre, Denver, CO (USA) – 9 February
Deep Ellum Live, Dallas, TX (USA) – 11 February
The Liberty Lunch, Austin, TX (USA) – 12 February
The Urban Art Bar, Houston, TX (USA) – 13 February
The New Daisy Theatre, Memphis, TN (USA) – 15 February
The Cat's Cradle, Carrboro, NC (USA) – 17 February
The Masquerade, Atlanta, GA (USA) – 18 February
The Stone Pony, Ashbury Park, NJ (USA) – 3 March
The Wust Music Hall, Washington, DC (USA) – 4 March
The Abyss, Virginia Beach, VA (USA) – 5 March
The Theatre of Living Arts, Philadelphia, PA (USA) – 7 March
The Academy, New York, (USA) – 8 March

GIGOGRAPHY

Lopo's, Providence, RI (USA) – 10 March
The Avalon, Boston, MA (USA) – 11 March
Club Soda, Montreal (Canada) – 12 March
The Phoenix Theatre. Toronto (Canada) – 14 March
The Odeon, Cleveland, OH (USA) – 15 March
St Andrew's Hall, Detroit, MI (USA) – 16 March
Tyndall Armory, Indianapolis (USA) – 18 March
The Vic Theatre, Chicago, IL (USA) – 19 March
The Orbit Room, Grand Rapids, MI (USA) – 20 March
First Ave, Minneapolis, MN (USA) – 24 March
Rave At Eagles, Milwaukee, WI (USA) – 25 March
The Cliffs Pavilion, Southend – 17 April
Le Bataclan, Paris (France) – 20 April
Sheffield Arena, Sheffield – 22 April